To Oli,
With best Wishes

Peter

January 2017

FROM OBSCURITY TO CLARITY IN PSYCHOMETRIC TESTING

'Professor Peter Saville's creativity, ingenuity, and profound impact on the field of applied psychology are reflected time and time again in this volume, which provides an indispensable and much-needed link between research and practice. For both the seasoned or budding applied psychologist, this volume constitutes essential reading.' Duncan J. R. Jackson, Birkbeck, University of London, UK.

The field of psychometrics has a long and varied tradition across the social sciences. A range of academics have sought to understand human consciousness more fully by statistically testing our abilities, personalities, attitudes and beliefs. But perhaps the area where psychometric techniques have had most impact on contemporary society is in employee recruitment, where a range of psychometric tests have become commonplace.

Professor Peter Saville is one of the pioneers of adapting psychometric testing to the field of occupational psychology and human resource management. In a career of nearly 40 years, his work has been adopted by hundreds of public and private organisations, assessing the suitability of prospective candidates through a range of questionnaires and tests. In this anthology of his work, including both keynote conference addresses and journal papers, Saville provides a masterly overview of the field of psychometrics, and the key issues and questions that it raises.

An ideal companion for any student or researcher of HRM, occupational or organisational psychology, or applied psychology in general, Peter Saville's selected works represent the thinking of one of the most influential psychologists of our time.

Professor Peter Saville, BA, MPhil, PhD, HonFBPsS, CPsychol, CSci, Academic FCIPD, FRSA, FIoD – Founder, SHL and Founder, Saville Consulting; Visiting Professor, Kingston Business School.

Tom Hopton, MA (Hons) (Oxon), MBPsS, CPsychol – Principal Consultant, Saville Consulting, A Willis Towers Watson Company; Visiting Fellow, Kingston Business School.

World Library of Psychologists

The *World Library of Psychologists* series celebrates the important contributions to psychology made by leading experts in their individual fields of study. Each scholar has compiled a career-long collection of what they consider to be their finest pieces: extracts from books, journals, articles, major theoretical and practical contributions, and salient research findings.

For the first time ever the work of each contributor is presented in a single volume so readers can follow the themes and progress of their work and identify the contributions made to, and the development of, the fields themselves.

Each book in the series features a specially written introduction by the contributor giving an overview of their career, contextualizing their selection within the development of the field, and showing how their thinking developed over time.

FROM OBSCURITY TO CLARITY IN PSYCHOMETRIC TESTING

Selected works of Professor Peter Saville

Professor Peter Saville
With Tom Hopton

Routledge
Taylor & Francis Group

LONDON AND NEW YORK

First published 2016
by Routledge
2 Park Square, Milton Park, Abingdon, Oxon OX14 4RN

and by Routledge
711 Third Avenue, New York, NY 10017

Routledge is an imprint of the Taylor & Francis Group, an informa business

British Library Cataloguing in Publication Data
A catalogue record for this book is available from the British Library

Library of Congress Cataloging in Publication Data
Names: Saville, Peter, 1946- author. | Hopton, Tom, author.
Title: From obscurity to clarity in psychometric testing : selected
    works of professor Peter Saville / Professor Peter Saville ; with
    Tom Hopton.
Description: Abingdon, Oxon ; New York, NY : Routledge, 2016. |
    Series: World library of psychologists
Identifiers: LCCN 2015048456| ISBN 9781138823433
    (hardback : alk. paper) | ISBN 9781315742083 (e-book)
Subjects: LCSH: Psychometrics.
Classification: LCC BF39 .S29 2016 | DDC 150.1/5195—dc23
LC record available at http://lccn.loc.gov/2015048456

ISBN: 978-1-138-82343-3 (hbk)
ISBN: 978-1-315-74208-3 (ebk)

Typeset in Bembo
by Swales & Willis Ltd, Exeter, Devon, UK

MIX
Paper from
responsible sources
FSC
www.fsc.org   FSC® C013604

Printed and bound by CPI Group (UK) Ltd, Croydon, CR0 4YY

CONTENTS

FIGURES

TABLES

NOTES ON CONTRIBUTORS

Professor Peter Saville, BA, MPhil, PhD, HonFBPsS, CPsychol, CSci, Academic FCIPD, FRSA, FIoD – Founder, SHL and Founder, Saville Consulting; Visiting Professor, Kingston Business School

Peter is a chartered psychologist and chartered scientist as well as holding numerous other honorary positions. His picture hung in the National Portrait Gallery, London, as the first Work Psychologist to be awarded the Centenary Life Time Achievement Award from the British Psychological Society for Distinguished Contributions to Professional Psychology. In his career, he has been a consultant to over 100 organisations and has presented in over 65 countries.

Peter founded SHL, taking it to full flotation on the London Stock Exchange, and then left the SHL board to found Saville Consulting in 2004. In 2015, Saville Consulting joined Towers Watson. Peter was listed as one of the UK's top entrepreneurs by Enterprise Magazine and was voted one of the UK's top ten psychologists, the only Industrial Psychologist listed. Already a Fellow, in 2012 he was awarded Honorary Fellowship of the British Psychological Society, joining an eminent list including Freud, Jung, Murray, Skinner and Chomsky. The citation states that 'he brought science to the workplace and set the global gold standard in psychometric testing'.

Tom Hopton, MA (Hons) (Oxon), MBPsS, CPsychol – Principal Consultant, Saville Consulting, a Willis Towers Watson Company; Visiting Fellow, Kingston Business School

Tom is a chartered psychologist, Principal Consultant at Saville Consulting and Visiting Fellow of Kingston University, London. He graduated from the University of Oxford as an experimental psychologist and is a consultant and trainer to a range of global clients. As well as working on the research and development of numerous workplace assessment tools, he is a published author and an established presenter on subjects such as assessment, performance and leadership.

FOREWORD

At the time of writing, I've had the immense pleasure of working with Professor Peter Saville for over eight years. He was formerly the founder and Chairman of SHL Group plc, which was floated on the main London Stock Exchange in 1997 and recently sold for over half a billion US dollars. After disagreeing with the then new SHL strategy, Peter started again and formed the Saville Consulting Group in 2004. In 2015, Saville Consulting became part of the global professional services company Towers Watson, reflecting the culmination of over a decade at the forefront of psychometric assessment under Peter's leadership.

Peter sits alongside such eminent psychologists as Sigmund Freud, Carl Jung and Charles Spearman in an elite group who have been awarded the Honorary Fellowship of the British Psychological Society for their pioneering and influential services to the discipline of psychology. Peter is acknowledged as a worldwide authority in the field of Industrial and Organisational Psychology and has been referred to as an 'assessment guru', 'one of Britain's most creative psychologists' and by Professor Binna Kandola as 'a genius in his field'.

Peter learnt his craft at the National Foundation for Educational Research where he became Chief Psychologist at the Test Division by the age of 27. It was here that Professor Stephen Wiseman noted his unusual combination of both an academic and entrepreneurial brain. In 1998, Peter was voted one of the UK's top entrepreneurs by *Enterprise Magazine* and in 2004 he was recognised as one of the UK's top ten psychologists – the only industrial psychologist cited. His picture hung in the National Portrait Gallery, London, when he was awarded the BPS Centenary Life Time Achievement Award for Distinguished Contribution to Professional Psychology in 2002.

Throughout his career, Peter has been an international consultant to a wide range of prestigious international organisations, including Mensa and the United

Nations. He is the author of over 250 academic papers and publications and has delivered speeches in over 60 countries worldwide.

For anybody interested in business success and workplace performance, as well as those who have experienced psychometric testing in any capacity, this book provides a unique opportunity to better understand the field of workplace psychology from the personal perspective of one of its greatest and most successful minds. I hope you enjoy reading it as much as we did preparing it.

Tom Hopton, November 2015

ACKNOWLEDGEMENTS

We'd also like to thank everybody who helped with the production of this book, including Rachel Walton, Richard Field, Sophie Pestell and Dominic Goodacre.

INTRODUCTION

My overarching concern when selecting the material for this anthology has been to provide an overview of the advances made in occupational psychology over the last 30 years and more. I have been privileged to have played a role in a number of the key developments in this field and want to furnish the reader with an accessible introduction to the history, present and future of this fascinating area of psychology.

In this book, Tom and I discuss the theoretical origins of modern workplace psychology, including my work creating and developing a number of the most well-known and frequently-used psychometric assessments. We also discuss modern advances in workplace assessment, including the latest technologies and the diverse applications of psychometrics, such as in the prediction of leadership and entrepreneurial potential.

In *From Obscurity to Clarity in Psychometric Testing*, we hope to provide you with a unique and intimate insight into my life's work. We've chosen to focus on 12 important examples which have shaped my career as a scientist, entrepreneur and business leader.

— *Professor Peter Saville, November 2015*

PART I
The origins of psychometrics

1

WHAT'S IT ALL ABOUT?

Introduction

This chapter is based on a keynote speech which I delivered at a conference in South Africa in 2008:

> Saville, P. (2008). Psychometrics in the workplace. Presented at the 14th South African Psychology Congress, Johannesburg, South Africa, August.

Here I will provide a brief introduction and overview of a number of concepts which will be discussed in greater depth throughout several of the chapters in this book.

Psychometrics in the workplace

There are a wide variety of different assessment methods that can be used. Just some examples include:

- Reading fluency.
- Spelling accuracy.
- Grammatical understanding.
- Verbal reasoning.
- Numerical reasoning.
- Abstract reasoning.
- Logical reasoning.
- Spatial reasoning.
- Mechanical reasoning.
- Clerical/error-checking ability.

- Manual dexterity.
- Physical strength.
- Tests of sensory abilities (e.g. sight, hearing).
- Application forms.
- Biographical data.
- Interviews.
- References.
- In-tray exercises.
- Group activities.
- Projective techniques (e.g. inferring characteristics about a person from how they interpret certain situations, images or even abstract shapes).
- 360-degree performance assessment (i.e. where various stakeholders all offer their assessments of one particular individual).
- Values/preference surveys.
- Personality/behavioural questionnaires.
- Observation/job simulation.
- Assessment centres (where multiple different kinds of assessments are used in one overall assessment period).

These various kinds of assessments have been used in countless different situations and applications. A number of them are to this day used in the workplace and some are used in other contexts too – educational or clinical environments, for example. Certain kinds of assessments are straightforward and transparent, whereas others may be more complex and require a greater degree of understanding to use and interpret appropriately.

We know, for example, that the observation of people at work has been used to assess many individuals in a vast number of different situations. A neurosurgeon once told me that in the 1800s, surgeons often insisted that their apprentices be present early on for especially gruesome operations such as sawing off somebody's leg. The rationale was that if the apprentice fainted or couldn't bear to watch, they wouldn't be hardy enough to train as a surgeon and so had to be dismissed early on.

Such 'job samples' have also taken other forms. I once heard that in Japan sales applicants to certain jobs would be required to climb to the top of a hill or other high place overlooking a large number of people. They would then be asked to scream the name of the product that they would be required to sell. The rationale was that if the individual was too scared to do this, they wouldn't be able to perform successfully in the role and so would have to be rejected. Other graduate applicants in Japan were reputed to have been required to clean a toilet as part of their application process. The rationale here was that this would demonstrate how motivated and detail-conscious they were. This particular group of assessors also observed the graduates during mealtimes. If they ate quickly and properly, they were kept in the applicant pool, but if they were messy or slow, they were rejected. In this case, their personality characteristics were being inferred from their eating style. Lastly, we also know that ancient Chinese civil servants were assessed not only on their intellect, but also on their creativity. This was sometimes assessed by giving them the first line of a poem or rhyming couplet and then asking them to provide the most original possible following line.

Speaking more specifically about 'psychometric' assessments, there is one particular sub-class of assessments which is often used in workplace contexts. So when we speak of psychometric assessments, what are we actually talking about? In broad terms, psychometrics are standardised assessments of psychological attributes. It can be useful to categorise them at the highest level into 'can do' assessments of maximal performance and 'will do' assessments of typical performance. In practical terms, this usually represents the distinction between assessments where there are right and wrong answers (e.g. IQ or ability tests) and those where there aren't explicit 'correct' responses (e.g. personality or preference questionnaires).

Personality or behavioural questionnaires are among the most widely used workplace assessments and I'd like to take this opportunity to provide a brief overview of the history of personality research.[1]

One of the earliest known attempts to define personality came around 3,000 years ago, when Buddhist writers outlined the five most important characteristics of elephant trainers (surprisingly close to the Big Five model of personality discussed later) as health, confidence, wisdom, diligence and sincerity.

We also know that descriptions of personality go back to the ancient Greeks. Plato postulated the need for society to have governors who were leaders and philosophers. He indicated that these individuals required specific qualities to succeed; they must be truthful and not at any time be cowardly.

The great ancient Greek physician Hippocrates first proposed the four temperamental characteristics 'Melancholic', 'Phlegmatic', 'Choleric' and 'Sanguine' which he called 'humors'. Hippocrates believed that these humors were caused by changes in certain bodily fluids, namely: black bile, blood, yellow bile and phlegm.

Hippocrates was therefore one of the first to conceptualise a personality theory. He proposed that only the proper mixture of these four humors would produce the condition of health. Temperament theory suggested that though the proportions of the humors may vary considerably from person to person, people could in essence be reduced to four types of temperaments according to the predominance of a given humor.

Since there were four humors, it was proposed that there could be four kinds of healthy equilibrium, not one, and that individuals could be subdivided into four psychological groups named after the prevalent humor: the sanguine, buoyant type; the phlegmatic, sluggish type; the choleric, quick-tempered type; and the melancholic, dejected type. These humors were, in turn, linked to the four fundamental elements of the universe: air, water, fire and earth, respectively. Hippocrates believed that personality and illness were dependent upon these four humors. Any imbalance in these humors would result in a personality problem or an illness.

Research has also brought to light that the Vikings actually had a competency-based system for selecting their leaders; it was not necessarily done through the blood line. As historian Paul Mortimer[2] has explained to me, if a king's son could not reach the standard required by the elders, they were put to one side and a more worthy individual would be put through the selection process, even if not of royal 'blue blood'. Such selection processes included measures of bravery (they had to show a reputation for exceptional achievements), job knowledge (they needed to have absorbed education from an expert), presence both on and off the battlefield (they had to show signs of wealth, eminence and were often taller than average), eloquence and persuasiveness (they needed to be good orators), a keen intellect, evidence that they had helped develop the young, being generous (they circulated their wealth and accolades), but the capacity to be cruel to anyone who challenged them.

They had a clear benefits and rewards system in the workplace. As Paul Mortimer continued: 'A stingy, niggling king did not last long.' Although the Vikings were often regarded as a rabble when fighting, in fact they were immensely skilled and adroit at strategy, which made them a formidable fighting force. Lastly, I should add that it is also a myth that they wore helmets with horns – they did not!

We also know that people have tried to find links between the biological and the mental. Shakespeare (1599) wrote in *Julius Caesar*:

> *Let me have men about me that are fat;*
> *Sleek-headed men and such as sleep o'nights;*
> *Yond Cassius has a lean and hungry look;*
> *He thinks too much;*
> *Such men are dangerous.*

Sheldon's (1942) constitutional approach to psychology also attempted to relate body type and personality. *Endomorphs* were seen as extrovert, fun-loving and out-going, while *mesomorphs* were seen as aggressive, risk-taking and athletic. Lastly, *ectomorphs* were seen as introverted, inhibited and shy. Although such broad generalisations may initially seem hard to sustain, more recently it has been suggested that there might be a physiological basis to this, relating to people's relative levels of neurotransmitters and hormones such as serotonin, testosterone and dopamine.

Clearly, there are many factors which impact on the development of human personality. These factors include genetics, biology, life experiences, trauma, situational factors, workplace culture, national, gender, ageing, family, educational and perhaps even constitutional factors.

In considering why there are numerous methods and styles of assessment available and to fully understand the history of assessment, it is important to look at the theories of personality from which these methods of assessment have evolved. Over the years, there have been many attempts to define and explain personality and there are considerable variations among psychologists as to the precise definition of the term 'personality'.

Carl Rogers (1959) defined personality as being about the self: an organised permanent subjectively perceived entity, which is at the very heart of all our experiences. Rogers was a strong believer in the notion that the way in which individuals perceive themselves influences both their behaviour and the way they see the rest of the world.

Gordon Allport is often called the father of personality theory. He was a trait theorist who believed in the individuality and uniqueness of the person, and that people have consistent personalities. His lexical approach (sometimes known as the Lexical Hypothesis) described many of the different characteristics or facets of personality. It was based on the idea that personality variables which are important to people's lives are manifest in the language they use. Allport and Odbert (1936) engaged in research where they categorised dictionary entries into various conceptual lists to produce nearly 20,000 items which were used to describe personality and behaviours. Allport believed that each person had traits of various types.

Raymond Cattell, author of the 16PF personality questionnaire, defined personality as being something which 'enables us to predict what a person will do in real life situations' (Cattell, 1946). This is a very useful definition as it says that questionnaires should be defined by their relationships to how people behave (and, by extension, how they perform at work). Cattell held that an individual's personality was composed of a set of various traits; his work could also be said to have been influenced by the lexical approach.

Perhaps the best-known theory of personality development was proposed by Sigmund Freud. *The Interpretation of Dreams*, probably his best known work, was published in 1900. Freud proposed that adult personality was shaped to a great degree by childhood experiences at various key formative stages in their development. He advanced the importance of various methods of gratification that were prevalent at each of these stages (oral, anal, phallic).

Freud identified three main components of personality, namely the *ego*, the *id* and the *super-ego*. The id was the source of subconscious urges in the individual, the ego was what stands between these urges and reality, and the super-ego represented the sense of conscience and guilt. These days, a good deal of Freud's approach is viewed with considerable scepticism. His writings and much of his theorising were based on a very limited sample group, made up primarily of middle-class Viennese women. It has been argued that a good deal of Freud's work is problematic as it is focused on the subconscious and hence is difficult to test – you cannot argue with the analyst! Those aspects of Freud's propositions which have been tested empirically have often provided little support for his theories. Nevertheless, his recognition that there are things which influence our behaviours without our conscious awareness remains an important contribution in the field of psychology.

Albert Bandura is considered as the leading proponent of social learning theory (Bandura, 1977), which focuses on the learning that occurs within a social context. It considers that people learn from one another, including such concepts as observational learning, imitation and modelling. Thus, the adult personality is formed by observing others and imitating their behaviour in childhood and later in life. Role models (parents, older children, characters on TV, etc.) become vital in shaping preferred behaviour. Since the conditions for learning vary among individuals, different people will reproduce the same behaviour differently. Differences in stereotypically male and female behaviour may come from social learning. Even in adulthood, the effect of a company culture on the behaviours of people in that company can be remarkable.

Behaviourism is a theory of animal and human learning which only focuses on so-called objectively observable behaviours. Behaviourists define learning as the acquisition of a new behaviour. Pavlov (see e.g. Pavlov, 1927) worked extensively with dogs in order to demonstrate that they could be conditioned to salivate at the sound of a bell. The 'conditioned reflex', as it was termed, was the demonstration of learned behaviour with an association being built up between the bell (a neutral stimulus) and the physical response of salivating in anticipation of being fed. This research into the relationships between stimulus and response was also the basis of the work of B. F. Skinner.

B.F. Skinner is now the name most prominently associated with the behaviourist school of thought. He carried out many years of laboratory experiments with rats in mazes and pigeons in Skinner boxes, investigating how learning occurred via operant conditioning (e.g. Skinner, 1938). This involved the use of rewards presented in a controlled manner (schedules of reinforcement) so as to shape behaviour. Skinner always recommended positive reinforcement (rewarding of desired behaviour) over negative reinforcement or punishment. A behaviourist in-joke describes a conversation between two rats in the midst of one such experiment; one turns to the other and remarks: 'Look how well I've conditioned that psychologist! Every time I press this button, he is compelled to give me a food pellet!'

In the workplace, certain behaviours are rewarded and others are punished. Positive and negative reinforcement is something that happens not only in an animal cage but also in everyday life. 'Carrot and Stick' approaches to motivation, based around rewards and punishments, are part of many people's daily lives. The founders or leaders of an organisation constantly shape its culture by encouraging and rewarding certain actions and discouraging or even prohibiting others.

Contrastingly, the focus of the humanistic perspective is on the self and 'your' perception of 'your' experiences. This view argues that you are free to choose your own behaviour rather than it constituting a mere reaction to environmental stimuli and reinforcers. Issues dealing with self-esteem, self-fulfilment and needs are paramount. The major focus is to facilitate personal development.

Humanistic personality theory evolved partly out of Carl Rogers' work as a clinical psychologist and his 'person-centred therapy'. His approach postulated that human behaviour is 'exquisitely rational' and the core of man's nature is essentially positive; he is a 'trustworthy organism'. Rogers stated that we all have a 'phenomenal field' which is made up of all the experiences available to us and, as we develop, a portion of this differentiates itself and becomes our sense of 'self'. This self develops through our interactions with other people. Each person operates from a unique frame of reference in terms of their self-concept (one's own beliefs about oneself).

Maslow, another proponent of the humanistic approach, stated that adult personality depends on the satisfaction of various needs as people go through life. Only after one need has been satisfied do people progress to the next, and not everyone progresses as far as others. Basic needs like warmth, food and shelter, once satisfied, lead to more elevated ones. Those who have reached the ultimate level are said to be self-actualised. Nevertheless, Maslow's 1943 work has frequently been criticised for methodological problems in the original research and a lack of empirical support for the theory.

In the 1940s, a number of competing models of personality emerged that led to the development of 'first generation' personality questionnaires, developed for general or clinical use. An early example of a questionnaire developed for clinical use is the Minnesota Multiphasic Personality Inventory (MMPI: Hathaway and McKinley, 1943). Hans Eysenck was one of the first psychologists to study personality using factor analysis, a statistical technique used by the famous British psychologist Charles Spearman. Eysenck's results suggested two main personality factors, the first being the tendency to experience negative emotions, referred to as Neuroticism (N). The second factor was the tendency to enjoy positive events, especially social events, and was named Extraversion (E). E and N provided a two-dimensional space to describe individual differences in behaviour (Eysenck and Eysenck, 1969). The third dimension, Psychoticism (P), concerns such characteristics as tough-mindedness, non-conformism and willingness to take risks, although a lot of people have found it difficult to define. It was added to the model in the late 1970s.

In common with Eysenck, Raymond Cattell used factor-analytical methods in the study of human personality. He did this manually in the 1930s and developed a detailed model of 16 personality factors and the corresponding 16PF questionnaire (see e.g. Cattell, 1946). These factors were termed 'source traits' by Cattell, providing the underlying source for the surface behaviours that are thought of as personality. As part of my PhD, I studied the measurement characteristics of the 16PF and used factor-analytic techniques in 1977 to condense the questionnaire into a structure that we now recognise as the Big Five (to be discussed shortly) plus intelligence (Saville, 1977). This was the foundation of the Pentagon model of the occupational personality questionnaire (OPQ) published in 1984 (Saville et al., 1984).

Most psychometric models see personality as a combination of traits. A trait can be any characteristic way of behaving, thinking, feeling or operating. The Eysenck Personality Inventory (EPI) and Cattell's 16PF are both based on trait theories. These give great flexibility of description, as everyone will have a somewhat different constellation of traits. Theoretically, anything which can be measured and shows differences between individuals can be considered a trait, so some psychologists feel that trait approaches lack a strong theoretical basis.

Type theories are those which divide people into distinct groups, generally consisting of a combination of preferred behaviours. Katharine Cook Briggs and her daughter Isabel Briggs Myers developed the Myers-Briggs Type Indicator (MBTI) at the Educational Testing Services organisation (ETS), based on their interpretation of Jungian thinking (Myers, 1980). The tool consists of four bipolar scales which broadly correspond to four of the Big Five factors (excluding Neuroticism) and define 16 personality types. Other typologies include Belbin's Team Roles (Belbin, 1981) and Holland's Vocational Types (Holland, 1973).

If type theories stress similarities, trait theories stress differences between individuals. A major concept in modern personality psychology is the Big Five factors of personality. Barrick and Mount (1991) outlined the research base for the broad trait factors that have frequently been found and replicated in personality research, and are known as the Big Five: Openness to Experience, Conscientiousness, Extroversion, Agreeableness and Neuroticism (the initial letters of which form the OCEAN mnemonic). Barrick and Mount traced the origins of the Big Five back to the work of Norman (1963) and acknowledged that over the years, different names had been used for what is now understood to be essentially the same set of personality factors. Neuroticism is increasingly referred to as 'emotional stability', while agreeableness and openness to experience are sometimes described using their opposite end, i.e. 'independence' and 'conventionality', respectively. The Big Five has been discovered in all cultures so far studied. Surprisingly, relatively little difference has been found in the personalities of different cultures.

The NEO-PI-R questionnaire (Costa and McCrae, 1985) is one of the most commonly used benchmark measures of the Big Five, although my team developed what was the first commercially available Big Five measure in the Pentagon model of the Occupational Personality Questionnaire (Saville et al., 1984). At that time, I defined personality as: 'A person's typical style of thinking, feeling and behaving.' The Wave questionnaire, developed in 2004 by my team at Saville Consulting, covers the Big Five across its scales with more workplace-focused titles. Wave's 'Influence' cluster covers extroversion, 'Thought' covers openness to experience, 'Delivery' covers conscientiousness and the final of Wave's four clusters, 'Adaptability', covers both of the Big Five factors of agreeableness and neuroticism. Our research found that this was the best way to capture the Big Five scales in a work-relevant, contemporary model.

Clearly, personality is more complex than just being composed of five different variables. There is a difference between friendliness and a need for friends, for example. Equally, there is a difference between being overtly and covertly sensitive to criticism. Nevertheless, the Big Five model is a useful general framework for assessing personality. It is important not to forget, however, that the subtle differences between people can often be the most interesting and useful – everybody is unique and should be valued.

A summary of some of the most commonly-used personality questionnaires is included below.

However, we must also acknowledge that not all personality questionnaires are created equal. On looking at the content of many personality questionnaires, it's hardly surprising that they are controversial in psychology. 'Pseudoscience', as one academic said at my old university. Many are inappropriate in the workplace and poorly worded at best, or downright stupid. Here are a few items from real questionnaires:

TABLE 1.1 A selection of the most well-known personality questionnaires

Questionnaire	Authors	Factors	Date
16PF	Cattell	16 scales	1949
EPI	Eysenck	3 factors	1947
MBTI	Briggs-Myers	16 types	1943
OPQ	Saville et al.	30 scales /32 scales	1984
NEO-PI-R	Costa & McCrae	5 factors & 30 facets	1992
Wave Styles	Saville et al.	36 dimensions & 108 facets	2004

1. 'I have a fear of being buried alive.'
2. 'There is something wrong with my sex organs.'
3. 'I would rather be Dr Crippen than Jack the Ripper.'
4. 'I believe in the Second Coming of Christ.'
5. 'I have no difficulty holding my bowel movements.'
6. 'I would like to be a Formula One racing driver.'
7. 'Given the circumstances there is absolutely nothing I wouldn't do.'
8. 'I often think about taking part in orgies.'
9. 'I would rather keep my desk tidy than kiss someone of the opposite sex.'
10. 'The sight of blood no longer excites me.'
11. 'Do more than 50% of Americans kiss on their first date?'
12. 'It's hard to concentrate in a roomful of mice.'
13. 'I never resent not getting my OWN way.'

Market researchers are often far better at writing questionnaire items than psychologists. They have to be. Clients employ them to predict pragmatic issues like sales of different products. If they get it wrong, they are out of business. In market research, good, clear items are written with the minimum of theory. Psychologists write silly items, but surround them with a web of intricate sounding so-called 'theory'. So are all personality questionnaires pseudoscience and snake oil? As one observer commented: 'What's wrong with snake oil? It did wonders for my mother's rheumatism . . . !'

Some years ago I came across a book on market research with a story on asking questions:

> *Two clergy people were discussing whether it was a sin to smoke at the same time as praying. They could not agree so decide to consult their respective superiors. On meeting again, the first said, 'My superior thought it was a sin.' The second said, 'That's very strange, my superior said it was fine. What exactly did you ask?' The first replied, 'I asked if it was a sin to smoke when praying.' 'Oh,' said the second, 'I asked if it was a sin to pray whilst smoking.'*

However, every single assessment method has its strengths and its limitations. For example, while many people would say that job interviews are one of the most useful methods for assessing workplace performance, research has shown that interviewers:

- Have different views on the person they need.
- Weight the same information differently.
- Decide intuitively (and not objectively).
- Talk too much and listen too little.
- Raise ratings of candidates if pressurised to make a selection.
- Make decisions early on.
- Over-rely on academic qualifications.
- Rate candidates comparatively to others rather than in a standardised, consistent manner.
- Prefer candidates like themselves.
- Influence candidates' behaviour.
- Influence candidates' responses.

One criticism often levelled at psychometric assessments in general – and personality questionnaires in particular – is that they can be manipulated and distorted to say what the respondent wants them to say.

To summarise some of the existing research in this area:

- If instructed, people can distort and be consistent in their distortion.
- In selection, applicants tend to distort less than is often expected.
- So-called 'subtle items' don't tend to work to reduce distortion.
- Social desirability and lie scales don't work to reduce distortion.
- Distortion doesn't necessarily lower validity according to some studies.
- There are issues associated with unsupervised online testing, so having a secure re-test form is important.
- Bayesian statistics don't help with identity deception.
- Randomised test banks of content and Item Response Theory provide no guarantee against identity deception.

So what can be done about distortion? A few useful approaches include:

- Not asking stupid questions and keeping it job-relevant.
- Giving feedback for both its positive reception and for probing for accuracy of responses (while this is not the default position in the USA, it is in the UK).
- Putting highly verifiable items in the questionnaire can help (e.g. asking about people's abilities).
- Warning the candidate that there are measures to detect cheating.
- Writing items lower in social desirability (e.g. 'I get nervous before important events' rather than 'I am a neurotic mess').
- Not relying on internet-delivered test forms alone and having a secure parallel form available for cross-checking.

- Using personally administered/proctored and paced testing at the final stage because people who take longer are more likely to distort.
- Using ipsative forms (because there is some evidence that these reduce distortion).
- Using a dynamic ipsative and normative format which keeps you on your toes. Our experience is that where the ipsative scores are much lower than the normative, the respondent may have exaggerated. This enables one to probe specific scales rather than relying on an overall social desirability scale that gives no direction or guidance on where to look.
- Remembering that all selection methods can be manipulated – over 70% of application forms contain serious errors of fact, interviews are subject to bias and references (where available) are next to useless.
- Treating the person like a human being – it's not an interrogation!

Whatever assessment method is being used, it is important to have validity evidence to back it up. The validity of any workplace assessment, not just psychometrics, is the degree of relevance that the assessment has in forecasting effectiveness at work. A valid assessment must be able to measure how the individual is likely to perform in a given job.

Clearly, the higher the validity, the better. The evidence shows that using assessment methods with higher validity means higher-performing individuals are more likely to be selected. This is illustrated in the three graphs which follow; as the validity of the predictor measure (e.g. a personality questionnaire) increases, the relative proportion of high-performing individuals who will be selected also increases.

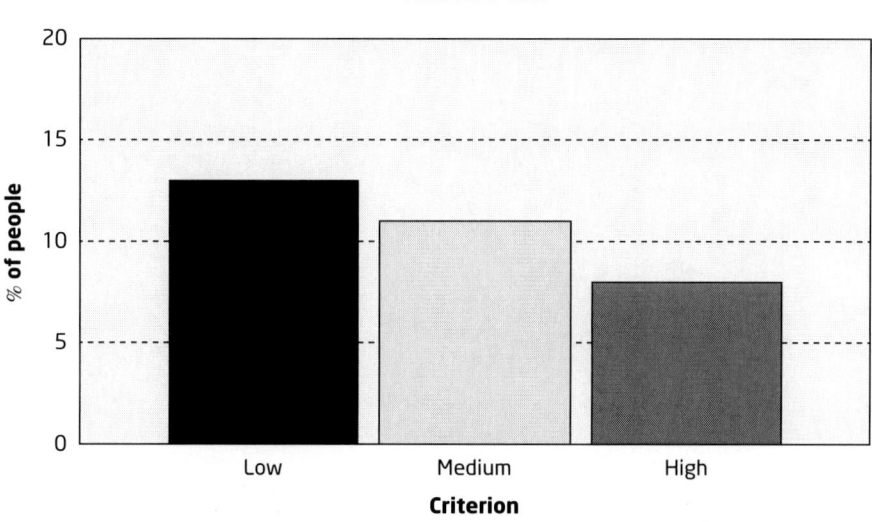

FIGURE 1.1 Expected proportions of low, medium and high performers selected on the basis of a predictor measure with low validity

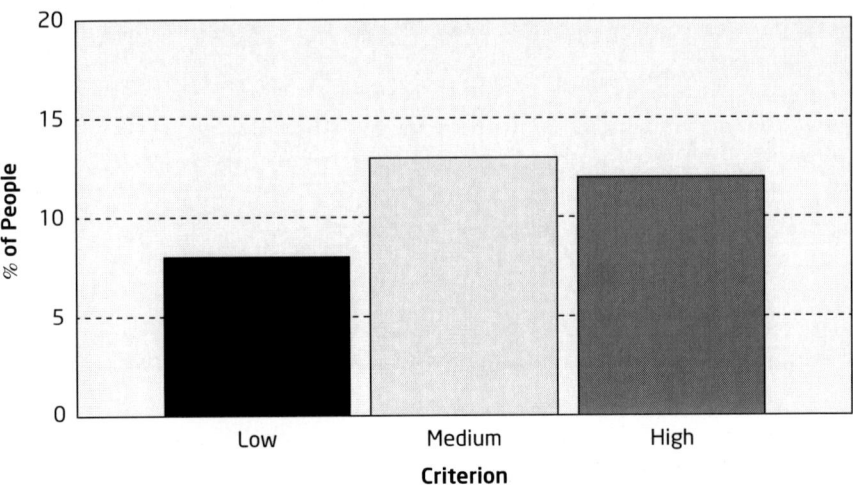

FIGURE 1.2 Expected proportions of low, medium and high performers selected on the basis of a predictor measure with medium validity

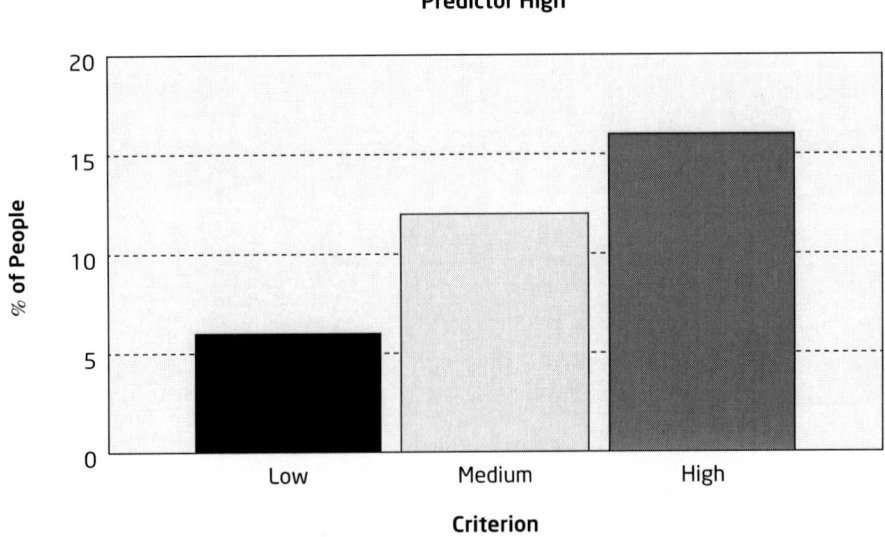

FIGURE 1.3 Expected proportions of low, medium and high performers selected on the basis of a predictor measure with high validity

Validity clearly matters. The costs of poor selection using invalid methods can include:

- Poor performance.
- Poor retention and staff turnover.
- Recruitment costs.
- Company failure.
- Reduced revenues.
- Lost training costs.
- Reduced morale.
- Lost opportunity costs.
- Personal misery.

In order to increase the validity of any assessment tool, there are a few principles that are worth following.

In Morgeson et al. (2007), Schmitt states:

> *If you are going to use personality measures make sure you know what the outcome is and direct your personality measure development toward that outcome, then you are also likely to be able to defend the use of that test if challenged.*

In other words, if you're going to measure workplace performance, produce a questionnaire which specifically targets this as your criterion. In developing the OPQ in 1984 with Lisa Cramp, Gill Nyfield, Bill Mabey and Roger Holdsworth (Saville et al., 1984), we used elementary job analysis, but mainly a deductive review of other questionnaires backed up with item analysis. We did this because there was little knowledge of the criterion space at the time. This is interesting because others still use Freudian, Jungian or even pathological traits when measuring in the work domain. We specifically avoided this.

Indeed, Morgeson et al. (2007) noted that there is poor item content in many work-based personality questionnaires. These include:

- Clinical items – intrusion into privacy.
- Ambiguous or embarrassing content.
- Use of bipolar items.
- Negations.
- Words like 'and', 'or' and 'always'.
- We discovered a distinct difference between 'what I enjoy' (motive) and 'what I am good at' (talent) – many items in the OPQ were mixed between these two concepts.

Taking all of these issues into consideration, progress has certainly been made in the psychometric assessment of personality and measurement of performance in the workplace. A number of studies (e.g. Schmitt et al., 1984; Barrick and Mount,

1991; Morgeson et al., 2007) have found that well-constructed, work-relevant personality questionnaires do have a role to play and can offer validity in the measurement of workplace performance.

Indeed, our own recent research has shown that a range of different assessments available on the market demonstrated value in forecasting likely workplace performance. It is particularly rewarding for me to be able to report that the questionnaires developed most recently by the team at Saville Consulting came out as the most valid amongst the competition and we will be publishing our results in full in the near future.

Notes

1 We discuss the history of intelligence testing in a separate chapter of this book.
2 Paul Mortimer would later go on to author *Woden's Warriors – Warfare, Beliefs, Arms and Armour in Northern Europe during the 6th–7th Centuries* (2011).

References

Allport, G. W. and Odbert, H. S. (1936). *Trait-Names: A Psycho-lexical Study*. Albany, NY: Psychological Review Company.
Bandura, A. (1977). *Social Learning Theory*. Englewood Cliffs, NJ: Prentice Hall.
Barrick, M. R. and Mount, M. K. (1991). The Big Five personality dimensions and job performance: A meta-analysis. *Personnel Psychology*, 44, 1–25.
Belbin, M. (1981). *Management Teams*. London, Heinemann.
Cattell, R. B. (1946). *The Description and Measurement of Personality*. New York: World Books.
Costa, P. T. and McCrae, R. R. (1985). *The NEO Personality Inventory Manual*. Odessa, FL: Psychological Assessment Resources.
Eysenck, H. J. and Eysenck, S. B. G. (1969). *Personality Structure and Measurement*. London: Routledge.
Freud, S. (1900). *The Interpretation of Dreams*. New York: Macmillan.
Hathaway, S. R. and McKinley, J. C. (1943). *Manual for the Minnesota Multiphasic Personality Inventory*. New York: Psychological Corporation.
Holland, J. L. (1973). Making vocational choices: A theory of vocational personalities and work environments. Englewood Cliffs, NJ: Prentice Hall.
Maslow, A. H. (1943). A theory of human motivation. *Psychological Review*, 50(4), 370–96.
Morgeson, F. P., Campion, M. A., Dipboye, R. L., Hollenbeck, J. R., Murphy, K. and Schmitt, N. (2007).
Reconsidering the use of personality tests in personnel selection contexts. *Personnel Psychology*, 60(3), 683–729.
Mortimer, P. (2011). *Woden's Warriors – Warfare, Beliefs, Arms and Armour in Northern Europe during the 6th–7th Centuries*. Cambridge: Anglo-Saxon Books.
Myers, I. B. (1980). *Gifts Differing: Understanding Personality Type*. Mountain View, CA: Davies-Black Publishing.
Norman, W. T. (1963). Personality measurement, faking, and detection: An assessment method for use in personnel selection. *Journal of Applied Psychology*, 47(4), 225–41.
Pavlov, I. P. (1927). *Conditioned Reflexes*. Oxford: Oxford University Press.
Rogers, C. (1959). A theory of therapy, personality and interpersonal relationships as developed in the client-centered framework. In S. Koch (ed.), *Psychology: A Study of a*

Science. Vol. 3: Formulations of the Person and the Social Context. New York: McGraw-Hill, pp. 184–256.

Saville, P. (1977). A critical analysis of the 16PF. PhD Dissertation. London: Brunel University.

Saville, P., Holdsworth, R., Nyfield, G., Cramp, L. and Mabey, W. (1984). *The Occupational Personality Questionnaire (OPQ).* London: SHL.

Schmitt, N., Gooding, R. Z., Noe, R. A. and Kirsch, M. (1984). Meta-analyses of validity studies. *Journal of Applied Psychology,* 70, 280–9.

Shakespeare, W. (1599). *The Tragedy of Julius Caesar.*

Sheldon, W. H. (1942). *The Varieties of Temperament.* New York: Harper & Brothers.

Skinner, B. F. (1938). *Behavior of Organisms.* New York: Appleton-Century-Crofts.

2

INTELLIGENCE TESTING

This chapter is based on a number of chapters from the user handbook which we wrote in 2010 to support our Analysis Aptitude Range of cognitive ability tests:

> Hopton, T., MacIver, R., Saville, P. and Kurz, R. (2010). *Analysis Aptitude Range Handbook*. Jersey: Saville Consulting Group.

This handbook is an important work because it pulls together in published form disparate areas, including the history of ability testing, the development of the Analysis Aptitude Range, and statistical and empirical evidence in order to support the fairest and most accurate possible use of these tests.

To provide an overview of the history, concepts and methods in intelligence testing, as well as the positioning of the Analysis Aptitude Range within this milieu, we have selected content from the following handbook chapters:

- Introduction to aptitude testing.
- Item types.
- Construction.
- Validity.

Excerpts from the *Analysis Aptitude Range Handbook*

From early on in recorded history, humans have been assessing each other. By the seventh century, the Chinese were formally testing civil servants using written tests of verbal ability and creativity. In the seventeenth century, Samuel Pepys devised sophisticated navigation tests for prospective lieutenants in the British Navy; it has been argued that these tests had a pivotal role to play in the success of the British fleet at that time, because her leaders were the brightest and best. Pepys was also tapping into the very useful area of job knowledge. He realised it simply wasn't enough for the lieutenants to be well-bred, confident and good at asserting themselves over others; they also needed to be good sailors themselves.

However, it was not until 1905 that modern psychology saw the first formally developed ability test. Alfred Binet and his physician pupil Théodore Simon were researching intellectual disability (then referred to as 'mental retardation') in French schoolchildren and produced a test of 30 items which assessed attention, memory and verbal skills. Following this research was the concept of 'mental age': the idea that intellectual ability increases with age throughout childhood.

The outbreak of World War I also saw the first use of intelligence tests in a work-related context. The Army Alpha and Army Beta tests came from an adaptation of Alfred Binet's test which Yerkes developed for groups of recruits in order to assess their suitability to deal with the mental requirements of serving in the US Army. The concept of IQ (Intelligence Quotient) soon followed, helping to compare people's intelligence across different groups. An average IQ is 100 and scores above 100 represent progressively higher levels of intelligence, while scores below 100 represent lower intelligence. Although IQ as a concept has been heavily criticised by a number of different people, IQ tests remain some of the most commonly used and well-known measures of intelligence.

The turn of the nineteenth century also saw the pioneering work of Charles Spearman, who noted that those who perform well on one test generally tend to do better than other people on similar tests. This is much like suggesting that a professional soccer player who plays as a striker is probably a much better defender or even goalkeeper than the average man or woman. Spearman proposed that there was a hierarchy to intelligence and the highest factor was 'g' or 'general intelligence'. This is a concept still used today and many of the modern ability tests are based on this important work by Spearman. Nevertheless, Louis Thurstone attacked 'g', claiming instead that there were seven separate primary mental abilities (verbal comprehension, word fluency, number facility, spatial visualisation, associative memory, perceptual speed and reasoning).

Although it may have seemed like a deadlock had been reached, it was Philip Vernon who, in the 1950s, reconciled the two views by suggesting that there was likely to be a hierarchy of specific skills through to broader abilities (e.g. educational and practical intelligence), with general intelligence right at the top of the pyramid. Another prominent name in this field of psychology is Raymond Cattell, who decided to cut the 'g' cake a little differently and in doing so helped to overturn the prevalent idea of the time that intelligence was purely inherited. Cattell distinguished between 'fluid intelligence' – that which is hypothesised to be genetically based, culture-free, declines with age and cannot be taught – and 'crystallised intelligence' – learned through life and built from knowledge and wisdom. A nice aspect of Cattell's theory is that there is something for everyone: young people have higher levels of fluid intelligence and older people have higher levels of crystallised intelligence.

The application of ability tests in work-relevant contexts is actually a relatively recent phenomenon. Until well into the latter half of the twentieth century, certainly in the UK, testing had been largely educational in nature. When Peter Saville started Saville and Holdsworth Limited, his team began to develop a range of tests designed for different users at different levels of a business. For example, they developed managerial tests of verbal, numerical and logical reasoning, as well as technical tests for people in engineering and practical roles which involved spatial and mechanical reasoning. This approach has been updated for the internet age in our current company, Saville Consulting, with a portfolio of over 30 different aptitude tests measuring a range of different abilities.

The Saville Consulting portfolio of aptitude tests provides content for the global and online age, featuring three principal ranges of tests: the Analysis Aptitude Range for higher-level assessment (e.g. professionals, managers and graduates); the Comprehension Aptitude Range for general-level use; and the Technical Aptitude Range for technical roles in production, construction, engineering and scientific jobs. Although these tests are very much designed for the twenty-first century and are built by leading experts in the field with extensive experience, including Dr Rainer Kurz, Rab MacIver, Peter Saville and Tom Hopton, they are founded on over 100 years of psychology research. For example, the Analysis and Comprehension Aptitude Ranges cover the ground of Vernon's Educational Intelligence, while the Technical Aptitude Range covers Practical Intelligence. The hierarchical modelling enabled the development of tests which combine different ability areas to measure Vernon's higher-order constructs.

Introducing the Analysis Aptitude Range

The Analysis Aptitude Range is a portfolio of modern and innovative assessments which are available online and in hard-copy (paper and pencil) formats. Online versions are available both for screening candidates unsupervised (Invited Access: IA) and, for greater security, for completion with a supervisor present (Supervised Access: SA). The different tests within the Analysis Aptitude Range measure verbal, numerical and diagrammatic analysis. All tests within the Analysis Aptitude Range are designed for high-level roles such as directors, managers, professionals, graduates and management trainees.

Swift Analysis Aptitude is a combined assessment which consists of three short sub-tests: Verbal, Numerical and Diagrammatic Analysis. The assessment can be completed in an IA format, or a parallel version can be undertaken in supervised conditions online (SA), or in hard-copy (HC) in 18 minutes.

Analysis Aptitudes (IA) is a range of three single tests of Verbal Analysis, Numerical Analysis or Diagrammatic Analysis, which are frequently used for online screening purposes. Verbal Analysis Aptitude, Numerical Analysis Aptitude or Diagrammatic Analysis Aptitude are also relatively quick to complete, with time limits of 24 minutes each.

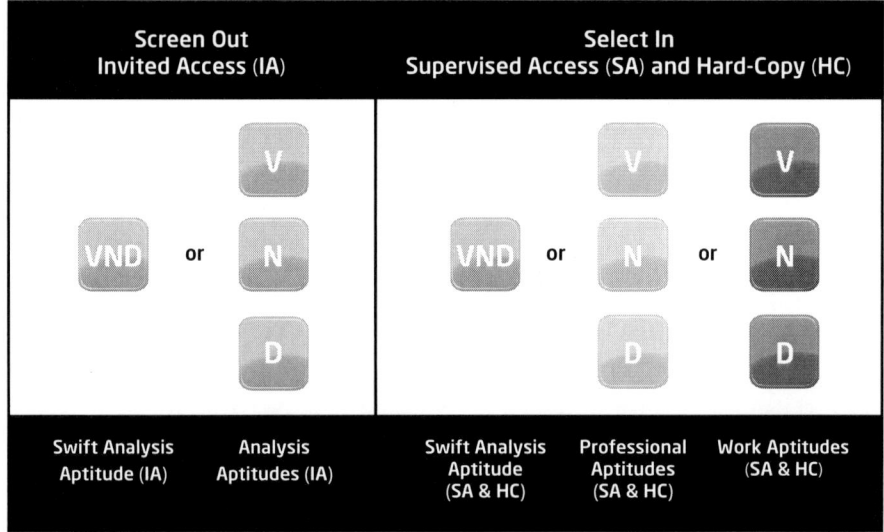

Screen Out Invited Access (IA)	Select In Supervised Access (SA) and Hard-Copy (HC)	
Swift Analysis Aptitude (IA) Analysis Aptitudes (IA)	Swift Analysis Aptitude (SA & HC) Professional Aptitudes (SA & HC)	Work Aptitudes (SA & HC)

V= Verbal Analysis   N = Numerical Analysis   D = Diagrammatic Analysis

FIGURE 2.1 Overview of the Analysis Aptitude Range

The Professional Aptitudes and Work Aptitudes parallel test series are available in supervised access online and hard-copy formats. The Professional Aptitudes series is designed for the highest-level managers, directors and professionals, and the parallel Work Aptitudes series targets graduates, trainees and technicians. Each single test within the Professional and Work Aptitudes series has a time limit of around 20 minutes.

The Analysis Aptitude Range has been researched and developed from first principles to provide a choice of assessments with impressive validity in predicting ability, performance and potential in high-level roles. It is scalable for use with specific individuals, right through to high-volume assessments. The range also benefits from being administered from a stable online environment and parallel versions of the tests exist for enhanced testing security in supervised conditions.

Rationale

The Saville Consulting Analysis Aptitude Range was designed specifically with a number of objectives in mind:

- To develop tests with modern, relevant content.
- To enhance feedback through valid and easily understood reports.
- To design tests which are internationally applicable and fair.
- To maximise the simplicity of the assessment process for test-users and test-takers.

- To provide flexibility for users of hard-copy and online formats.
- To create high-validity tools for selection.
- To create tests which differentiate performance and potential in high-level roles.
- To deliver tests from a highly reliable online environment.
- To have online versions suitable for online screening.
- To have supervised versions for secure administration.
- To provide tests suitable for volume screening.
- To increase the security of tests for online use.

Saville Consulting Wave® Performance Culture Framework

At the heart of all Saville Consulting assessments is the Wave Performance Culture Framework. This is an extensively researched model of the key characteristics which underpin success at work across different occupations. It is an important starting point for Saville Consulting's new product developments, because extensive validation evidence has demonstrated that its elements are important correlates of work performance. The Saville Consulting Wave Performance Culture Framework is made up of Behaviour, Ability and Global areas, as shown below.

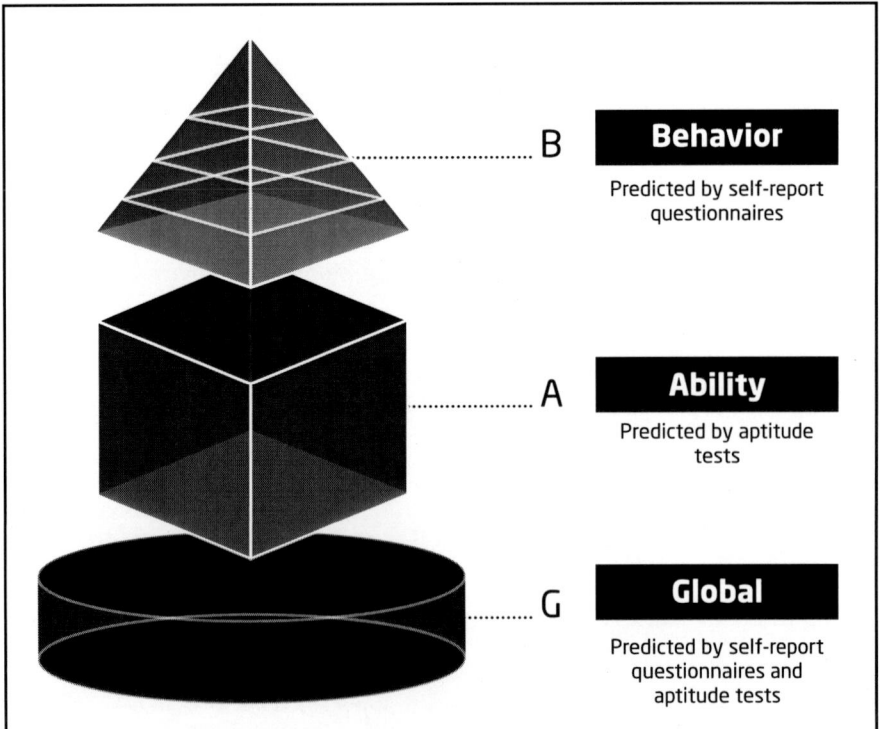

FIGURE 2.2 Overview of the structure of the Wave Performance Culture Framework

'Behavior' refers to behavioural styles and competencies at work. The Saville Consulting Wave Professional Styles and Focus Styles questionnaires were developed to indicate the respondent's self-reported potential to perform in these behavioural areas. These behavioural areas can also be directly assessed using the Saville Consulting Wave Performance 360 questionnaire.

'Ability' refers to an individual's capability to perform certain intellectual or cognitive tasks. Working with words, numbers, details, systems, designs or equipment are ability areas that can be assessed using Saville Consulting tools. These capabilities can be predicted using the Saville Consulting portfolio of aptitude assessments, of which the Analysis Aptitude Range forms one part.

'Global' describes the broad overall effectiveness characteristics of performance at work. The Saville Consulting Wave Performance Culture Framework includes a hierarchical model of Global work performance, which can be assessed using Saville Consulting assessment tools. This refers to a person's overall performance at work and differentiates key areas such as Applying Expertise, Accomplishing Objectives and Demonstrating Potential.

The Saville Consulting ability hierarchy

Saville Consulting's model of ability in the workplace is based on a hierarchy of abilities which may be required in the workplace in order for effective performance to be realised. These abilities are captured in the Saville Consulting aptitude assessments, including the Analysis Aptitude Range.

The cluster at the top of the hierarchy is related to overall ability at work. This can be thought of as aligned to Spearman's construct of 'g' – a general factor of intelligence. This overall factor, Reasoning at Work, is defined by Kurz (2000) as the sum of scores on tests across six aptitude areas (verbal, numerical, error checking, diagrammatic, spatial and mechanical reasoning). The overall factor, Reasoning

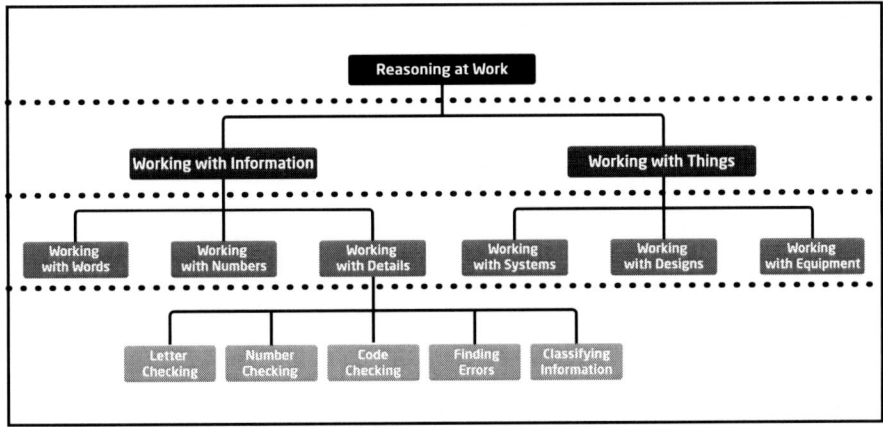

FIGURE 2.3   The Saville Consulting ability hierarchy

at Work, splits into two sections which are similar to Vernon's 'Academic' vs. 'Practical' factors of ability. The two sections are Working with Information and Working with Things. There are six dimensions at the next level in the hierarchy (Working with Words, Working with Numbers, Working with Details, Working with Systems, Working with Designs and Working with Equipment).

The six dimensions are assessed using Verbal, Numerical, Error Checking, Diagrammatic/Abstract, Spatial and Mechanical tests, respectively. The six areas are similar to both Thurstone's 'Primary Mental Abilities' and Guilford's 'Content' areas. To give a more precise definition of the content assessed in each of the dimensions and the Saville Consulting tests which assess them, each dimension is further broken down into five more detailed facets. For example, in Figure 2.3 we can see that the dimension Working with Details is split into five facets, namely Letter Checking, Number Checking, Code Checking, Finding Errors and Classifying Information. The 30 facets in the Saville Consulting ability hierarchy are the starting point of what is measured by the tests in the Saville Consulting aptitude assessment portfolio.

Test-taking information and item types

Saville Consulting's aptitude test reports provide information about how a candidate approached a test. This allows users to go beyond the total score information and to use additional data about the test completion process during feedback and the interpretation of test scores. The differentiation of item types is an important characteristic of the Analysis Aptitude Range. It allows the test-user to have a clearer, more accurate definition of what a given test is assessing. The availability of a range of item types provides reassurance that a test has been designed from first principles to broadly sample important characteristics of an individual's aptitudes. Having different item types also ensures that the tests can mitigate individual method effects which may result from the prevalence of just one item type, as is common in many aptitude tests.

Intelligence, ability and aptitude tests have traditionally measured just one aptitude area and it has often taken 30 minutes or more to achieve an accurate assessment of an area such as verbal reasoning. The Analysis Aptitude Range includes short tests for high-level roles. With tests having time limits ranging from 18 to 24 minutes, it is possible to measure distinct aptitude areas (verbal analysis, numerical analysis and diagrammatic analysis), as would be required in a number of high-level roles, in less time than the industry standard. Swift Analysis Aptitude's revolutionary approach is to create one overall score from a combined test of Verbal Analysis, Numerical Analysis and Diagrammatic Analysis Aptitude, which takes just 18 minutes to complete. This makes Swift Analysis Aptitude an effective and well-rounded volume screening tool which is particularly useful when it would be inappropriate to give candidates lengthy assessments at the start of a selection procedure.

Aptitude area scores

Swift Analysis Aptitude is designed to be a revolutionary measure, leading to one overall aptitude score based on a number of different ability areas. The combination of the three sub-tests (Verbal, Numerical and Diagrammatic) allows for a reliable, valid assessment of an individual's ability in just 18 minutes. As well as producing an overall score within the Swift Analysis Aptitude assessment, it's also possible to produce scores for each of the three sub-areas in this combined test (Verbal, Numerical and Diagrammatic sub-test scores).

Multiple item types

All Saville Consulting aptitude assessments are built around groups of questions which are defined as different item types. This format brings a number of advantages. From a psychometric point of view, having multiple item types allows the assessor to profile multiple aptitude areas and skills within an efficient assessment process. From the candidate's point of view, it provides variety and realism in the test completion, ensuring that the tests maximise the positive nature of the candidate experience and serve as a realistic and work-relevant task.

Item type sub-scores

In the Professional and Work Aptitudes assessments designed for supervised use (both online and hard-copy), a total score for each of the different item types can also be profiled, which helps provide more specific feedback about an individual's areas of strength and weakness. In high-stakes assessment where supervised testing is required, the item type sub-scores can help test-takers to better understand and learn from their test performance and equally can help test-users or administrators in the in-depth exploration of a respondent's strengths and weaknesses.

Test-taking information

Saville Consulting has recently developed a new approach to measuring the test-taker's completion pace, as well as other test-taking information, which is now being incorporated into the new reports for its suite of randomised tests.

Randomised (–R) tests

Many of the Saville Consulting aptitude assessments feature variable test content whereby statistically comparable tests from large banks of questions are constructed according to pre-determined rules. The advantage of using this banking methodology is that it improves the security of online tests, as it becomes much harder to learn the answers to a test if many alternative but comparable assessments can be presented to different candidates.

A brief introduction to test security and testlet banking

More and more tests are being delivered in unsupervised formats around the world. This increase in unsupervised test usage is accompanied by heightened security concerns. A small percentage of candidates may try to take advantage of the unsupervised nature of an assessment process, for example, by trying to get access to the correct answers before they sit the test. The most direct way to address such security concerns is to assess candidates in supervised environments where their identity and test completion can be monitored. Saville Consulting would recommend that candidates who make it to the final stage of a high-stakes assessment process involving aptitude tests are retested under supervised conditions prior to appointment.

Yet, as it may not always be possible or desirable to test all candidates under supervised conditions (for example, where the number of applicants is very high), one way to reduce the impact of content being compromised in an unsupervised test is to present different questions in different orders to different candidates. When lots of variants of a test can be produced, it becomes extremely unlikely that different candidates will experience exactly the same test. This makes it harder for candidates to familiarise themselves in advance with the actual test content that they are going to experience. Content randomisation is used to increase the security of test content delivered under unsupervised conditions. Item Response Theory (IRT) is one method used to ensure that the different test variants produced are statistically comparable (and that these variants are therefore fair and accurate assessments).

What does IRT do?

IRT takes into account a number of different factors which help provide an estimate of an individual's performance. For example, it takes into account the difficulty of each question (item) to ensure that different candidates experience different tests of comparable difficulty. Rather than defining test performance in terms of the overall number of correct answers given in a test (as is done in 'traditional' testing), IRT is more sophisticated and focuses on the level of each individual item in a test. It provides various types of statistical information about how much each item is contributing to overall test performance (e.g. an estimation of each item's difficulty).

Why do we use IRT?

The main advantage of this is that IRT becomes a suitable means of delivering, scoring and comparing many different tests drawn from an overall bank of content. By applying IRT rules to an item bank, we ensure that we deliver statistically comparable versions of a test, even though the actual test content itself can vary. IRT-driven item banks ensure that the score each candidate receives from the particular test they completed can then be fairly compared against the scores of other candidates on different tests. Another major advantage of IRT is that we can add new questions and retire old questions without having to update our norm groups each time.

Does banking mean that supervised tests are no longer needed?

Although banking can help with a number of issues, such as people learning the answers or being exposed to questions they have seen before, it does nothing to guarantee candidate identity. Candidate identity deception cannot be prevented by any level of sophistication in the test itself. Saville Consulting's message remains that while content randomisation is an important means to address a number of test security issues, supervised follow-up testing prior to appointment remains a reliable method for ensuring that able candidates are recruited.

Is it possible to get information on the number of questions attempted/correct for the randomised (–R) tests?

Saville Consulting's current policy is not to show these scores because they can be misunderstood in IRT-scored tests. Because IRT takes into account the difficulty of each individual test item (among other item properties), a person who correctly answered a smaller number of difficult items may actually have a higher ability than a person who correctly answered a greater number of easier items, for example. The classic 'total number of questions correct' figure that is often taken as a candidate's ability level can therefore be misleading. 'Number correct' or 'number attempted' scores are actually less sophisticated because they work on the assumption that all items contribute equally to determining a person's overall ability, which is not really true.

Randomised (–R) tests are currently available for unsupervised use (IA) across the Analysis Aptitude Range, as outlined below:

- Swift Analysis Aptitude–R (IA).
- Swift Analysis Verbal and Numerical Aptitude–R (IA).
- Verbal Analysis Aptitude–R (IA).
- Numerical Analysis Aptitude–R (IA).
- Diagrammatic Analysis Aptitude–R (IA).

Randomised (–R) versions also exist for the following two tests which are closely related to the Analysis Aptitude Range:

- Swift Executive Aptitude–R (IA).
- Abstract Reasoning Aptitude–R (IA).

This section outlines the new information that is now included in the latest randomised test reports.

Aptitude and Pace information

With online tests, we can go beyond simply counting the number of questions a candidate attempted in the time available (the Speed score) and can use our online platform to measure the actual time that they spent on each question, in milliseconds. This is particularly useful when comparing how quickly candidates have worked when they have seen different questions from each other (e.g. as in the online –R tests).

The new Pace score is based on the candidate's response time for the questions they completed compared to the average response time for the same questions. It can be defined as how quickly a candidate has responded compared to the average for the same questions. All randomised aptitude tests contain aptitude and Pace scores for each of the areas in the test.

For the multiple-component tests (Swift Analysis Aptitude–R and Swift Analysis Verbal and Numerical–R), the Pace score compares time usage per question across each of the sub-tests to the average time usage on the same questions. The aptitude score is the total score across each of the sub-tests. For the single-component tests (Verbal Analysis Aptitude–R, Numerical Analysis Aptitude–R, Diagrammatic Analysis Aptitude–R), the Pace score compares time usage per question across the whole test to the average time used on the same questions.

The aptitude score is the total score across the whole test. The aptitude and Pace scores are compared in a graph, using a 1–10 sten scale. Pace is shown from 'slow' at the bottom of the graph to 'fast' at the top. Aptitude runs from 'low' on the left of the graph to 'high' on the right. Individuals working at a high pace have spent less time on the questions that they saw than the average for the same questions; individuals working at a low Pace have spent more time on the questions that they saw than the average for the same questions.

1. Summary of the key benefits of the Pace score

- Simple to calculate and makes use of the measurement of response times in milliseconds through the online Oasys system.
- Simple to explain to test-users.
- Pace can be displayed graphically alongside aptitude scores.
- Enhanced sophistication of measurement:

  - the Pace score is tailored to the specific questions seen by a candidate;
  - Pace comparisons can be made between candidates who saw different questions;
  - the Pace score can differentiate between candidates who complete the test within the time limit (people with maximum Speed – i.e. who attempt all the questions – may vary in their actual time usage);
  - the Pace score can be profiled in depth at the sub-score level (e.g. Swift tests).

2. Online test access summary

Some new reports also contain supplementary information about the candidate's individual completion experience. This information is intended for use by assessors to aid their interpretation of candidate scores:

- Initial Access – the date and time that the candidate first accessed the test.
- Responses Saved – the date and time when the candidate's responses were saved following test completion.
- Administrator Resets – the number of administrator resets required during the completion of the test. This information can be useful to report to users because an individual who has had several resets may start to accrue more experience of the test format and this familiarity could give them an advantage when completing the test. Having this information flagged up may also indicate if there were any potential technical problems or other issues which could have impacted on the performance of the test-taker.
- Candidate Aborts – the number of times a candidate left the test during its completion. Like Administrator Resets, this information can be useful to report to users because an individual who has aborted several times may start to accrue more experience of the test format and this familiarity could give them an advantage when completing the test. Having this information flagged up may also indicate if there were any potential technical problems or other issues which could have impacted on the test-taker's performance.
- Time Adjustment – where extra time has been manually added for the candidate, or the time limit has been turned off, this is shown as a percentage time increase, e.g. +10%. It is possible to adjust the time limits on the online Saville Consulting aptitude assessments. Reasonable adjustments may be made for candidates with special requirements (e.g. dyslexic candidates may receive some extra time at the recommendation of a suitably qualified medical professional). If a time adjustment has been made, the percentage change in time provided to the test-taker is displayed so that the user of the report is aware of this. This information can be useful when comparing candidates who may have had more or less time than others in the same assessment process.

It is important to note that if a time adjustment has been made, Pace information will not be displayed in the feedback report. This is to avoid confusion in interpreting the pace of candidates who had a different time available to them compared to others.

Non-randomised (fixed-form) tests

The suite of Supervised Access tests in the Analysis Aptitude Range, both the online supervised and hard-copy versions (SA and HC), will continue to make use of the original feedback report with test-taking style information instead of Pace information. This is to maintain consistency/comparability with the hard-copy format, which does not permit the online calculation of Pace information:

- Accuracy – concerns the proportion of answers that were correct.
- Speed – concerns the number of questions answered.

These scores are based on the work of one of the Analysis Aptitude Range's lead authors, Rainer Kurz (see Kurz, 2005). A Caution score is also profiled on these tests, which is computed as the difference between the individual's accuracy and speed scores. The following tests in the Analysis Aptitude Range use the SA and HC compatible reports:

- Swift Analysis Aptitude[1] (SA and HC).
- Professional Verbal Analysis (SA and HC).
- Professional Numerical Analysis (SA and HC).
- Professional Diagrammatic (SA and HC).
- Work Verbal Analysis (SA and HC).
- Work Numerical Analysis (SA and HC).
- Work Diagrammatic (SA and HC).

Analysis Aptitude Range development goals

The starting point for the development of any assessment must be a clear under-standing of the criterion (outcome) it is designed to measure. An apparently elegant, sophisticated or plausible theory is of little use if it has no impact on real-world behaviours. For example, with aptitude assessments it is important to be clear on exactly which outcomes an assessment is designed to predict.

Work-relevant assessments are usually designed to measure overall work effec-tiveness through general areas such as applying specialist expertise, accomplishing objectives and demonstrating potential, or specific individual abilities (e.g. effec-tiveness at working with words).

The primary assessment goal of all the Saville Consulting aptitude assessments is to accurately forecast people's performance at work. In the Saville Consulting Aptitude Assessment Portfolio, this is achieved by maximising the criterion-related validity of the tests through the accurate measurement of key characteristics which research has shown underpin performance at work. In addition to this goal of hav-ing strong validity, the Saville Consulting aptitude assessments were also designed to be as fair as possible in their application and to be internationally applicable. Fairness includes providing advice on taking tests which will not disadvantage individual test-takers.

Security of the assessment process must also be a key aspect of test development. Saville Consulting's portfolio features aptitude tests designed for unsupervised online use (LA) and others designed for supervised use online (SA) or supervised use offline (HC). Testing is increasingly done online in unsupervised conditions and so the invited access tests are designed for screening, and feature content randomisation to increase the security of test content.

Saville Consulting's aptitude assessments are designed to combine maximum breadth of work-relevant content with shorter administration times than the industry standard. This helps make these tests particularly powerful, as they deliver high levels of validity in a short amount of time. In the achievement of these goals, the Saville Consulting aptitude assessments have been designed to provide measurable value and return on investment to organisations by virtue of the improved workforce productivity and performance which comes from using these assessments to select the best performers for any given job.

Saville Consulting believes that attaining the highest possible levels of assessment validity should be the main developmental focus for test publishers. This is also a priority for the people who use such tests, both assessors and assessees alike. Tests with higher validity are more accurate and can lead to fairer decisions being made about the performance of respondents who have completed them.

Every assessment should also be easy to use, accessible to participants, attractive and applicable to today's modern workplace. The Saville Consulting assessments are designed to ensure that their validity is easily accessible and understood by the end user in terms of administration, scoring and reporting. This is achieved by providing the user with clear, well-researched links between the aptitude assessments and measures of effectiveness in the workplace. Validation is fundamental to the development of the Analysis Aptitude Range and in the other Saville Consulting aptitude assessments. Focusing on maximising an assessment's criterion-related validity while it is still in the design and development phase is arguably the most effective way to overcome any obstacle. In the context of the workplace, test designers should strive to measure aptitudes which have been empirically demonstrated to lead to effective performance. That is, assessments of workplace performance should be able to tell us how effective someone is in those behaviours which have been demonstrated to matter for performance.

Timeline of the development process

In October 2004, Saville Consulting began development of the Swift Analysis Aptitude assessment and the Professional and Work Aptitudes. In November 2005, the Professional Aptitudes and Work Aptitudes series were launched as Verbal, Numerical and Diagrammatic Analysis tests in HC format. In February 2006, the Swift Analysis Aptitude combined test followed in HC format, and in May 2006, its Invited Access online counterpart was available. A Supervised Access version of the HC Swift Analysis Aptitude test content was launched in October 2006. By October 2007, international versions of the Swift Analysis Aptitude instrument were available in 12 languages. In March 2009, SA online versions of Professional Aptitudes became available, followed by Work Aptitudes in 2010.

As Saville Consulting moved from fixed versions of tests to creating individual tests which are drawn from item banks according to a series of rules, IRT was introduced. This is an alternative way of analysing and scoring test data compared to classical methods and makes use of new technological advances. It works by drawing individual sub-tests from large item banks according to a series of randomisation rules. This means that the content of a test is not fixed and can be randomised according to desired criteria. The single Analysis Aptitude Invited Access tests were launched in March 2010 in an online invited access format. Swift Analysis Verbal & Numerical–R was developed, trialled and put live in 2011.

Establishing desired test features and characteristics

During the development of the Analysis Aptitude assessments, the following features and characteristics were focused on:

- Security for Online Use – the provision of online and separate supervised versions of tests, both in single and combination formats, helps to ensure that online administrations can be followed up by supervised secure use prior to appointment. This provides a mechanism for safeguarding against the selection of individuals who cheat by getting others to take tests for them online.
- Flexible Administration Mode – in practice, people who use online administrations may also want the option of having a paper-and-pencil version, both for individual and bulk volume supervised administrations, which does not require them to provide a computer for each test-taker.
- High Face Validity, User-Friendliness and High Quality Design – users of tests should be impressed by the quality of test materials, supporting documentation and feedback reports as the standard of these materials can influence their perception of the organisation using the tests. For this same reason, test items should also appear relevant to workers. The Saville Consulting Analysis Aptitude assessments were designed to be modern, user-friendly and of the highest quality for users.
- Validity – the item types, quality and content of the tests were designed to focus on those characteristics which differentiate success in roles of the relevant level.
- Fairness – care was taken to include only materials suitable for test-users regardless of their culture, country of origin, age, gender, ethnicity, sexual orientation or religious belief. This includes avoiding content which might favour one test-taker over another (e.g. colloquialisms).
- Assessment of Aptitudes – the Analysis Aptitude tests were designed to assess an individual's aptitudes for a range of high-level roles using only knowledge and methods that candidates at this level would be expected to know (e.g. the numerical questions are based on multiplication and addition rather than logarithmic functions). The assessments therefore measure ability in specific areas relevant to the role and are not designed to assess general knowledge.

- Reliability – various methods can be employed to assess reliability. The alternate form and test-retest methods are considered the most appropriate for establishing the reliability of Saville Consulting assessments, and where it is not possible to use these methods, internal consistency measures are used.

- Appropriate Difficulty Level – tests were, and are, designed so that the majority of individuals could attempt all or most of the questions, with the average number of correct answers tending to be around half or more of the items correct. This helps ensure that the test can differentiate effectively between the best and worst candidates at the intended level of difficulty. If the average candidate answers about half of the questions correctly, this means that the test will have a good distribution of scores and suggests that it was rigorous but not overly difficult. In addition, respondents are likely to feel positively about a test which is neither too difficult nor too easy.

- Mixed Item Types – tests are and were designed to ensure that different content areas are sampled effectively, giving appropriate breadth of measurement. The items are written to sample different aspects of an individual's aptitudes; this is achieved using different item sub-types within the test. The presence of different item sub-types also helps to mitigate against method effects which often arise as a result of overreliance on, or exclusive use of, one particular item format (e.g. restriction to 'True/False/Cannot Say' questions).

- Shorter Assessments – the Analysis Aptitude Range was designed to consist of valid single tests which are shorter than the industry standard and which can be combined to create even shorter combination tests (e.g. Swift Analysis Aptitude). This makes for a more efficient assessment process and more effective use of candidate time.

- Power and Speed – tests were based on specific groups of items to allow for online versions which would have individually timed testlets, typically consisting of four items. The time allowed was calibrated to ensure that the majority of candidates could complete the test and that the main differentiating factor for candidates was their accuracy in answering the questions rather than their cognitive processing speed.

Generation of item type templates

One of the key aims of the Analysis Aptitude assessments was to develop different item types. The purpose of this was to broaden the range of aptitudes measured, to increase the variety for the candidates and to provide richer information for feedback. Example passages were written based on different item types as a starting point for reviewers to write questions. Numerous existing high-level tests were reviewed to evaluate the strengths and weaknesses of what was available at the time. To create an effective, well-balanced test without specific method effects, different item types were created. These templates formed the basis of item writing.

Item writing

Inspiration for the test content was taken from an array of materials used by professionals on a daily basis. Modern, relevant graphics were created to accompany the questions; these included graphics based on broadsheet newspapers, emails, company presentations and documentation, industry-specific magazines, press releases and web pages. The design of the tests was also very important for ensuring their face validity. The development goals discussed earlier drove the test development process. Initially, several different item writers produced content for the item trial versions of each of the tests. Item writers were given guidelines by three highly experienced psychometricians on how to produce different types of items.

Item writing of the Professional Aptitudes tests began in October 2004 and the Work Aptitudes tests followed in January 2005. The Swift Analysis Aptitude assessment was collated as a sub-set of items from the Professional and Work Aptitudes materials. Different but comparable items were created to ensure that the Swift Analysis Aptitude combined assessment could serve as a suitable alternative to the longer Professional and Work Aptitudes single tests. Item writing for the Swift Analysis Aptitude and single Analysis Aptitude tests which are based on IRT began in April 2008, with the aim of creating parallel versions of the existing tests. Swift Analysis Verbal and Numerical Aptitude–R, which is also based on IRT, was created in 2011.

Item review and selection

An independent team of experts reviewed the items for effectiveness. The review concentrated on meeting the requirements of the desired test characteristics and, in addition, focused on:

- Motivation – ensuring that each item was a relevant question.
- Closed Format – avoiding ambiguity in the keyed answer (item writers were only supplied with the key after the initial item–review phase).
- Suitability of Content – ensuring that the content was neither esoteric nor offensive to anyone.
- Difficulty Level – ensuring that the content was neither too difficult nor too easy and that there was a gradation of difficulty levels, both within blocks of questions (testlets) and throughout the test as a whole.
- Efficiency – ensuring that the questions were simple in format and did not require an extensive number of calculations or take too much time to complete. Items which fulfilled these criteria were selected for item trialling.

Trialling

Swift Analysis Aptitude, Professional and Work Aptitudes

From December 2004 to January 2005, a mix of 200 graduates and professionals completed the first versions of the Professional and Work Aptitudes assessments.

During these sessions, participants were instructed to insert timing marks at certain intervals to indicate what point in the test they had reached within certain time limits. This was done so that the effect of varying time limits could be analysed. After this initial trial, item content was revised and more specific Professional Aptitudes item trials took place in March and April 2005.

A 108-item version of Professional Verbal Analysis was piloted on 35 volunteers with a time limit of 60 minutes. Subsequently the test was shortened to 82 questions and 153 candidates completed this version, again with a time limit of 60 minutes.

A 60-item version of Professional Numerical Analysis was piloted on 16 volunteers with a time limit of 60 minutes. Following minor revisions, a version featuring six items for each of 10 testlets was trialled on 138 volunteers. Candidates also had 60 minutes to complete the test.

An early 32-item version of Professional Diagrammatic Analysis was entered into the item trial and was completed by 158 participants. Candidates had 30 minutes to complete the test. This test version required candidates to infer all rules from a complex diagram where various paths were marked by lines and arrows of differing colours.

The item trial version of Work Verbal Analysis consisted of 65 questions (nine testlets with seven or eight questions) to be completed in 40 minutes. A total of 95 participants completed this item trial alongside Professional Verbal Analysis.

The item trial version of Work Numerical Analysis consisted of 54 questions (nine testlets with six questions) to be completed in 40 minutes and again 95 participants completed this item trial along with the Professional Numerical Analysis assessment.

The item trial version of Work Diagrammatic Analysis consisted of 28 questions (seven testlets with four questions) developed largely as parallel variations of those in Professional Diagrammatic Analysis. The cloned items were piloted with a small group of 32 participants who completed these alongside Professional Diagrammatic Analysis.

The original fixed-form Swift Analysis Aptitude combined assessments were created as sub-sets of the trial data from the longer Professional and Work Aptitudes single tests. The content in the original fixed-form version of Swift Analysis Aptitude (IA) was purposefully not included in any of the SA or HC assessments going forward. Those items trialled with the appropriate characteristics for a shorter, combined test were selected and integrated into the Swift Analysis Aptitude tests.

This trialling process helps to ensure that both the combined and single tests within the Analysis Aptitude Range are measuring the same areas of aptitude.

Swift Analysis Aptitude–R, Verbal Analysis Aptitude–R, Numerical Analysis Aptitude–R, Diagrammatic Analysis Aptitude–R

The Analysis Aptitude–R tests were trialled in July 2009 by 1,992 participants. They completed tests with eight blocks (testlets) of five items, making a total of

40 items. The testlets were assigned a time limit of 3 minutes 30 seconds in order to give triallists enough time to complete the questions. In order to undergo item analysis, the sample of 552 individuals who completed the Analysis Aptitude single tests was combined with Swift Analysis Aptitude data which was collected from 3,289 individuals to give a total sample of 3,841. From these initial data, item banks of content could be assembled to produce the –R tests.

Data analysis

Swift Analysis Aptitude, Professional and Work Aptitudes

The data obtained during the 2005 trialling was analysed based on item partials, competency self-assessment, educational criteria validation data (exam scores) and participant feedback. The best items and content were then selected for the standardisation versions. Content representative of senior level roles (Level 5 in the UK National Vocational Qualifications (NVQs)) was allocated to Professional Aptitudes, while more generic content was allocated to Work Aptitudes aimed at intermediate (NVQ 3) and higher-level roles (NVQ 4).

At this point, all content was reviewed internationally to help ensure that it was understood around the world and that the style of test was internationally acceptable. The 20-minute timing data suggested that this time limit should produce good score distributions and reliabilities for single tests of 28–32 items. Two particularly discriminating testlets were placed third and fifth position with a view to becoming 'link testlets' which would feature across the different HC and SA test versions.

The Swift Analysis Aptitude combined assessments were created as sub-sets of the data from the longer Professional and Work Aptitudes single tests. Those items trialled as part of the Professional and Work Aptitudes assessments with the appropriate characteristics for a shorter, combined test were selected and integrated into the Swift Analysis Aptitude tests.

The trialling process through the Professional and Work Aptitudes helps to ensure that both the combined and single tests within the Analysis Aptitude Range are measuring the same areas of aptitude.

Swift Analysis Aptitude–R, Verbal Analysis Aptitude–R, Numerical Analysis Aptitude–R, Diagrammatic Analysis Aptitude–R

In 2009, Swift Analysis Aptitude–R was developed with an item bank using IRT. This bank of content also formed the basis of the single Analysis Aptitude–R tests of verbal, numerical and diagrammatic aptitudes. The test data were initially analysed using classical methods to identify poor items or potential problems with the answer key. Items which had low partials or for which high scorers were frequently giving incorrect responses were excluded from further analyses. For those tests based on IRT principles, a factor analysis was carried out in order to check whether IRT was appropriate for the multi-item type design of the tests. The data were then further analysed to identify which IRT model was the most appropriate.

Standardisation and development of norms

Professional and Work Aptitudes

Standardisation trials for the Professional Aptitudes test took place between February and April 2005, and for the Work Aptitudes test between May and July 2005. The standardisation version of Professional Verbal Analysis was completed by 354 participants. The standardisation version of Professional Numerical Analysis was completed by 363 participants. The standardisation version of Professional Diagrammatic Analysis was completed by 359 participants. The initial standardisation versions featured 40 items and were completed by a group of 83 participants. The final version with 28 questions was completed by 109 participants.

Each standardisation version test in Work Aptitudes was designed as a 'Parallel Form' of its Professional Aptitudes counterpart with 28 questions and a time limit of 20 minutes. A total of 339 participants completed the standardisation version of all three Work Aptitudes single tests.

For Professional and Work Aptitudes, participants had to complete all three tests in the series (Verbal, Numerical and Diagrammatic) for inclusion in a norm group. For the Work Aptitudes Standardization Norm 339 individuals were included and for the Professional Aptitudes Standardization Norm 300 were included. 'Multicultural Professionals and Graduates' Professional (N = 281) and Work (N = 139) Aptitudes norms were also created, based on individuals with limited English language proficiency.

The original Swift Analysis Aptitude online Invited Access version was standardised in April 2006 on 275 participants from the UK. This version of the test consisted of a total of 24 items. The initial norm group was created through combining Professional Aptitudes and Work Aptitudes standardisation groups with the subsequent scoring of Swift Analysis Aptitude items. This version was launched in February 2006 and was superseded by usage-based norms from 2008 onwards.

Swift Analysis Aptitude–R, Verbal Analysis Aptitude–R, Numerical Analysis Aptitude–R, Diagrammatic Analysis Aptitude–R

For the single and Swift Analysis Aptitude assessments designed using IRT in 2009 (the –R tests), testlets were created to be of similar average times and to increase in difficulty through the test. The reporting of scores for IRT-based tests gives a more sophisticated estimate of ability than a simple count of the total number of items correct. The IRT test norms created in 2009 were calibrated versions of the norms used for the original version of the Swift Analysis Aptitude combined assessment. This is possible because the Swift Analysis Aptitude test and estimations of respondent abilities were also scaled in 2009 using IRT methods. Any item-level set of respondent data can be calibrated using these methods. Additional –R test norms have been created since this original standardisation, which are based on live usage.

Swift Analysis Verbal & Numerical–R

Swift Analysis Verbal & Numerical–R was developed in the summer of 2010, drawing items from the Swift Analysis Aptitude–R, Verbal Analysis–R and Numerical Analysis–R item banks.

Supporting materials

Hard-copy materials

Question booklets

All booklets were designed to be reusable and include instructions printed inside for the candidate to follow while they are read aloud by the administrator.

Administration instructions

The instructions are uniform across the Verbal, Numerical and Diagrammatic test formats. Each example answer is revealed, together with a rationale for the answer (which helps both test administrators and candidates to better understand the examples).

Answer sheets

Integrated answer sheets were designed with a report on the back, so that there is a carbonated scoring key and profile chart within a sealed unit. This allows the test administrator to score up the responses and plot the output reports on the profile chart. This can be detached from the answer sheet and given to the test-taker or test-user as required. The profile chart features pre-printed T-scores, sten scores and text verbalisers aligned to percentile scores. This allows the user to easily compare the respondent's scores to the comparison group.

Technical documentation

This latest version of the *Handbook* and the supporting Analysis Aptitude Range–R Technical Summary now supersede all previous technical documentation.

Online assessment materials

The online environment

The online assessment tools originally used Adobe Flash Player as the delivery mechanism to ensure accurate timing and saving of responses in the case of internet connection failure. The Saville Consulting Oasys platform determines whether the software and hardware of the candidate's computer meet the minimum specification requirements for the presentation of the test, and lets candidates know if there is anything which will prevent them from accessing the assessment. If the internet connection is interrupted, the Flash Player saves a copy of the responses inputted up until that point in time.

In 2014, the latest HTML5 technology became the preferred delivery mechanism for the Saville Consulting aptitude tests. HTML5 offers comparable functionality to Adobe Flash Player, plus some additional technical benefits. Adobe Flash Player is still supported by the Oasys platform for individuals running existing projects before HTML5 was introduced.

Based on extensive experience with MS-DOS, Windows and web-based online assessments, the interface of the online Analysis Aptitude tests was designed to be intuitive and easy to use. Candidates use large arrow buttons to move between pages and select radio buttons to indicate their answer. The design aims for simplicity and consistency of layout across the different tests within the range.

Online instructions

The instruction sequence is comprehensive and designed for unsupervised use. Example questions are timed as in the actual tests and can be completed as often as the candidate requires. Automated example feedback confirms correct answers with a short rationale, gives hints for incorrect answers or indicates that the candidate did not answer the question before running out of time. Throughout the first instructions and examples sequence, an 'abort' button is available to allow candidates to exit and re-access the test again later.

Once a candidate has started the first testlet, they are obliged to complete the whole test. Any invalid exit (for example, by closing the browser window) blocks access to the test. In such a case, the candidate has to contact the project administrator for the test to be reset.

Practice tests and preparation guides

Hard-copy preparation guides are available for offline assessment preparation. One preparation guide can be used for each type of test in the Analysis Aptitude Range, regardless of whether it is in an online or hard-copy test format. The Verbal Analysis preparation guide can thus be used for all Verbal Analysis components, the Numerical Analysis preparation guide for all Numerical Analysis components, and the Diagrammatic Analysis preparation guide for all tests with Diagrammatic Analysis components within the Analysis Aptitude Range. Preparation guides were developed from content used in item trials.

The examples are designed to make the candidate familiar with the format of the test. The questions tend to be representative of the easier questions at the beginning of a test, as the inclusion of difficult items may increase test-taking anxiety. The first page of each preparation guide provides a rationale for the use of the given test, as well as example questions, with the back page providing correct answers, advice on how to prepare for testing and tips for improving abilities.

Online practice tests have also been developed in order to give candidates a chance to become familiar with the style of test and types of questions they will be presented with when completing a Saville Consulting aptitude test online. Candidates using the online practice test facility will see the same examples that are used in the hard-copy preparation guides and will be instructed to try to complete the questions in the time they would have available in the testing situation. Once the practice test has been completed, feedback is provided in response to the individual's answers.

Validity

In order to allow us to make better decisions about people based on assessments they have completed, it is essential that the assessments can provide evidence of their validity. First is an introduction to, and orientation in, the concept of validity. This introduction helps explain why the Analysis Aptitude assessments are different from traditional aptitude assessments in certain respects. While validity itself can be thought of as a unitary concept, this section will cover two aspects of validity with regard to the Analysis Aptitude Range: criterion-related validity and construct validity.

What is validity?

How do we know that a test or an assessment works and actually does what it claims to do? How do we know if the inferences and decisions made using one assessment are any better than another? How can we know which assessment tools are most accurate and will maximise the amount of benefit derived from the information provided? Which tool is the best investment for an organisation? These and other related questions are fundamental to the development and continuous improvement of assessment in the workplace. These questions directly relate to the validity of an assessment. All Saville Consulting aptitude assessments are designed to maximise their validity in forecasting effectiveness at work, in terms of both overall performance and in relation to specific workplace competencies.

The validity of an assessment is its most important property. For an assessment developed for use in the workplace, validity is essentially concerned with how well the assessment actually relates to, or predicts, the relevant aspects of work performance. Even if an assessment can accurately measure an obscure psychological theory, this is of little importance if the assessment is unrelated to performance at work. Assessments, such as aptitude tests, used to make selection and performance decisions in the workplace must forecast the important aspects of workplace performance. The interpretation of scores on an assessment, as well as the resulting inferences and decisions, should be valid. In the words of the *Standards for Educational and Psychological Testing* (1999), of the American Psychological Association:

Validity is a unitary concept. It is the degree to which all the accumulated evidence supports the intended interpretation of the test scores for the proposed purpose.

This section considers two different forms of accumulated evidence: criterion-related validity and construct validity.

Criterion-related validity is often seen as one of the most important properties of an assessment. For our application, it is the relationship between a score on an assessment and the relevant measure of performance at work. The criterion-related validity shows an assessment's appropriateness for the intended application. It is typically assessed by having independent raters judge the performance of the test-taker at work and then evaluating the strength of the relationship between these judgements and scores on the test. Where independent performance ratings are provided at the same time as the test is completed, concurrent validity is being assessed. Measurement of the relationship between an assessment score and a later measure of job performance assesses predictive validity.

Construct validity is the extent to which an assessment measures a hypothetical construct or area of human performance. The scores from an assessment with good construct validity would be expected to behave as if the underlying construct was directly being measured. In essence, an assessment needs to provide a good reflection of the construct it is measuring. Where constructs are well-defined and used, such as in an aptitude assessment, a common and useful method for measuring construct validity is by comparison with other assessments which aim to measure the same or similar constructs. Correlations between different assessments are presented to support the construct validity of the Analysis Aptitude assessments.

Construct validity focuses on convergent and discriminant evidence, looking for instances where relationships which are expected to occur are present (convergent evidence) and instances where relationships which are not expected to occur are absent (discriminant evidence). By pre-hypothesising where we would expect to see relationships between two or more scales and where we would not, we can build up an idea about the construct validity of the assessment in question. For example, if an established personality questionnaire has a scale measuring 'reasoning', we would expect a person's score on this scale to correlate with their scores on Saville Consulting's aptitude tests. However, it is perhaps less likely that there will be a strong relationship between a person's level of optimism and their score on the Saville Consulting aptitude tests. In fact, the presence of such a relationship could point towards construct irrelevant variance being present in the aptitude test. Amassing construct validity evidence is therefore a continuing scientific pursuit to build up a body of evidence about how an assessment instrument works in practice rather than simply something that a test possesses or does not possess (Landy, 1985).

It is worth mentioning two other types of validity which are relevant to assessments: content validity, which looks at how representative the questions in an assessment are of real workplace tasks; and face validity, which is a measure of how job-relevant an assessment is perceived, at face value, to be. Although these aspects are commonly measured through less quantitative methods than construct validity, they are nonetheless very important, since they provide an indication of an assessment's relevance to the content domain in question.

Validity and inferences from assessment scores

Validity has at its heart the notion of the validation of inferences made from assessment scores. Many inferences can be explicitly stated as hypotheses and tested empirically. For example, it may be believed that individuals who score highly on a particular aptitude assessment scale are likely to be more analytical than people who score lower on the scale. Testing such inferences can provide information that a scale is meaningful and that drawing inferences about a person's analytical ability based on such a scale is appropriate. Assessments which are demonstrated to be valid can be used to make specific inferences about people's behaviours and likely performance.

Each assessment within the Analysis Aptitude Range is designed to predict a different area of workplace performance. Verbal Analysis is designed to measure potential for Working with Words, Numerical Analysis is designed to measure potential for Working with Numbers and Diagrammatic Analysis is designed to measure potential for Working with Systems. These three criterion areas form part of the Saville Consulting Wave Performance Framework. In all instances, criterion-related validity is crucial. We believe that assessment users benefit from having clear links between the predictors (the assessment) and the criteria (workplace performance). The validity of an assessment helps to ensure that it is used appropriately.

The justification for using an assessment is derived partly from the extent to which it can measure the required criteria of workplace performance. Such evidence provides us with confidence that the item is meaningful and the inference or interpretation we then draw using the item score is appropriate. General inferences such as these can be explicitly stated as hypotheses and tested empirically. If a test or assessment score is shown to be a valid measure of a technical skill, such as mechanical reasoning, and if we learn from a job analysis study that a skill like mechanical reasoning is important to successful job performance, then we may want to use the test or assessment score to identify which people are more adept at mechanical reasoning than others.

A summary of the validity of the Analysis Aptitude Range

Criterion-related validity

Table 2.1 below summarises key evidence of the criterion-related validity of the Analysis Aptitude Range.

Construct validity

Table 2.2 below summarises key evidence of the construct validity of the Analysis Aptitude Range.

TABLE 2.1 The validity of Swift Analysis Aptitude against various performance criteria

Analysis Aptitude Test	Correlate Used	Sample Size	Correlation (Uncorrected)	Correlation (Corrected)
Validity of Swift Analysis Aptitude with Ability Criteria				
SAA Total	Sum of Scores on Working with Words, Numbers and Systems Competencies	308	.29	.54
SAA Verbal	Score on Working with Words Competency	308	.27	.48
SAA Numerical	Score on Working with Numbers Competency	308	.20	.34
SAA Diagrammatic	Score on Working with Systems Competency	308	.10	.24
Validity of Swift Analysis Aptitude with Various Other Criteria				
SAA Total	Accountancy Exam - Mean Correlation Across 9 Modules	178	.24	.31
SAA Total	Selection Center Score - Group Exercise	188	.28	.36
SAA Total	Selection Center Score - Written Exercise	188	.23	.30
SAA Total	Selection Center Score - Simulation Exercise	188	.32	.41

Note: The correlations between Swift Analysis Aptitude and the Ability Criteria were adjusted for criterion unreliability based on the inter-rater reliability of peer ratings on these criteria (Overall Sum of Competencies = .29, Working with Words =.31, Working with Numbers = .34, Working with Systems = .18). N=263. The correlations between Swift Analysis Aptitude and the other criteria were adjusted according to an attenuation estimate of .60.

Validity summary

This section has provided validity evidence for both the Swift combined and in-depth single tests in the Analysis Aptitude Range. Swift Analysis Aptitude achieves impressive levels of criterion-related validity for an assessment that can be completed in 18 minutes. Given that it samples the same domains as the in-depth single tests, it is appropriate to assume that Swift Analysis Aptitude provides a conservative lower-bound estimate of the validity of the longer tests within the Analysis Aptitude Range.

The tests within the Analysis Aptitude Range show appropriate and expected correlations with other test scores. The level of correlations between total scores of other tests suggests that the broad domains of performance being assessed have

TABLE 2.2 The construct validity of the Analysis Aptitude Range tests

Analysis Aptitude Test	Correlate Used	Sample Size	Correlation (Uncorrected)
Validity of Swift Analysis Aptitude with other Ability Tests			
SAA Total Score	Swift Comprehension Aptitude (IA) - Total Score	308	.54
	Swift Technical Aptitude (IA) - Total Score	308	.53
	Work Aptitudes (HC) - Overall (Combined) Total Score	339	.91
	Operational Aptitudes (HC) - Overall (Combined) Total Score	103	.69
	Practical Aptitudes (HC) - Overall (Combined)Total Score	103	.65
Validity of Professional Aptitudes with other Ability Tests			
Professional Verbal Analysis - Total Score	Score on Raven's Advanced Progressive Matrices	58	.50
Professional Numerical Analysis - Total Score		58	.46
Professional Verbal Analysis - Total Score	Score on Watson-Glaser Critical Thinking Appraisal	70	.61
Professional Numerical Analysis - Total Score		70	.46
Validity of Work Aptitudes with other Ability Tests			
Work Aptitudes - Overall (Combined) Total Score	SHL Aptitude Test - Combined Verbal, Numerical and Diagrammatic Score	98	.79
Work Verbal Analysis - Total Score	SHL Aptitude Test - Verbal Score	98	.60
Work Numerical Analysis - Total Score	SHL Aptitude Test - Numerical Score	98	.63
Work Diagrammatic Analysis - Total Score	SHL Aptitude Test - Diagrammatic Score	98	.65
Validity of Professional Aptitudes with GCSE Scores			
Professional Aptitudes - Overall (Combined) Total Score	UK GCSE English, Mathematics and Science Combined Score	227	.53
Validity of Work Aptitudes with GCSE Scores			
Work Aptitudes - Overall (Combined) Total Score	UK GCSE English, Mathematics and Science Combined Score	273	.62

some overlap as expected, but equally provide a good degree of unique performance measurement. The matched correlations between the sub-test areas (e.g. Verbal Analysis in Swift Analysis Aptitude and Verbal Comprehension in Swift Comprehension Aptitude) are reflective of the expected level of construct overlap between these sub-tests.

The relatively moderate correlations between the different sub-areas within the Analysis Aptitude Range tests are also indicative of their measuring sufficiently different aspects of workplace performance.

Note

1 A non-randomised version of Swift Analysis Aptitude is also available on request for unsupervised online use. This version also uses the original feedback report with Accuracy, Speed and Caution information instead of Pace and Online Test Access Summary information.

References

Binet, A. and Simon, T. (1907). *Les enfants anormaux*. Paris: A. Colin. Published in English as *Mentally Defective Children Mentally Defective Children*. New York: Longmans, Green & Co, 1914.

Cattell, R. B. (1963). Theory of fluid and crystallised intelligence: A critical experiment. *Journal of Educational Psychology*, 54, 1–22.

Guilford, J. P. (1967). *The Nature of Human Intelligence*. New York: McGraw-Hill.

Kurz, R. (2000). The facets of occupational testing: General reasoning ability, residual aptitudes & speed-accuracy balance. Doctoral dissertation, Manchester: University of Manchester Institute of Science and Technology.

Kurz, R. (2005). Convivence of personality, motivation, interest & ability theories in competency. Paper presented at EAWOP Congress, Istanbul, May.

Landy, F. (1985). Stamp collecting versus science: Validation as hypothesis testing. *American Psychologist*, 41(11), 1183–92.

Spearman, C. (1904). General intelligence objectively determined and measured. *American Journal of Psychology*, 15, 201–93.

Thurstone, L. L. (1938). *Primary Mental Abilities*. Chicago: University of Chicago Press.

Vernon, P. E. (1950). *The Structure of Human Abilities*. London: Methuen.

Yoakum, C. S. and Yerkes, R. M. (1920). *Army Mental Tests*. New York: H. Holt and Company.

PART II
Constructing psychometrics

3
THE 'TRADITIONAL' APPROACH

The core of this chapter is based on the published UK standardisation of Raymond Cattell's 16 Personality Factor Questionnaire (16PF), which I carried out at the National Foundation for Educational Research (NFER) in 1972.

This standardisation, praised by Raymond Cattell (as can be seen in the preface included in this chapter), is one of the publications which resulted from a period of research that I carried out on the 16PF. Ultimately, data from this standardisation and other strands of 16PF research culminated in my PhD thesis, which was published in 1977:

Saville, P. (1977). A critical analysis of the 16PF. PhD Dissertation, London: Brunel University.

During this period of research, I looked at age trends across all factors of the 16PF for both versions of the questionnaire (Form A and Form B) and for both genders. I have included some age trend graphs in an appendix to this chapter, as a supplement to the main body of text. These graphs provide just a few highlights of the rich data which I investigated. I have included these in the form of modern graphical displays because I think they provide a useful summary of the key findings from the 16PF questionnaire.

Initially, however, we focus on the core of this chapter, my UK standardisation of the 16PF, which featured in my PhD.

The British standardisation of the 16PF: supplement of norms

Author's note

This supplement, based on the results of a large survey conducted by the Technical Department of the NFER Publishing Company during 1971, forms one part of a larger standardisation programme involving tests which have originated from various sources and authors.

Although further analyses of these data are to be undertaken, it was considered undesirable to delay a normative report which will have practical significance for the many users of the Sixteen Personality Factor Questionnaire both in Britain and abroad.

Preface by Professor Raymond B. Cattell

At first glance, a psychologist may see nothing more in a test standardisation than a public service at its best faithfully but banausically performed. If that is all he sees, he is – like someone who sees a railroad as just so many sleepers and rails – denied the gift of imagination. For a standardisation is also literature and sociology and history. To the understanding person, it has some qualities of a good novel because it opens his eyes to the personalities of the rest of his fellow men. It is sociology because it corrects our knowledge of classes, subcultures and age groups; it is history because comparisons of today's standardisation with that 20 years hence will tell us – more reliably than history can yet specify – what the trends in human adjustment over time actually are.

Of course, this spectacle would be narrow, and of small relevance, if the standardisation concerned some narrow specific ability, especially one arbitrarily defined. But the 16PF by construction and design covers a spectrum of 15 primary and fundamental dimensions of personality, plus intelligence. And there is general scientific value in the scales which measure them because they are not arbitrary, but rooted in 25 years of systematic research by 50 or more psychologists on the basic structure of personality. In this last respect too, the scientist of imagination and vision will see in the present standardisation something far more significant than the calibrating of just any psychometric testing scale. For if, as is claimed on good evidence, the primary and second-order source traits in the 16PF, derived by repeated factor analyses, are the natural genetic and culturally developed structures in the normal personality, then the analyses of age, sex, social class and occupation which this standardisation will permit is a substantial contribution to the general psychology of personality. In the same way, but on a narrower theme, the substantial standardisation in America of the Stanford Binet Intelligence Test a generation ago was a contribution to our knowledge of intelligence, ably interpreted and used for example by Terman in illuminating the social and biological associates of intelligence.

The standardisation of a test with 16 independent factors (not to mention its involving two distinct equivalent forms) is a more complex undertaking than that of a single intelligence test. It is not surprising, therefore, that except for the USA and Germany, the standardisations of the 16PF in the various countries in which it is in use – Argentina, Australia, Belgium, Brazil, Chile, Czechoslovakia, France, Holland, India, Italy, Japan, Mexico, New Zealand, the Philippines, Poland, Sweden and Taiwan – have been relatively unambitious as to numbers and stratification requirements. Nevertheless, they have been very effective and useful to many psychologists. The standardisation in one country will not do for another because it is part of the sensitivity of the instrument that it registers statistically significant differences of profile (see Cattell, Eber and Tatsuoka, 1970) among these cultures – therefore requiring separate standardisations. This statement should not be misunderstood. When independent factor analyses have been made – as in Brazil, Germany, India, Japan and New Zealand – the *same* essential factor *structures* have been found. The scales are dealing with virtually *universal* trait dimensions in human nature, and it is this which makes comparison of individuals and countries mathematically possible and psychologically meaningful. What we are stating is that the *average* scores of various national population samples on traits such as surgency, ego strength, dominance, anxiety, etc. show systematic differences, as the work of Alvarez, Lynn, Nichols, Schröder, Tsujioka, Vaughan, Warburton and several others demonstrates.

Cultural anthropologists, sociologists, historians and social psychologists will be able to make full use of these findings in their theories, however, only when the within-country sampling for these standardisations reaches the levels of precision happily reached by the work of Saville and his technical associates in Britain at the NFER. Being in touch with the greater part of the above developments, the present writer is compelled to say that not even in America itself, where research support is apt to be more lavish, has any one of these standardisations quite reached the closeness to the ideal model that has now been achieved for Britain in this undertaking.

The conception of *random location sampling*, the success in getting percentages in sampling which so faithfully match the sub-totals for existent geographical, class, sex and other divisions in the country, the attention given to possible selection by testing procedures, etc. evoke the pleasure of seeing good craftsmanship in a job well done. At the same time, one gets assurances from other directions – for example, the agreement of roughly 90% of the significant sex differences with those found in America and elsewhere – that one can thump the chest of this creature and be rewarded by the notes of sound health. It is indeed a standardisation that NFER in Britain, and the Institute for Personality and Ability Testing in America, may advantageously keep focused as a model for procedures with other tests.

A very brisk research activity in cross-cultural comparisons has kept American psychologists in particular busily engaged over this decade. As just mentioned, the 16PF and its younger brother the High School Personality Questionnaire have yielded some striking differences of national culture profiles. However, all such comparisons are sound only to the extent that other countries can produce standardisations as carefully representatively sampled as this. If that is done, then such apparently coldly statistical documents as this become gold mines of information for the social psychologist. Even for within-country social analysis, there is enough in these tables to provide researchers in several fields with findings stimulating to many important theories. It is happily evident that Peter Saville and his colleagues are already aware of this, in telling us that 'research will be continuing'.

While imagination could readily move over the possibilities, one must not forget that the primary purpose of the standardisation is to give the most dependable service in the use of the 16PF in education, clinical psychology, vocational guidance and other fields of applied psychology. Through the sten[1] scores which this supplement will permit the practising psychologist to derive from his raw scores, he is assured of 'placing' the given individual much more accurately than was possible before. That individual can be focused in a perspective of sex, class and age ranges to permit richer understanding and better prediction from his test performance. NFER and Peter Saville are to be congratulated on a well-planned and highly valuable contribution to psychology in Britain.

Laboratory of Personality Analysis, University of Illinois, July 1972.

Acknowledgements

A standardisation exercise of this order could not have been possible without the co-operation and continued support of the great many individuals involved in the project.

Special thanks are extended to Bill Mabey, Senior Research Executive, and Susan Badger, Research Executive of the British Market Research Bureau, who were closely involved in the total organisation of the standardisation. I would like to acknowledge the co-operation and assistance of Robert Fletcher, Associate Director, and Joan Macfarlane-Smith, Field Director of BMRB.

The excellent work of the staff of the NFER Publishing Company and the BMRB field-force is greatly appreciated.

The writer also wishes to thank Miss Jill Tarryer of the NFER for her invaluable advice and Miss Janice Hare of the Technical Department of the Company.

Finally, grateful acknowledgement is made to the Institute for Personality and Ability Testing, Champaign, Illinois for the permission to reproduce data in this report.

Introduction

In recent years, the Sixteen Personality Factor Questionnaire, developed by R. B. Cattell, H. W. Eber and M. M. Tatsuoka and published by the Institute for Personality and Ability Testing in the USA, has been increasingly employed in the UK – indeed, only the personality measures of Eysenck can seriously rival the popular currency of the 16PF in British psychology.

In view of the wide clinical, educational and industrial applications of the questionnaire, the 1968 editions of Forms A and B were amended in terms of item content by the NFER Publishing Company during 1970. The Anglicised editions of Forms A and B of the 16PF were designed to remove obvious Americanisms and incorporated some minor idiomatic and grammatical, lexical and spelling modifications.

It was also at this time that the inherent problems of using American testing procedures in the UK were recognised by the publication of a series of Test

Information Sheets, which detailed the results obtained from the testing of various specific British groups. However, the representativeness of the samples could not be ensured and the data were necessarily of limited applicability.

Because of the need for more adequate data, early consideration was given to the respective merits of various methods of standardising the 16PF in Britain. The prohibitive cost of full-scale random sampling was weighed against other factors: the absence of background demographic information and insufficient numbers of subjects ruled out the possibility of collecting and utilising existing data; the very nature of the instrument to be standardised and questions of test security made a postal survey totally inappropriate and group sessions are known to produce severe deficiencies in the sample. Thus, as the best method of overcoming these difficulties, it was finally decided that a sampling technique developed by the British Market Research Bureau over a number of years and known as Random Location Sampling would be employed and that specially trained interviewers would administer Forms A and B of the 16PF actually in the homes of the standardisation group.

The methods and procedure of standardisation

Random Location Sampling involves the drawing up of a representative sample of 200 Parliamentary constituencies in England and Wales and those parts of Scotland south of the Caledonian Canal, selected with probability proportional to their population size. These constituencies were selected at random using the cumulative sum and fixed sampling interval technique, after stratification by the distribution of votes cast at the 1970 General Election (as an indicator of economic status) within conurbation or urban or rural area, within standard region. For each of the 200 constituencies, the polling districts in it were placed in random order within ward, the wards in random order within administrative areas and the administrative areas in random order within constituency. Groups of streets were then selected with probability proportionate to the electorate in a way which was consistent with polling district. Interviews were then spread uniformly over these streets.

In this particular application a number of further controls were necessary and those making up the standardisation sample therefore possess the following characteristics:

1. All testees were in the 16 to 70 age range.
2. All testees were literate and capable of reading the booklet for themselves. If required, help was given with occasional words and sentences. In the case of the subject being unable to read either through illiteracy or severe physical or mental infirmity, the interview was diplomatically terminated.
3. All testees held a six-month residence qualification in the British Isles prior to November 1971. This was imposed in order to exclude overseas visitors and temporary/recent immigrants.

A total of 200 experienced female interviewers were specially selected from the field-force of the British Market Research Bureau and were trained at five regional centres (Birmingham, Bristol, Glasgow, London and Manchester) in the administration of the 16PF. On the evidence of two previously conducted pilot studies, where answer sheet coding errors (especially among older subjects) were found, the questionnaires were completed by individuals ringing their responses directly in the booklets. In the main survey this resulted not only in the eradication of transcription mistakes, but also in a considerable

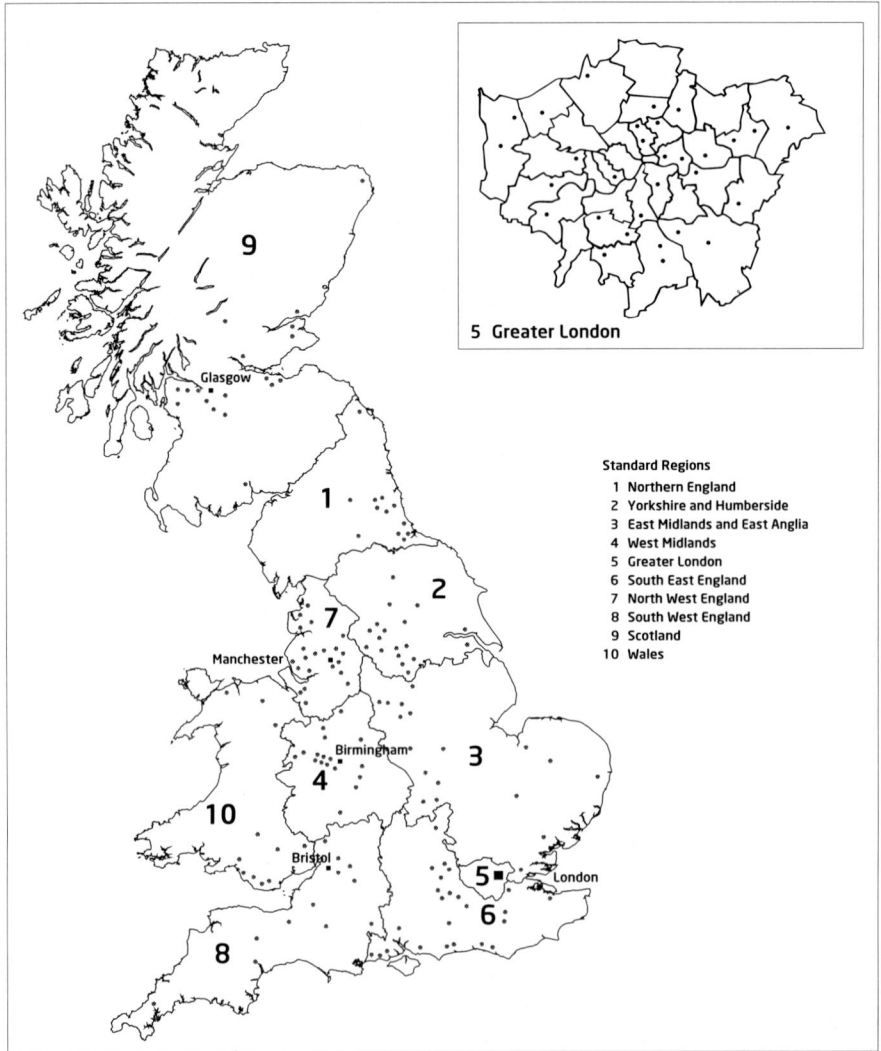

FIGURE 3.1 The sampling units and standard regions of the 16 PF British standardisation sample (N = 2,227)

reduction in the duration of the average interview from 100 to 80 minutes. Since all subjects were giving up their own time by co-operating in the research, this was of considerable importance. Despite this measure, however, the interview still amounted to something over three hours at the maximum to a minimum of 30 minutes.

The two forms of the 16PF were systematically alternated by the interviewer, resulting in either a Form A + B or a Form B + A administration procedure for each subject. Having completed both questionnaires, detailed information on a number of socio-economic and demographic variables was collected. These included the occupation of the head of household and the age, marital status, working hours and terminal education age of the respondent. Further to these data, subjects were classified by the ten standard geographical regions illustrated below.

On completion of the fieldwork, which was conducted during November 1971, materials were returned via the regional centres to the Technical Department of the NFER Publishing Company for subsequent data analysis.

The standardisation sample

The demographic and socio-economic characteristics of the British 16PF standardisation sample are given in Table 3.1. The population estimates come either from the Target Group Index (TGI) – a national survey conducted by the British Market Research Bureau of some 25,000 adults – or, where possible, by way of statistics derived from the Registrar General's Annual Estimates and the National Readership Survey.

In order that the reader may more meaningfully interpret Table 3.1, greater information on the variables used in the standardisation is given below.

Standard region

Apart from the East Midlands and East Anglia, which were treated as one unit, the ten geographical regions employed in the study were those of the Census General. The total standardisation group was made up of testings conducted in the following 48 British counties:

- *Northern England*: County Durham, the North Riding of Yorkshire and Northumberland.
- *Yorkshire and Humberside*: the East and West Ridings of Yorkshire and Lincolnshire.
- *East Midlands and East Anglia*: Derbyshire, Leicestershire, Northamptonshire, Nottinghamshire, and Cambridgeshire, Norfolk and Suffolk.
- *West Midlands*: Shropshire, Staffordshire and Warwickshire.
- *Greater London*: testings were conducted in a total of 30 Parliamentary constituencies within the administrative boundaries of the Greater London Council.

TABLE 3.1 The 1971 British standardisation sample

		% Total Adult Population	% Sample	% Male Adult Population	% Sample	% Female Adult Population	% Sample
	Region						
	Northern England	6.2	6.4	6.3	6.4	6.2	6.4
	Yorkshire and Humberside	9.0	8.6	9.0	8.9	8.9	8.2
Registrar General's 1971 Estimates and the National Readership Survey: Derived Statistics	East Midlands and E. Anglia	9.4	9.3	9.4	9.6	9.2	9.2
	West Midlands	9.5	8.9	9.8	8.8	9.3	9.0
	Greater London	14.9	15.4	14.7	14.8	15.2	15.0
	South East England	17.8	16.7	17.6	16.5	18.0	17.0
	North West England	12.5	13.1	12.3	13.2	12.7	13.0
	South West England	6.8	7.2	7.0	6.9	6.6	7.6
	Scotland	8.7	9.3	8.7	9.3	8.7	9.2
	Wales	5.1	5.5	5.1	5.7	5.1	5.3
	Social Group						
	AB	12.6	15.9	12.5	15.7	12.7	16.3
Target Group Index 1971	C1	19.6	21.8	19.3	21.9	19.9	21.7
	C2	40.4	36.6	42.1	37.8	38.7	35.2
	DE	27.4	25.2	26.1	24.1	28.7	26.2
	Marital Status						
	Married	73.4	72.5	77.8	75.5	69.4	69.6
Target Group Index 1971	Widowed/Divorced/Separated	9.2	7.5	3.7	4.4	4.2	10.6
	Single-Engaged	2.5	2.3	2.4	1.6	2.6	3.0
	Single-Not Engaged	15.0	17.5	16.2	18.5	13.8	16.6
	Working Hours						
Target Group Index 1971	Working 30 Hours or More	52	56	79	81	26	31
	Working 8-29 Hours	6	7	1	1	11	14
	Not Working	42	36	20	18	63	55
	Terminal Education Age						
	15 Years or Under	70	63	69	64	70	62
	16 Years	12	15	12	15	12	15
	17 Years	5	6	5	4	5	8
Target Group Index 1971	18 Years	3	3	3	3	3	3
	19 Years	1	1	1	1	1	1
	20 Years	1	1	1	1	1	1
	21-23 Years	3	4	3	4	2	3
	24 or More	1	2	1	3	1	1
	Still Studying	4	5	4	5	4	7
	Head of Household						
Target Group Index 1971	Yes	47.2	46.4	82.0	81.4	15.4	11.6
	No	52.8	52.9	18.0	17.9	84.6	87.7
	Age						
Registrar General's 1971 Estimates and the National Readership Survey: Derived Statistics	15-24 Years	21.5	23.0	21.9	22.1	21.1	24.0
	25-34 Years	18.1	24.3	18.6	22.2	17.7	26.3
	35-44 Years	17.6	17.6	18.2	17.4	16.9	17.9
	45-54 Years	18.4	15.0	18.3	16.5	18.5	13.5
	55-69 Years	24.5	20.0	23.0	21.8	25.8	17.1

Missing data due to subjects refusing to provide some information cause certain columns not to total exactly 100%

- *South East England*: Bedfordshire, Berkshire, Buckinghamshire, Essex, Hampshire, Hertfordshire, Kent, Oxfordshire, Surrey and Sussex.
- *North West England*: Cheshire and Lancashire.
- *South West England*: Cornwall, Devon, Dorset Gloucestershire, Somerset and Wiltshire.
- *Scotland*: Aberdeenshire, Angus, Dumfriesshire, Dunbartonshire, East Lothian, Fifeshire, Lanarkshire, Midlothian, Perthshire and Renfrewshire.
- *Wales*: Brecknockshire, Denbighshire, Glamorgan, Monmouthshire and Radnorshire.

Social grade

Rather than rely on information such as economic standing, educational level and racial origin, which undoubtedly affect social class in varying degrees but which are often difficult to assess objectively, social grading has been based upon the occupation of the head of the family unit as the single factor most responsible for the social status of the family. For this reason, detailed information was collected on the job, position, type and size of organisation, and any professional qualifications of the senior breadwinner. Social class was then carefully assessed by way of a detailed guide, of which the following serves as an illustration:

- *Social Grade A*: The Upper-Middle Class
  Professional and Semi-Professional: Doctor, Solicitor, Senior Civil Servant (Principal and above), University Professor, Chartered Accountant, Airline Pilot.

  Commerce and Industry: Proprietor, Senior Executive, Company Director and Manager of large business (25 or more in establishment), Senior Industrial Scientist.

  Police and Armed Forces: Superintendent, Chief Con-stable, Lieutenant Colonel, Wing Commander, Commander (RN) and above.

- *Social Grade B*: The Middle Class
  Professional and Semi-professional: School Teacher, University Lecturer, Executive Grade Civil Servant, Journalist.

  Commerce and Industry: owner of medium-sized business or shop, Manager of small branch office of bank or insurance company (10–24 in establishment), Manager of a department in a large factory or business.

  Police and Armed Forces: Inspector and Commissioned Officers in the Armed Forces.

- *Social Grade C1*: The Lower-Middle Class
  Professional and Semi-professional: Junior Civil Servant, Bank or Local Government Clerk, Pharmacist, all Students other than Apprentices.

  Commerce and Industry: Lower Managerial and Supervisory Grades, Clerk, Typist, Laboratory Technician.

- *Social Grade C2*: The Skilled Working Class
  All skilled manual workers: Foreman (manual), Deputy (mining), Chargehand, Overlooker, Overseer (manual), Superintendent (manual), Supervisor (manual).

- *Social Grade D*: The Semi-skilled and Unskilled Working Class
  Most semi-skilled and unskilled workers. Most adult female manual workers. Unskilled assistants, labourers and mates of the occupations in grade C2, all apprentices to skilled trades.

- *Social Grade E*: Those at the Lowest Level of Subsistence
  Social grade E is assigned only to those households which are dependent on state pensions, etc. and where no member of the household is working.

Marital status

Marital status was classified by one of four categories:

a.   Married.
b.   Widowed, divorced or separated.
c.   Single and engaged.
d.   Single but not engaged.

   In passing, it should be pointed out that this variable is a good example of the bias, albeit small, from which self-report questionnaires may sometimes suffer. On the basis of TGI estimates in Table 3.1, there are 89,000 (0.2%) more females than males engaged to be married in the adult population! Nevertheless, these unfortunate misapprehensions do not usually constitute intentional falsification, unlike deliberate sabotage, which is fairly easily detected by experienced interviewers in the face-to-face situation with the respondent.

Working hours

Information was gained on whether the respondent was working full-time, part-time or not working at the time of the study.

Terminal education age

The age at which the subject completed full-time education was established. If a respondent had worked for a period between uninterrupted education, the most recent age was coded.

Head of household

The head of household was defined as the member who owns or is responsible for the accommodation occupied by members of the household. Suitable criteria were laid down to ensure correct evaluation in the event of unusual household composition.

Age

Subjects were required to give their age in years at their last birthday; if this was refused, as was the case in approximately 20 instances, age was estimated and then coded by one of five intervals.

The 16PF standardisation samples differ from both TGI and the Registrar General's Estimates by the exclusion of the illiterate and more seriously infirm. Obviously these constraints will have their influence on a number of further demographic and socio-economic variables, not least of which is the lesser likelihood of the aged being included in the study. For this reason, the population estimates provided in Table 3.1 can only be regarded as the best available and not the most relevant statistics. The sample and the population clearly do not share identical parameters and direct comparison on some variables could therefore be misleading. Accordingly, we would be in error to apply any weighting values to the obtained sample. Indeed, whilst bias due to non-response is also involved here, the greater proportion in the sample of those of older terminal education age and higher social grade, and the smaller numbers of non-working as against working respondents reflect to some extent the controls employed in the standardisation. Even on the evidence of Table 3.1, however, which, if anything, serves to underestimate the adequacy of the sample, the standardisation groups are thought to be good representations of the British adult population.

Demographic adequacy apart, careful consideration was also given to a major problem which besets all studies of this kind: the unknown nature of bias in results introduced by those refusing to co-operate in research. Certainly, the introductory statement to the individual, which requested his assistance in an important social research project to be conducted with complete anonymity of participants, a gift pen and the opportunity to win Premium Bonds up to the value of £100, acted as efficient incentives. Moreover, the procedure was made as flexible as possible by interviewers making appointments with respondents as and when necessary. That only 21 of 2,227 subjects prematurely terminated the interview is evidence of the value of these incentives and of the skill and determination of the interviewers.

The important practical consideration that adults have to be willing to co-operate in research means that it is virtually impossible to apply true random sampling. Accordingly, to investigate the problem of non-response further, a small study of 194 subjects was carried out after completion of the main survey. Here the refusal rate approximated 28% (it was evident that some of these refusals had stemmed from a noticeable hostility towards the 1971 Census – a prejudice that was difficult to break down). On the basis of interviewers' estimates, an analysis of these refusals showed that non-co-operators tended more usually to be female and older, and of a lower socio-economic group than participants in the research. Although the nature and extent of this trend is unknown, it is not thought that the bias is large.

British sex differences in personality

The means and standard deviations for the male and female samples on Forms A + B of the 16PF are to be found in Table 3.2. It should be mentioned that although the male group is 2.7 years older than the female, it is doubtful that this would invalidate the basic findings.

The differences between British men and women show a close similarity to those reported for comparable American groups. Ten of the 16 factors (A, E, F, H, I, L, O, Q1, Q3 and Q4) demonstrate differences which are congruent with US results, based on samples corrected to 35 years. Unlike the non-significant differences of North America, however, British males achieved significantly higher mean scores on Factors B, C and Q2. Also worthy of note is the non-significant difference in means on Factor G for the British groups. Finally on Factor M, with British males higher, and on Factor N, with British females higher, a reversal of sex differences in personality between America and Britain is evident.

The differences on Forms A + B are in fact consistent across both Form A and Form B, except for Factors G (males higher on Form A, females higher on Form B), N (females higher on Form A, no significant difference on Form B) and Q2 (no significant difference on Form A, males higher on Form B). Why these factors should fluctuate in such a manner is not immediately apparent. It may be significant, however, that as measured by coefficients of equivalence between Forms A and B, Factors G, N and Q2 are three of the least reliable source traits (Cattell, Eber and Tatsuoka, 1970).

It should be remembered that these sex differences are based upon groups with a mean age of approximately 38 years. The nature and extent of these differences should therefore only be generalised to other ages with great caution. There is evidence that the 16PF personality factor age-changes in the American culture at least show dissimilar patterns for the sexes (Cattell, Eber and Tatsuoka, 1970). For example, Crystallized Intelligence demonstrated a slight fall in women on Forms A + B in the 1961–2 Edition of the 16PF which was not discernible for males.

Cross-national differences

Because the British samples are of somewhat older mean age than the American standardisation base of 30 years, it was not possible to test for cross-national differences without first having taken account of age discrepancies. Accordingly, to bring all mean factor scores to a common age, the British group means were corrected on the American quadratic model provided in the Tabular Supplement No. 1 to the 16PF Handbook (IPAT, 1971).

TABLE 3.2 Significant personality differences between British men and women

		A	B	C	E	F	G	H	I	L	M	N	O	Q1	Q2	Q3	Q4
Male	Mean	17.58	14.65	30.80	25.00	26.27	24.63	27.25	17.63	17.72	22.94	20.96	19.69	18.86	20.40	24.86	23.77
	S.D.	5.85	3.47	6.99	7.30	9.23	5.90	10.30	5.76	4.95	5.63	4.80	7.79	4.97	5.76	6.00	9.20
Female	Mean	21.72	14.16	28.07	19.09	26.42	24.79	23.48	25.01	15.89	21.75	22.34	25.35	16.49	19.68	23.13	28.78
	S.D.	5.02	3.44	6.67	6.69	8.61	5.46	10.36	4.58	4.94	5.92	4.71	7.58	4.71	5.59	5.73	8.16
Difference in Means (Positive if Male Higher)		-4.14	0.49	2.73	5.91	-0.15	-.016	3.77	-7.38	1.83	1.19	-1.38	-5.66	2.37	0.72	1.73	-5.01
T Value		17.02	3.18	8.96	18.92	0.38	0.63	8.18	31.78	8.29	4.62	6.50	16.50	10.97	2.84	6.61	12.91
Significance of Difference, P		<.001	<.01	<.001	<.001	NS	NS	<.001	<.001	<.001	<.001	<.001	<.001	<.001	<.01	<.001	<.001

After the application of the relevant weights, it is evident from Table 3.3 that British females were significantly higher than American females on Factors L (p < .01), N (p < .05), Q2 (p < .001) and Q4 (p < .01), and significantly lower on Factors G (p < .001), H (p < .001) I (p < .05) and M (p < .001). Differences were not significant on the remaining eight factors. In Table 3.4 the respective American and British male standardisation groups are compared. Eleven of the 16 source traits are in fact significantly different at the 5% level or above, British males being higher on Factors B (p < .001), E (p <.05), L (p <.001), Q1 (p <.001), Q2 (p <.001) and Q3 (p <.01), and lower on A (p <.001), G (p <.001), I (p <.001), M (p <.001) and O (p <.001).

As was noted above, differences between means were tested for significance after the British results had first been adjusted to a base age level of 30 years. It should be pointed out, however, that a more adequate approach, but one which is beyond the intended scope of this preliminary report, would be to correct by bringing the American data up and the British data down to the mean age of the two groups. This procedure would have taken account of both American and British age trends.

A further and probably the most satisfactory procedure would have been significance testing for national differences across each age interval. Nevertheless, this design would still suffer from the inherent differences in the American and British standardisation methods, the former being based on samples drawn from data submitted from a large number of American test users and the latter involving a specially undertaken study. For this reason, any cross-national comparisons should be treated with some caution.

TABLE 3.3 Significant personality differences between the American and British standardisation groups adjusted to age 30 years: females

		A	B	C	E	F	G	H	I	L	M	N	O	Q1	Q2	Q3	Q4
British	Adjusted Mean	23.29	14.16	30.04	21.08	26.80	24.97	23.48	25.18	14.85	23.05	21.99	23.61	16.49	20.22	23.41	27.39
	S.D.	5.02	3.44	6.67	6.69	8.61	5.46	10.36	4.58	4.94	5.92	4.71	7.58	4.71	5.59	5.73	8.16
American	Mean	22.88	14.08	30.73	21.39	26.57	26.44	25.69	25.78	14.05	24.54	21.44	23.18	16.24	18.44	22.93	25.96
	S.D.	5.91	3.72	8.39	7.22	7.35	5.61	10.49	5.22	5.33	6.79	4.53	8.33	5.01	6.02	6.38	8.93
Difference in Means (Positive if British Higher)		0.41	0.08	-0.69	-0.31	0.23	-1.47	-2.21	-0.60	0.80	-1.49	0.55	0.43	0.25	1.78	0.48	1.43
T Value		1.30	0.39	1.56	0.79	0.53	4.72	3.78	2.13	2.74	4.08	2.14	0.95	0.91	5.40	1.39	2.94
Significance of Difference, P		N.S.	N.S.	N.S.	N.S.	N.S.	p<.001	p<.001	p<.05	p<.01	p<.001	p<.05	N.S.	N.S.	p<.001	N.S.	p<.01

TABLE 3.4 Significant personality differences between the American and British standardisation groups adjusted to age 30 years: males

		A	B	C	E	F	G	H	I	L	M	N	O	Q1	Q2	Q3	Q4
British	Adjusted Mean	19.29	14.65	34.19	27.38	28.48	25.38	30.75	16.87	16.11	24.98	19.98	15.04	18.86	20.40	25.96	20.20
	S.D.	5.85	3.47	6.99	7.30	9.23	5.90	10.30	5.76	4.95	5.63	4.80	7.79	4.97	5.76	6.00	9.20
American	Mean	20.36	14.08	34.69	26.71	28.40	26.88	30.30	18.25	14.78	25.86	19.76	17.60	18.20	18.25	25.24	20.61
	S.D.	6.32	3.72	8.18	6.37	7.45	5.78	10.26	5.75	5.48	6.36	4.37	8.49	4.88	5.78	6.01	9.41
Difference in Means (Positive if British Higher)		-1.07	0.57	-0.50	0.67	0.08	-1.50	0.45	-1.38	1.33	-0.88	0.22	-2.56	0.66	2.15	0.72	-0.41
T Value		4.16	3.75	1.56	2.29	0.22	6.05	1.03	5.65	6.03	3.47	1.12	7.44	3.15	8.78	2.83	1.04
Significance of Difference, P		p<.001	p<.001	N.S.	p<.05	N.S.	p<.001	N.S.	p<.001	p<.001	p<.001	N.S.	p<.001	p<.001	p<.001	p<.01	N.S.

The use of the appropriate British norm tables

The N–Sten norms on Forms A and B of the 16PF for British males and females are presented in Tables 3.5–3.13. The nature of the type of standard score employed has been discussed by Tatsuoka (1969). Despite there being rather more females than males in the British adult population (52.2% as against 47.8%), it should be noted that the Male + Female tables are here based upon equal numbers of the sexes.

As with the comparable American tables, the sizes of the samples and the means and standard deviations of the factor raw scores have been provided. However, until British age trends are adequately researched, results have not been centred on age 30 years, but are based upon groups with given age means and standard deviations. Nevertheless, the British test user may on certain occasions wish to take account of the American age corrections.

As a final recommendation regarding the relatively small magnitude of the differences between the British and American norms, it would seem unlikely from these Form A and Form B results that the use of the American Form C and D tables would give a greatly distorted picture of the British subject. However, this still remains to be checked against future studies. Meanwhile, research is continuing on further analyses of these data which will be incorporated into an account more detailed than this preliminary report.

TABLE 3.5 British general population female: Form A, N = 1,113 (mean age 37.6 years, SD 15.7)

Factor	Sten Score 1	2	3	4	5	6	7	8	9	10	Factor	Mean	S.D.
A	0-5	6	7-8	9	10-11	12	13	14-15	16	17.20	A	11.09	2.78
B	0-2	3	4	5	6	7	8	9-10	11	12-13	B	6.85	2.10
C	0-6	7-8	9-10	11	12-13	14-15	16-18	19	20-21	22-26	C	14.03	3.83
E	0-2	3	4-5	6-7	8-9	10-11	12-13	14-15	16-18	19-26	E	9.45	4.00
F	0-3	4-5	6-7	8-9	10-12	13-14	15-17	18-20	21-22	23-26	F	12.34	4.93
G	0-4	5-6	7-8	9-10	11-13	14	15	16	17	18-20	G	12.05	3.37
H	0-2	3	4-6	7-8	9-11	12-14	15-17	18-20	21-22	23-26	H	11.70	5.30
I	0-7	8-9	10	11	12-13	14	15-16	17	18-19	20	I	13.33	2.79
L	0-1	2	3	4-6	7	8-9	10-11	12-13	14-15	16-20	L	7.87	3.41
M	0-4	5-6	7-8	9	10-11	12-13	14-15	16-17	18-19	20-26	M	11.65	3.60
N	0-5	6	7-8	9-10	11	12-13	14	15-16	17-18	19-20	N	11.81	3.18
O	0-4	5-6	7-8	9-10	11-12	13-14	15-16	17-18	19-20	21-26	O	12.58	4.01
Q1	0-2	3	4	5-6	7	8-9	10-11	12	13-14	15-20	Q1	8.11	3.08
Q2	0-4	5	6-7	8-9	10-11	12-13	14-15	16	17-18	19-20	Q2	11.40	3.53
Q3	0-5	6-7	8	9-10	11-12	13	14-15	16	17	18-20	Q3	11.94	3.11
Q4	0-4	5-7	8-9	10-12	13-14	15-16	17-19	20-21	22	23-26	Q4	14.31	4.56
	1	2	3	4	5	6	7	8	9	10			
	Sten Score												

TABLE 3.6 British general population female: Form B, N = 1,010 (mean age 36.8 years, SD 15.6)

Factor	Sten Score										Factor	Mean	S.D.
	1	2	3	4	5	6	7	8	9	10			
A	0-3	4-5	6-7	8-9	10	11-12	13	14-15	16	17-20	A	10.63	3.15
B	0-2	3-4	5	6	7	8	9	10	-	11-13	B	7.24	1.95
C	0-6	7-8	9	10-11	12-13	14-15	16-17	18-19	20-21	22-26	C	13.97	3.86
E	0-2	3-4	5	6-7	8-9	10-11	12-13	14-15	16-18	19-26	E	9.63	3.73
F	0-5	6-7	8-9	10-11	12-13	14-16	17-18	19-21	22-23	24-26	F	13.91	4.57
G	0-6	7-8	9	10-11	12	13-14	15	16-17	18	19-20	G	12.79	2.97
H	0-1	2-3	4-5	6-8	9-11	12-14	15-18	19-21	22-23	24-26	H	11.76	5.78
I	0-6	7	8	9-10	11	12-13	14	15	16-17	18-20	I	11.63	2.85
L	0-2	3-4	6	6	7-8	9	10	11	12-13	14-20	L	8.09	2.63
M	0-3	4	5-6	7-8	9	10-11	12-13	14-15	16-17	18-26	M	10.00	3.63
N	0-5	6	7	8-9	10-11	12	13	14	15-16	17-20	N	10.63	2.77
O	0-3	4-5	6-8	9-10	11-12	13-15	16-17	18-19	20-21	22-26	O	12.79	4.51
Q1	0-3	4	5	6	7-8	9	10-11	12	13-14	15-20	Q1	8.33	2.90
Q2	0-2	3	4	5-6	7-8	9	10-11	12-13	14	15-20	Q2	8.39	3.11
Q3	0-3	4-5	6-7	8-9	10-11	12-13	14	15-16	-	17-20	Q3	11.22	3.57
Q4	0-4	5-7	8-9	10-12	13-14	15-16	17-19	20-21	22-23	24-26	Q4	14.47	4.58
	1	2	3	4	5	6	7	8	9	10			
		Sten Score											

TABLE 3.7 British general population female: Form A + Form B, N = 1,005 (mean age 36.8 years, SD 15.6)

Factor	Sten Score										Factor	Mean	S.D.
	1	2	3	4	5	6	7	8	9	10			
A	0-10	11-13	14-16	17-19	20-21	22-24	25-26	27-28	29-30	31-40	A	21.72	5.02
B	0-6	7-8	9-10	11-12	13-14	15	16-17	18-19	20	21-26	B	14.16	3.44
C	0-15	16-18	19-21	22-24	25-28	29-31	32-34	35-38	39-41	42-52	C	28.07	6.67
E	0-8	9	10-12	13-15	16-18	19-21	22-25	26-30	31-34	35-52	E	19.09	6.69
F	0-10	11-14	15-17	18-21	22-26	27-30	31-35	36-40	41-44	45-52	F	26.42	8.61
G	0-13	14-16	17-19	20-22	23-25	26-27	28-30	31-32	33-34	35-40	G	24.79	5.46
H	0-4	5-8	9-12	13-17	18-22	23-28	29-35	36-40	41-44	45-52	H	23.48	10.36
I	0-15	16-18	19-20	21-22	23-25	26-27	28-29	30-31	32-34	35-40	I	25.01	4.58
L	0-6	7-8	9-10	11-13	14-15	16-18	19-20	21-23	24-25	26-40	L	15.89	4.94
M	0-11	12-13	14-15	16-18	19-21	22-24	25-27	28-31	32-35	36-52	M	21.75	5.92
N	0-12	13-15	16-17	18-20	21-22	23-24	25-26	27-29	30-31	32-40	N	22.34	4.71
O	0-10	11-13	14-17	18-21	22-25	26-29	30-32	33-36	37-40	41-52	O	25.35	7.58
Q1	0-8	9-10	11	12-13	14-16	17-18	19-20	21-24	25-27	28-40	Q1	16.49	4.71
Q2	0-8	9-11	12-13	14-16	17-19	20-22	23-25	26-27	28-30	31-40	Q2	19.68	5.59
Q3	0-11	12-14	15-17	18-20	21-23	24-26	27-29	30-31	32-33	34-40	Q3	23.13	5.73
Q4	0-11	12-15	16-20	21-24	25-29	30-33	34-36	37-41	42-44	45-52	Q4	28.78	8.16
	1	2	3	4	5	6	7	8	9	10			
		Sten Score											

TABLE 3.8 British general population male: Form A, N = 1,104 (mean age 39.8 years, SD 16.2)

Factor	Sten Score										Factor	Mean	S.D.
	1	2	3	4	5	6	7	8	9	10			
A	0-2	3-4	5-6	7	8-9	10	11-12	13-14	15	16-20	A	9.35	3.09
B	0-1	2	3	4-5	6	7	8	9	10	11-13	B	7.17	2.14
C	0-7	8-9	10-11	12-13	14-15	16-17	18-19	20-21	22-23	24-26	C	15.25	3.88
E	0-3	4-5	6-8	9	10-12	13-14	15-16	17-18	19-21	22-26	E	12.28	4.28
F	0-2	3-5	6-7	8-9	10-12	13-14	15-17	18-20	21-22	23-26	F	12.39	5.05
G	0-3	4-6	7-8	9-10	11-12	13-14	15-16	17	18-19	20	G	12.47	3.73
H	0-2	3-4	5-7	8-10	11-13	14-16	17-19	20-21	22-23	24-26	H	13.25	5.51
I	0-2	3-4	5	6-7	8	9-10	11-12	13-14	15-16	17-20	I	9.16	3.42
L	0-2	3	4-5	6	7-8	9-10	11-12	13-14	15	16-20	L	8.64	3.43
M	0-5	6-7	8	9-10	11-12	13-14	15	16-17	18-19	20-26	M	12.37	3.45
N	0-4	5-6	7	8	9-10	11-12	13	14-15	16	17-20	N	10.52	3.06
O	0-2	3-4	5	6-7	8-10	11-12	13-14	15-16	17-19	20-26	O	10.27	4.27
Q1	0-4	5	6	7-8	9-10	11	12-13	14-15	16	17-20	Q1	10.12	3.23
Q2	0-4	5-6	7-8	9	10-11	12-13	14-15	16	17	18-20	Q2	11.60	3.48
Q3	0-5	6-7	8-9	10-11	12	13-14	15-16	17	18-19	20	Q3	12.79	3.30
Q4	0-2	3-4	5-6	7-9	10-12	13-14	15-17	18-19	20-21	22-26	Q4	11.99	4.99
	1	2	3	4	5	6	7	8	9	10			
	Sten Score												

TABLE 3.9 British general population male: Form B, N = 1,011 (mean age 39.5 years, SD 16.1)

Factor	Sten Score										Factor	Mean	S.D.
	1	2	3	4	5	6	7	8	9	10			
A	0-1	2	3-4	5-6	7-8	9-10	11-12	13	14-15	16-20	A	8.22	3.68
B	0-2	3-4	5	6	7	8	9	10	11	12-13	B	7.44	2.00
C	0-6	7-9	10-11	12-13	14-15	16-17	18-19	20-21	22-23	24-26	C	15.50	4.14
E	0-4	5-6	7-8	9-10	11-12	13-14	15-16	17-18	19-20	21-26	E	12.67	4.01
F	0-3	4-6	7-8	9-10	11-13	14-16	17-19	20-21	22-23	24-26	F	13.80	4.99
G	0-5	6-7	8-9	10	11-12	13	14-15	16	17	18-20	G	12.27	3.05
H	0-2	3-5	6-7	8-10	11-14	15-17	18-19	20-22	23-24	25-26	H	13.93	5.63
I	0-2	3	4-5	6	7-8	9-10	11	12-13	14-15	16-20	I	8.48	3.28
L	0-3	4-5	6	7	8-9	10	11	12-13	14	15-20	L	9.05	2.68
M	0-3	4-5	6	7-8	9-10	11-12	13-14	15-16	17-18	19-26	M	10.52	3.78
N	0-4	5	6-7	8	9-10	11	12-13	14	15-16	17-20	N	10.47	3.01
O	0-1	2	3-4	5-6	7-9	10-11	12-14	15-16	17-19	20-26	O	9.51	4.53
Q1	0-3	4	5	6-7	8	9-10	11	12-13	14-15	16-20	Q1	8.72	3.01
Q2	0-2	3	4-5	6-7	8	9-10	11-12	13	14-15	16-20	Q2	8.75	3.35
Q3	0-4	5-6	7-8	9-10	11-12	13-14	15	16-17	18	19-20	Q3	12.10	3.46
Q4	0-2	3-4	5-6	7-8	9-11	12-14	15-17	18-19	20-21	22-26	Q4	11.75	5.05
	1	2	3	4	5	6	7	8	9	10			
	Sten Score												

TABLE 3.10 British general population male: Form A + Form B, N = 1,004 (mean age 39.5 years, SD 16.1)

Factor	Sten Score										Factor	Mean	S.D.
	1	2	3	4	5	6	7	8	9	10			
A	0-6	7-8	9-11	12-14	15-17	18-20	21-23	24-26	27-29	30-40	A	17.68	5.85
B	0-7	8-9	10-11	12	13-14	15-16	17-18	19	20	21-26	B	14.65	3.47
C	0-16	17-20	21-23	24-27	28-30	31-34	35-38	39-41	42	43-52	C	30.80	6.99
E	0-11	12-14	15-17	18-20	21-24	25-28	29-32	33-36	37-39	40-52	E	25.00	7.30
F	0-8	9-12	13-17	18-20	21-25	26-30	31-36	37-40	41-45	46-52	F	26.67	9.23
G	0-11	12-15	16-18	19-21	22-24	25-27	28-30	31-33	34	35-40	G	24.63	5.90
H	0-7	8-11	12-16	17-21	22-27	28-33	34-38	39-42	43-46	47-52	H	27.25	10.30
I	0-7	8-9	10-11	12-14	15-17	18-20	21-23	24-26	27-30	31-40	I	17.63	5.76
L	0-8	9-10	11-12	13-14	15-17	18-19	20-22	23-25	26-28	29-40	L	17.72	4.95
M	0-12	13-14	15-17	18-19	20-22	23-25	26-28	29-31	32-34	35-52	M	22.94	5.63
N	0-11	12-13	14-16	17-18	19-20	21-23	24-25	26-28	29-30	31-40	N	20.96	4.80
O	0-5	6-8	9-11	12-15	16-19	20-23	24-27	28-32	33-36	37-52	O	19.69	7.79
Q1	0-9	10-11	12-13	14-16	17-18	19-20	21-23	24-27	28-29	30-40	Q1	18.86	4.97
Q2	0-8	9-11	12-14	15-17	18-20	21-23	24-26	27-28	29-32	33-40	Q2	20.40	5.76
Q3	0-12	13-15	16-18	19-21	22-25	26-28	29-31	32-33	34-35	36-40	Q3	24.86	6.00
Q4	0-6	7-9	10-14	15-18	19-23	24-28	29-33	34-37	38-41	42-52	Q4	23.77	9.20
	1	2	3	4	5	6	7	8	9	10			
	Sten Score												

TABLE 3.11 British general population male + female: Form A, N = 2,220 (mean age 38.7 years, SD 15.9)

Factor	Sten Score										Factor	Mean	S.D.
	1	2	3	4	5	6	7	8	9	10			
A	0-3	4-5	6-7	8-9	10	11	12-13	14	15-16	17-20	A	10.22	3.06
B	0-2	3	4	5	6-7	8	9	10	11	12-13	B	7.01	2.13
C	0-7	8	9-10	11-12	13-14	15-16	17-18	19-20	21-22	23-26	C	14.64	3.90
E	0-3	4	5-6	7-8	9-10	11-12	13-15	16-17	18-20	21-26	E	10.86	4.38
F	0-3	4-5	6-7	8-9	10-12	13-14	15-17	18-20	21-22	23-26	F	12.36	4.99
G	0-4	5-6	7-8	9-10	11-12	13-14	15	16-17	18	19-20	G	12.26	3.56
H	0-2	3-4	5-6	7-9	10-12	13-15	16-18	19-20	21-23	24-26	H	12.47	5.46
I	0-3	4-5	6-7	8-9	10-11	12-13	14-15	16	17-18	19-20	I	11.25	3.75
L	0-1	2-3	4	5-6	7-8	9	10-11	12-13	14-15	16-20	L	8.25	3.44
M	0-5	6	7-8	9-10	11	12-13	14-15	16-17	18-19	20-26	M	12.02	3.55
N	0-4	5-6	7	8-9	10-11	12	13-14	15	16-17	18-20	N	11.16	3.18
O	0-3	4-5	6	7-9	10-11	12-13	14-15	16-17	18-20	21-26	O	11.44	4.30
Q1	0-3	4	5	6-7	8	9-10	11-12	13-14	15-16	17-20	Q1	9.11	3.31
Q2	0-4	5	6-7	8-9	10-11	12-13	14-15	16	17-18	19-20	Q2	11.50	3.51
Q3	0-5	6-7	8-9	10	11-12	13-14	15	16-17	18	19-20	Q3	12.36	3.23
Q4	0-3	4-5	6-8	9-10	11-13	14-15	16-18	19-20	21-22	23-26	Q4	13.16	4.92
	1	2	3	4	5	6	7	8	9	10			
	Sten Score												

TABLE 3.12 British general population male + female: Form B, N = 2,019 (mean age 38.2 years, SD 15.8)

Factor	Sten Score 1	2	3	4	5	6	7	8	9	10	Factor	Mean	S.D.
A	0-1	2-3	4-5	6-7	8-9	10-11	12	13-14	15-16	17-20	A	9.42	3.63
B	0-2	3-4	5	6	7	8	9	10	-	11-13	B	7.34	1.98
C	0-6	7-8	9-10	11-12	13-14	15-16	17-18	19-20	21-22	23-26	C	14.73	4.08
E	0-3	4-5	6-7	8	9-10	11-13	14-15	16-17	18-20	21-26	E	11.16	4.16
F	0-4	5-6	7-9	10-11	12-13	14-16	17-18	19-21	22-23	24-26	F	13.85	4.79
G	0-6	7	8-9	10-11	12-13	14	15	16	17-18	19-20	G	12.53	3.03
H	0-2	3-4	5-6	7-9	10-12	13-16	17-19	20-21	22-23	24-26	H	12.83	5.80
I	0-3	4	5-6	7-8	9-10	11	12-13	14-15	16	17-20	I	10.06	3.45
L	0-3	4	5	6-7	8	9	10-11	12	13-14	15-20	L	8.57	2.70
M	0-3	4	5-6	7-8	9-10	11	12-13	14-16	17-18	19-26	M	10.27	3.73
N	0-4	5-6	7	8-9	10	11-12	13	14	15-16	17-20	N	10.55	2.90
O	0-2	3	4-5	6-8	9-11	12-13	14-16	17-18	19-20	21-26	O	11.16	4.81
Q1	0-3	4	5	6	7-8	9	10-11	12-13	14-15	16-20	Q1	8.53	2.96
Q2	0-2	3	4-5	6-7	8	9	10-11	12-13	14-15	16-20	Q2	8.58	3.25
Q3	0-4	5	6-7	8-9	10-11	12-13	14-15	16	17	18-20	Q3	11.66	3.54
Q4	0-3	4-5	6-7	8-10	11-13	14-15	16-18	19-20	21-22	23-26	Q4	13.11	5.01
	1	2	3	4	5	6	7	8	9	10			
	Sten Score												

TABLE 3.13 British general population male + female: Form A + Form B, N = 2,012 (mean age 38.2 years, SD 15.8)

Factor	Sten Score 1	2	3	4	5	6	7	8	9	10	Factor	Mean	S.D.
A	0-7	8-10	11-13	14-16	17-19	20-22	23-25	26-28	29-30	31-40	A	19.64	5.83
B	0-7	8-9	10	11-12	13-14	15-16	17-18	19	20	21-26	B	14.41	3.47
C	0-15	16-19	20-22	23-26	27-29	30-32	33-36	37-40	41-42	43-52	C	29.43	6.97
E	0-8	9-11	12-14	15-17	18-21	22-25	26-29	30-34	35-38	39-52	E	22.05	7.60
F	0-9	10-13	14-17	18-21	22-26	27-30	31-35	36-40	41-44	45-52	F	26.34	8.92
G	0-12	13-15	16-18	19-22	23-25	26-27	28-30	31-32	33-34	35-40	G	24.71	5.69
H	0-6	7-9	10-14	15-19	20-25	26-30	31-36	37-41	42-45	46-52	H	25.36	10.50
I	0-8	9-11	12-14	15-17	18-21	22-24	25-27	28-30	31-33	34-40	I	21.32	6.38
L	0-7	8-9	10-11	12-14	15-16	17-19	20-21	22-24	25-27	28-40	L	16.80	5.03
M	0-11	12-14	15-16	17-19	20-21	22-24	25-28	29-31	32-35	36-52	M	22.36	5.81
N	0-11	12-14	15-16	17-19	20-21	22-24	25-26	27-28	29-30	31-40	N	21.65	4.80
O	0-6	7-10	11-13	14-18	19-22	23-26	20 7-30	31-34	35-38	39-52	O	22.53	8.20
Q1	0-9	10	11-12	13-14	15-17	18-19	20-22	23-25	26-28	29-40	Q1	17.68	4.98
Q2	0-8	9-11	12-13	14-17	18-20	21-23	24-25	26-28	29-32	33-40	Q2	20.05	5.69
Q3	0-11	12-14	15-17	18-21	22-24	25-27	28-30	31-32	33-34	35-40	Q3	24.00	5.93
Q4	0-7	8-11	12-16	17-21	22-26	27-31	32-35	36-39	40-42	43-52	Q4	26.28	9.04
	1	2	3	4	5	6	7	8	9	10			
	Sten Score												

Note

1 Sten stands for 'Standard Ten' and is a standardised scale which runs from 1 to 10. A score at the middle of this scale, i.e. 5.5, represents an average score for the particular group of people in question.

References

British Market Research Bureau (1971). *Target Group Index (T.G.1.)*. London.

Cattell, R. B. and Eber, H. W. (1968). *The Sixteen Personality Factor Questionnaire (16 P.F.) Forms A and B*. Champaign, IL: Institute for Personality and Ability Testing (Anglicised editions distributed in the UK by the NFER Publishing Company Limited, Windsor).

Cattell R. B., Eber, H. W. and Tatsuoka, M. M. (1970). *Handbook for the Sixteen Personality Factor Questionnaire (16 P.F.)*. Champaign, IL: Institute for Personality and Ability Testing. Distributed in the UK by the NFER Publishing Company Limited, Windsor.

General Register Office (1971). *Registrar General's Annual Estimates of the Population of England and Wales (and of Local Authority Areas)*. London: HMSO.

General Register Office – Scotland (1970). *The Annual Report of the Registrar General for Scotland 1970. No.16, Part 11: Population and Vital Statistics*. London: HMSO.

Joint Industry Committee for National Readership Surveys (1971). *National Readership Survey 1971*. London.

MacFarlane-Smith, J. (1972). *Interviewing in Market and Social Research*. London: Routledge & Kegan Paul.

NFER Publishing Company Limited (1971). *Collected Test Information Sheets October 1970– December 1971*, Windsor: NFER.

Tatsuoka, M. M. (1969). *Selected Topics in Advanced Statistics – Standardised Scales: Linear and Area Transformations*. Champaign, IL: Institute for Personality and Ability Testing. Distributed in the UK by the NFER Publishing Company Limited, Windsor.

Appendix: supplementary 16PF age trends - looking back

In Figure 3.2, Intelligence (16PF Factor B) on both Forms A and B follows a similar pattern for males and females. Males scored marginally higher than females but, although the difference reaches statistical significance, it is so small it is not of real practical importance. The items making up the scale were untimed and mainly of verbal and numerical reasoning. One 16PF intelligence item in the 1968 version was so poor that it actually correlated negatively with the remaining items reinforcing the view that no conclusions on female and male differences should be drawn here. Regarding the question of whether there is any decline with age: by looking at the z-score scale, a lower mean score did not occur until about 50 years of age. As these are cross-sectional, not longitudinal, data collected in the early 1970s, we could not be sure that this lower mean would occur at this age in future generations. And again the difference between ages 20 to 50 years, by modern standards of interpretation, are not great.

As is shown in Figure 3.3, Conscientious (Factor G) shows increased values by age for both men and women which is in line with modern research on this personality variable.

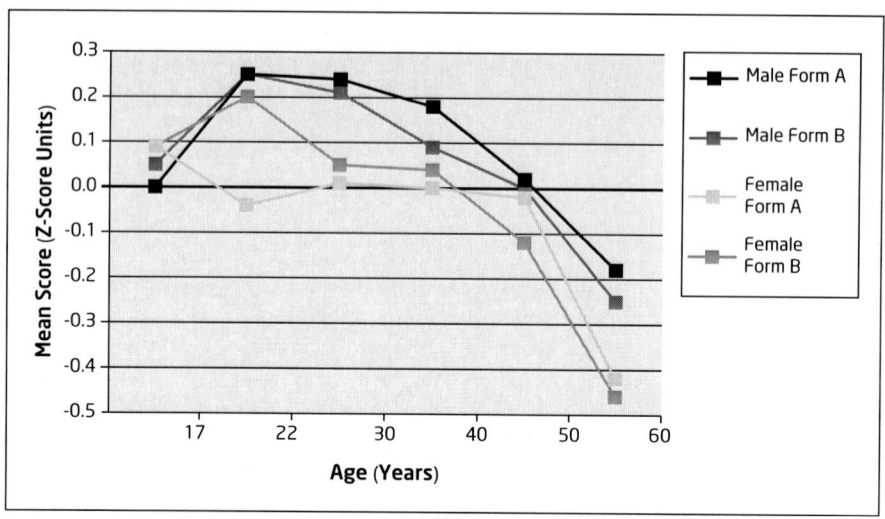

FIGURE 3.2   Age trends in personality: intelligence (16PF Factor B)

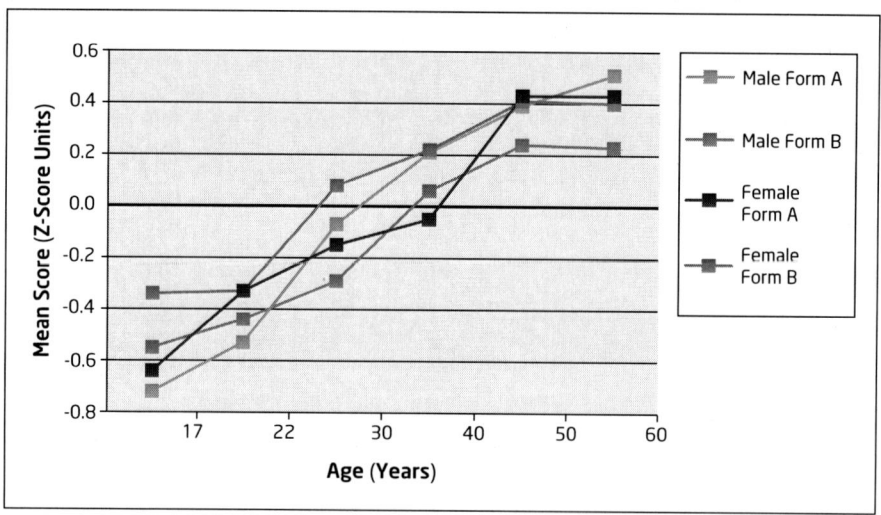

FIGURE 3.3   Age trends in personality: conscientious (16PF Factor G)

In Figure 3.4, Experimenting (Factor Q1), shows a very marked decrease with age with a medium effect size of men being somewhat more Experimenting by self-report than women. What is extremely curious is that Cattell, the author of the 16PF, stated in the then technical manual that this variable had absolutely no relationship with age in his research. This is not supported here and is against most of the prevailing literature from then and since. On detailed item analysis for one item on this scale there appeared to be an error on the publisher's scoring

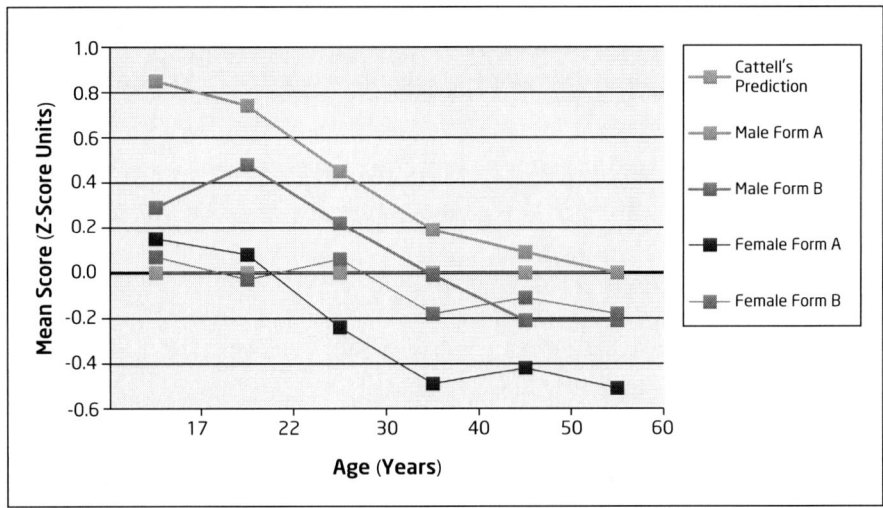

FIGURE 3.4 Age trends in personality: experimenting (16PF Factor Q1)

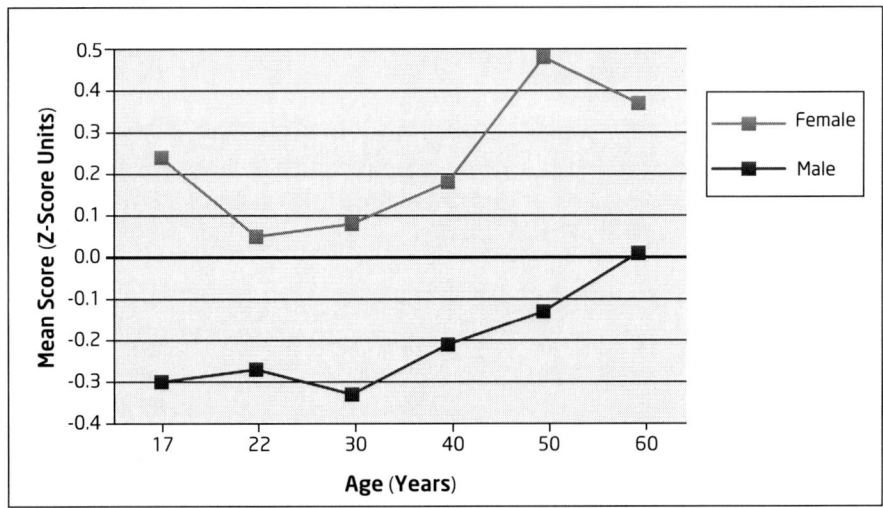

FIGURE 3.5 Age trends in personality: anxiety (16PF Factors C, O and Q4)

key where one item had an inverse relationship with all the other items on the Experimenting personality scale.

In terms of Anxiety, shown in Figure 3.5, males are lower (by self-report at least) at all ages than females. There are little age differences seen overall.

Figure 3.6 represents Extraversion and is made from 16PF Factors F and Q2.

Figure 3.7 represents Openness to Experience, measured through 16PF Factors I and M. Females are shown to be higher here, but this may be due to very

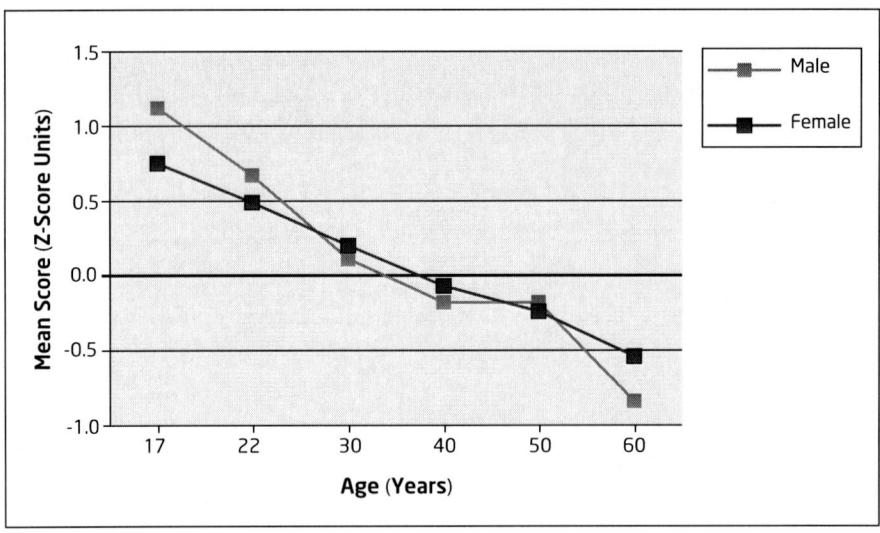

FIGURE 3.6 Age trends in personality: extraversion (16PF Factor F and Q2)

gender-specific items involving job choice at the time. For example, "I would like to be a mechanical engineer" was much more highly endorsed by males than females at the time of the study. Such answers would lead to lower openness to experience scores. It is the author's opinion that this has resulted in higher scores for females and demonstrates the need for the very much more careful consideration of content at the item level. It is worth noting that this is a practice which did not materially emerge until a decade later.

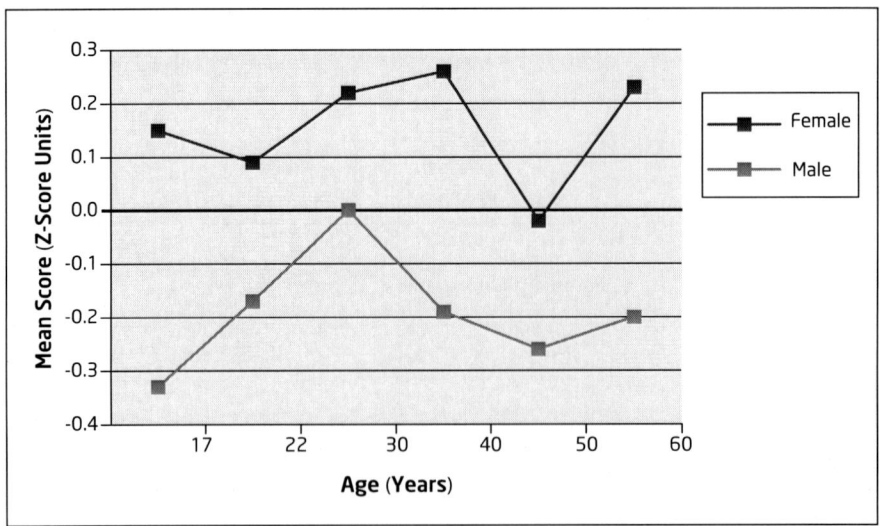

FIGURE 3.7 Age trends in personality: openness (16PF Factors I and M)

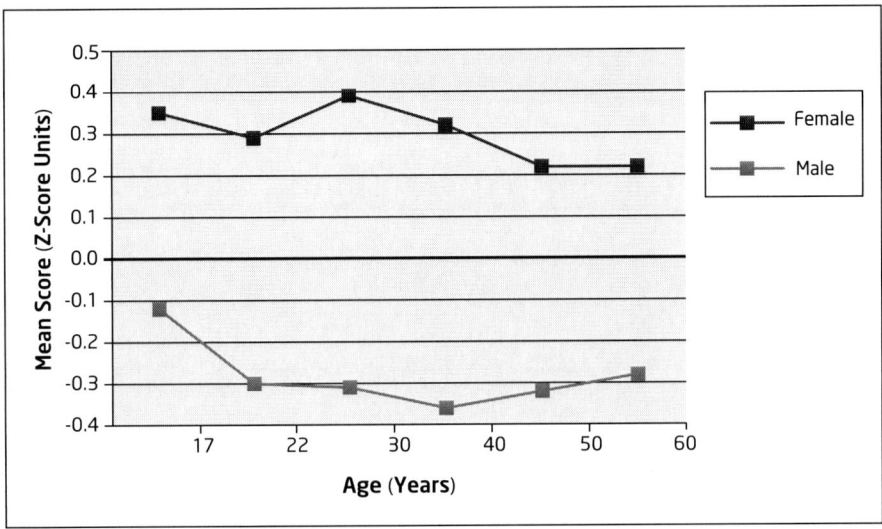

FIGURE 3.8   Age trends in personality: agreeableness (16PF Factor A)

Figure 3.8, measuring Agreeableness, also contains gender stereotypic item content which could be exaggerating the difference between men and women.

Figure 3.9 represents Conscientiousness defined more reliably by adding in Factors Q1 and Q3 alongside Factor G. When defined this way, the personality variable increases with age for both males and females. It is worth noting here that the alternate form reliability of many of the original 16PF primary traits between Forms A and B were not impressive. My data set revealed reliabilities as low as

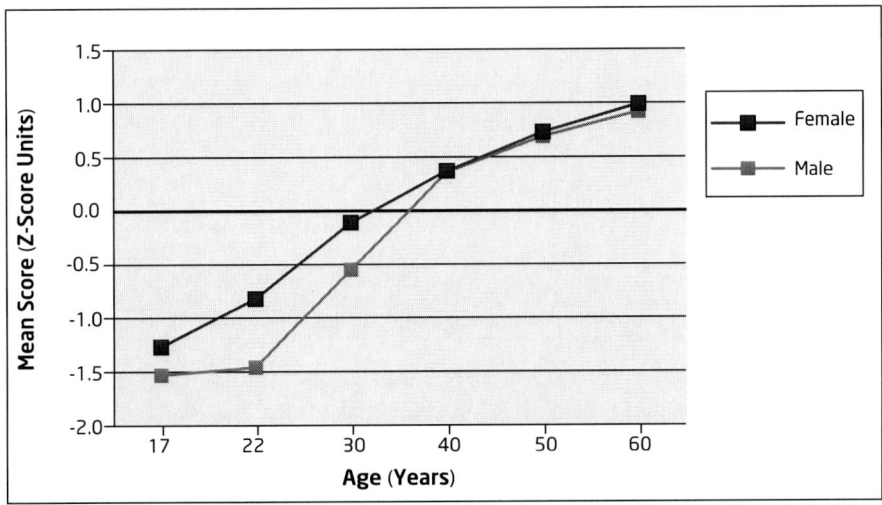

FIGURE 3.9   Age trends in personality: conscientiousness (16PF Factors G, Q1 and Q3)

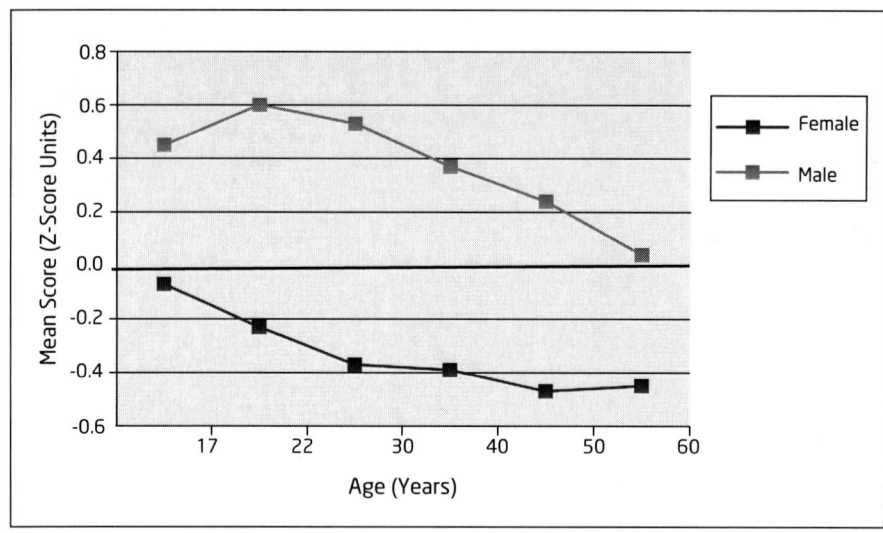

FIGURE 3.10   Age trends in personality: drive (16PF Factor E)

+0.2 for certain scales (for example, Factors such as L, M, N and Q1). Such levels of reliability are little above chance and may be due to content that was ambiguous or, even rather bizarre, in some cases.

Lastly, Figure 3.10 represents Drive and shows little change in practical terms over the different age groups measured.

4

REFLECTIONS ON THE DEVELOPMENT OF AN INDUCTIVE WORK-BASED QUESTIONNAIRE

The OPQ®

This chapter is based on a presentation I gave in 2005:

> Saville, P. (2005). Personality & job success. Public lecture presented at the University of the West Indies, Barbados, November.

Personality and job success

I'd like to take this opportunity to reflect on the development of the Occupational Personality Questionnaires (OPQ), one of the most important developments in workplace assessment.[1]

The demand for a range of new personality questionnaires was very much client-led. At Saville and Holdsworth Limited (SHL), we had launched a new range of ability and aptitude tests for the world of work in 1980. Clients had rapidly taken these up as more relevant and up-to-date than most of the other materials which were then available. It was their suggestion, therefore, that we should turn our attention to developing a range of personality questionnaires which were more related to the workplace than the materials currently in use in the 1980s. The first consideration was how to fund the origination, norming and validation of such a range. As a commercial organisation, government grants weren't readily available to us and the cost of the entire project could run into hundreds of thousands of pounds.

Funding the development of the OPQ

Thinking through the options, I went to our major clients and suggested a sponsorship arrangement, whereby each organisation would pay a fee of some £5,000 to £10,000 and in return would receive free training and materials for the instruments, and would not be required to pay an intended annual licence fee for five years. They also agreed as part of the agreement that each organisation would help in the trialling of some 1,500 personality scale items. During the period of 1980–1, seminars were held in London describing the intended research programme and over 50 major organisations sponsored the project. They included British Telecom (BT), Deloitte, Littlewoods, the then Manpower Services Commission, NatWest Bank, the Post Office, Prudential plc, Sainsbury's plc, Scottish & Newcastle Breweries and BP. Looking back on the list, it is fascinating to observe how many of the large sponsors have been merged into even larger conglomerates.

Objectives of the research

The OPQs were to be devised for use in administration, industry, commerce and the public sector in a wide range of roles, including managerial, professional, banking, accountancy, administrative, sales, supervisory, clerical, IT, technical apprentice and graduate jobs. The original OPQ was designed to be suitable for use by psychologists and HR professionals in selection, development, counselling, management assessment, succession planning and team building. It was considered important that the materials would be acceptable to candidates and not regarded in any way as clinical or an intrusion into privacy. The kinds of items which existed at the time in well-known questionnaires and which it was felt had to be avoided included:

1. 'I would rather be a colonel than a bishop' (measuring Tough v Tender-minded).
2. 'More than 50% of Americans kiss on their first date' (measuring Mating Urge).
3. 'I have fear of being buried alive' (measuring Anxiety).

The items below, from existing assessments at the time, were designed to measure mental health issues. Many job applicants considered them an intrusion into privacy, as those companies which used questionnaires that included such items were to discover, at their legal cost (and especially in the USA):

4. 'There is very little love or companionship in my family.'
5. 'I believe in the second coming of Christ.'
6. 'There is something wrong with my sex organs.'

Such content brings up so many issues of biases relating to gender, age and minority groups that it is scarcely conceivable that they were ever used at all.

A further objective of the development of the OPQ was that a range of questionnaires of different lengths would be developed. They were to vary from 15 to 60 minutes in length. There was also the need that the materials were professionally designed. Many questionnaires looked like they were printed at the turn of the century, yet many clients had pointed out that the appearance of materials used in selection was a reflection of the organisation. If selection materials look dated, it was a poor advertisement for the organisation; good design was an essential factor when it came to the publication of the questionnaires.

Above all, the OPQs were to meet the best technical standards in terms of norms, reliability and, most importantly, validity.

The main stages in the OPQ development

When developing any questionnaire, three methods of construction can be distinguished:

a. **The Deductive.** With this approach, the test author proposes a theory of personality and writes items according to this theory. An example would be the Myers-Briggs Type Indicator (MBTI), which is claimed to be based on Jungian theory. However, Burisch (1984) noted that complex theories did not yield higher validities than those based on relatively straightforward concepts.

b. **The Inductive.** Here the objective is to produce the most parsimonious or simple solution to personality measurement, with a minimum of variables, often based on some form of the statistical technique of factor analysis. An example questionnaire is Cattell's 16PF, an inventory I knew well on an item-by-item basis (e.g. Saville, 1977). In this case, the best scales had relatively short items, not long complex ones. Other questionnaires developed in this manner include many 'Big Five' measures of personality which measure openness to experience, conscientiousness, extraversion, agreeableness and the unfortunately named neuroticism.

c. **The Empirically Keyed.** This involves a great many items of personality and ability being written, then being administered to specific occupational groups such as computer programmers. The individual is then measured to the extent to which their responses are similar to the given group. Probably the best-known questionnaires of this kind are the Minnesota Multiphasic Personality Inventory (MMPI), which measures different psychiatric conditions, and the Strong Vocational Interest Bank, which is designed to measure occupational choice. The Empirically Keyed approach was not used in the development of the OPQ. Such measures are extremely difficult to score without computer assistance and there is very little evidence that they provide, in the world of work at least, particularly good validity. Moreover, the items which distinguish between different occupations are not particularly subtle or surprising. For example, the Engineer scale on the Strong Vocational Interest Bank asked the respondent whether they enjoyed repairing automobiles.

I decided, therefore, that both the Deductive and Inductive approaches would be used in the development of the OPQ, but that the Empirically Keyed approach would not. Moreover, controversial, offensive and contentious content should be avoided, as should items which would show gender or high social desirability bias – the tendency to portray oneself in a favourable light.

To gain a list of potential personality variables to be included in the questionnaires, Lisa Cramp and I undertook a review of the major personality tests of the time. This included instruments like Cattell's 16PF (which I had studied in my own doctorate), the California Personality Inventory (Gough, 1957), the Edwards Personal Preference Schedule (Edwards, 1959; a useful instrument, based upon Henry Murray's (1938) personality theory, but including the unfortunate variable of heterosexual sex drive), the MMPI (Hathaway and McKinley, 1943), designed for clinical use, but nevertheless still used in the workplace, and the Eysenck Personality Questionnaire (EPQ; Eysenck and Eysenck, 1975). The Guilford-Zimmerman Temperament Survey (1949) and the MBTI were also considered, though both were little used in the UK at the time. From these, a list of potentially useful personality constructs was assembled. Literature reviews of personality terms from academic papers were listed, as were assessment centre criteria used in organisations, as well as personality variables used in company appraisal systems.

To add to our database of personality constructs, Repertory Grid studies (Kelly, 1955) were undertaken, where managers were asked to write on separate cards ten high-performing individuals and ten low performers in a given job. Three cards were chosen at random and the manager requested to describe which two were alike and different from the third. From this we could elicit personality variables which distinguish between high and low performance. Flanagan's (1954) Critical Incident technique was also used in questionnaire form and completed by supervisors and managers where they described how a job holder dealt with a difficult task and handled it well or badly. From this, further aspects of personality relevant to job success were deduced. Group discussions then refined these variables and amalgamated them where there was clear overlap.

This gave an initial model of personality which consisted of 45 bipolar scales. In the analysis, each pole was considered independently, arriving at 90 variables in all. This first model is shown below.

From these accumulated data, an adjective checklist study was conducted where the respondent provided a self-rating, a rating of a colleague and a rating of 'how I would like to be'. The third task was to provide a measure of the social desirability of the adjectives. The adjective checklist was completed by some 500 working adults.

The 400-adjective questionnaire was analysed into 90 homogeneous item clusters (HICs) of four items each and 40 further variables. Further HICs were added to give 45 scales and a 98 × 98 correlation matrix was calculated. Each individual item was correlated with each of the 45 scales. Much of this and the ensuing statistical work was conducted and organised by one of our directors, Gill Nyfield, who also wrote new computer programmes to help with the enormous generation of item data that the project was to produce. Factor analysis, using the SPSS and Promax programmes set to extract factors with eigenvalues greater than one, were also employed. Following this adjective checklist study, the model was further refined and 32 personality scales were proposed for writing full-length items.

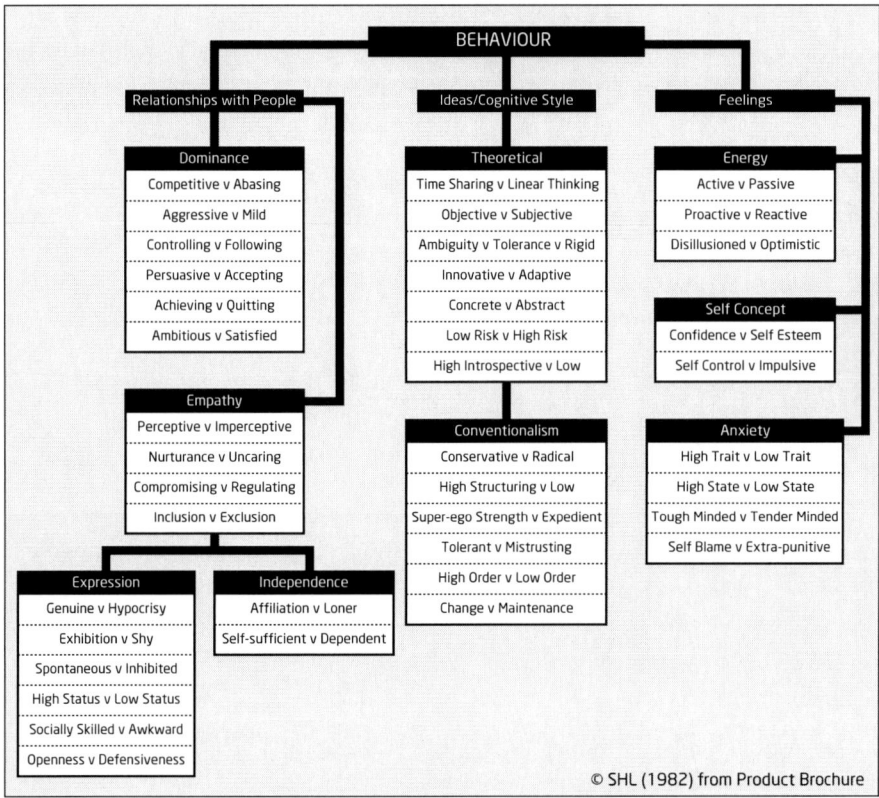

The diagram shows the following structure:

BEHAVIOUR

Relationships with People

Dominance
- Competitive v Abasing
- Aggressive v Mild
- Controlling v Following
- Persuasive v Accepting
- Achieving v Quitting
- Ambitious v Satisfied

Empathy
- Perceptive v Imperceptive
- Nurturance v Uncaring
- Compromising v Regulating
- Inclusion v Exclusion

Expression
- Genuine v Hypocrisy
- Exhibition v Shy
- Spontaneous v Inhibited
- High Status v Low Status
- Socially Skilled v Awkward
- Openness v Defensiveness

Independence
- Affiliation v Loner
- Self-sufficient v Dependent

Ideas/Cognitive Style

Theoretical
- Time Sharing v Linear Thinking
- Objective v Subjective
- Ambiguity v Tolerance v Rigid
- Innovative v Adaptive
- Concrete v Abstract
- Low Risk v High Risk
- High Introspective v Low

Conventionalism
- Conservative v Radical
- High Structuring v Low
- Super-ego Strength v Expedient
- Tolerant v Mistrusting
- High Order v Low Order
- Change v Maintenance

Feelings

Energy
- Active v Passive
- Proactive v Reactive
- Disillusioned v Optimistic

Self Concept
- Confidence v Self Esteem
- Self Control v Impulsive

Anxiety
- High Trait v Low Trait
- High State v Low State
- Tough Minded v Tender Minded
- Self Blame v Extra-punitive

© SHL (1982) from Product Brochure

FIGURE 4.1 The first OPQ model

A range of psychologist item writers of different ethnic groups, genders and age ranges were used to ensure a broad coverage of approach. Over 2,000 items were written, from which the best 1,500 were selected.

As we were unsure which type of item format in a questionnaire would prove more or less valid, four types of item were researched:

1. **A five-point normative Likert scale** – from 'strongly agree' to 'strongly disagree'; containing 384 items.
2. **A three-point normative items scale** – where the respondent answered (a) agree, (b) uncertain, (c) disagree; again, a total of 384 items.
3. **Pairs of words and phrases using an ipsative forced**-choice format – where the respondent had to choose between options in what was referred to as the 'Relating' domain and which were more attitudinal than behavioural in content; 320 pairs in total.
4. **A ranking task** – where four different aspects of personality had to be ranked in terms of 'which comes easiest to you'. This consisted of 107 blocks of four, took about an hour to complete and was necessarily ipsative in design.

For the field trials, 700 people organised through our sponsors were asked to complete two item banks. Biographical data such as gender, age, job category and other information were also collected. In total, there were approximately 800 questions. To save respondent time, these were printed in an attractive booklet to encourage a high response rate, which the individual completed without the use of a separate answer sheet ready for key entry into a computer. All possible combinations of two banks were printed, half in one order and the over half in reverse order. Each respondent was given four weeks to complete the task before returning to us for item analysis. As computer power was not as it is today, we often let the computer run through the night from 7 p.m. to 8 a.m. the next morning.

The criteria for an item to be accepted into the final form of the OPQ was that it was written for the specific personality scale, made psychological sense as judged by others, and mathematically had a high point-biserial correlation with the rest of the items in its own scale (to avoid spurious overlap), but an appreciably lower correlation with every other scale. Most of the attitudinal items failed this test and that entire bank had to be discarded. Examples of items which failed this scrutiny are given below, with the item-scale correlation in parentheses. I have modified them slightly to make my point more clearly. We refer to these as 'zombie' items.

Examples of 'zombie' OPQ items which failed to make the final form

1. 'People should learn to help themselves' (Caring, –01).
2. 'Most projects need a leader' (Controlling, .22).
3. This item had a higher correlation with Conscientious, at .28.
4. 'In a restaurant I like to: (a) Decide what to have quickly, (b) Not sure, (c) Wait for others, then have what they choose' (Decisive, .06).
5. 'I have been asked to make last minute talks without warning' (Outgoing, .28) This item correlated .38 with Controlling, .34 with Persuasive, .42 with Social Confidence and .31 with the Innovative scale.

In the first example, one can see that one could agree with the item if one was caring or uncaring; the result is virtually a zero correlation with its own scale.

For Example 2, one could agree with the statement that every project needs a leader, but not actually be the leader oneself. In fact, the item is shown to be a better measure of conscientiousness, with a correlation of .28.

For Example 3, perhaps choosing a meal is too situational (it depends on the menu or who is paying!), whilst options (a) and (c) are not really opposites. One might wait for others to choose, but then not have the same as them.

For Example 4, whilst the item does correlate +.28 with the remaining items of the Outgoing scale, it is a better measure of Controlling Behaviour (.38), Persuasive (.34) and Innovative (.31), and correlates highest with Social Confidence (.42). It is just too mixed an item to measure the single facet of personality for which it was written.

Ideally we were looking for a correlation of about +.60 of an item with its own scale and a near-zero correlation with the remaining 29 scales of this version of the OPQ. This should ensure good reliability of each scale of personality, but low correlations with all other scales to increase both fidelity and bandwidth. In turn, this should help to maximise validity.

The original OPQ scales were subdivided under the three Personality Domains:

1. Relating with People (9 scales).
2. Thinking (11 scales).[2]
3. Feelings (10 scales).

Overall, this gave 30 variables, plus one scale of Social Desirability. We named this the OPQ Concept Model of Personality. Our definition of personality given in the first OPQ manual of 1984 was 'that concerned with the person's typical ways of relating with people, thinking and feeling'. The scales of the OPQ model, with descriptions, are listed below.

Three versions of the Concept Model of the OPQ were published in 1984. These were the normative Concept 5, which consisted of six Likert items from 'strongly agree' to 'strongly disagree', the normative Concept 3, which were items of three-option multiple choice, and the ipsative Concept 4, which consisted of 107 blocks of four items, where the respondent was required to rank in order what was most to least true of them.

In 1986, an analysis was run where only the most and least true of the four statements needed to be endorsed, ignoring the two middle responses which carried the values of two and three. By giving both these middle responses the value of 2.5, the 'most true' the value of 1 and 'least true' the value of 4, it was found that the correlation by this simplified response format of merely choosing most and least true correlated +.97 to +.99 with ranking all of the four statements in each block, thus losing virtually no useful data. This version became known as Concept 4.2 (CM4.2) and brought down administration time from 60 to 50 minutes with virtually no loss of fidelity.

The opportunity was also taken at this stage to amend some items which contained British idioms and caused problems in the 40 languages into which the OPQ had been translated. These included items such as 'Chancing your arm' which was changed to 'Taking risks' and 'Beating the opposition', a measure of Competitiveness which in some cultures was taken literally!

In addition to the Concept Model, factor analysis was undertaken and the shorter Factor Model, consisting of 14 scales, the Octagon Model with eight scales and the Pentagon Model with five scales were all produced. Each of these instruments had parallel forms, giving six further questionnaires. It was, however, the Concept Model of 30+1 scales which was to prove the most popular, particularly the ipsative CM4.2, both in the UK and internationally.

In 1999, a team of Saville, Nyfield, MacIver, Baron and Miles revised the OPQ Concept Model by removing scales such as 'Artistic' and 'Practical', as it was felt

TABLE 4.1 The OPQ Concept Model

Relationships with People	
PERSUASIVE	enjoys selling, changes opinions of others, convincing with arguments, negotiates
CONTROLLING	takes charge, directs, manages, organises, supervises others
INDEPENDENT	has strong views on things, difficult to manage, speaks up, argues, dislikes ties
OUTGOING	fun loving, humorous, sociable, vibrant, talkative, jovial
AFFILIATIVE	has many friends, enjoys being in groups, likes companionship, shares things with friends
SOCIALLY CONFIDENT	puts people at ease, knows what to say, good with words
MODEST	reserved about achievements, avoids talking about self, accepts others, avoids trappings of status
DEMOCRATIC	encourages others to contribute, consults, listens and refers to others
CARING	considerate to others, helps those in need, sympathetic, tolerant

THINKING STYLE	
PRACTICAL	down-to-earth, likes repairing and mending things, better with the concrete
DATA RATIONAL	good with data, operates on facts, enjoys assessing and measuring
ARTISTIC	appreciates culture, shows artistic flair, sensitive to visual arts and music
BEHAVIOURAL	analyses thoughts and behaviour, psychologically minded, likes to understand people
TRADITIONAL	preserves well proven methods, prefers the orthodox, disciplined, conventional
CHANGE ORIENTATED	enjoys doing new things, seeks variety, prefers novelty to routine, accepts changes
CONCEPTUAL	theoretical, intellectually curious, enjoys the complex and abstract
INNOVATIVE	generates ideas, shows ingenuity, thinks up solutions
FORWARD PLANNING	prepares well in advance, enjoys target setting, forecasts trends, plans projects
DETAIL CONSCIOUS	methodical, keeps things neat and tidy, precise, accurate
CONSCIENTIOUS	sticks to deadlines, completes jobs, perseveres with routine, likes fixed schedules

FEELINGS AND EMOTIONS	
RELAXED	calm, relaxed, cool under pressure, free from anxiety, can switch off
WORRYING	worry when things go wrong, keyed-up before important events, anxious to do well
TOUGH MINDED	diffi cult to hurt or upset, can brush off insults, unaffected by unfair remarks
EMOTIONAL CONTROL	restrained in showing emotions, keeps feelings back, avoids outbursts
OPTIMISTIC	cheerful, happy, keeps spirits up despite setbacks
CRITICAL	good at probing the facts, sees the disadvantages, challenges assumptions
ACTIVE	has energy, moves quickly, enjoys physical exercise, doesn't sit still
COMPETITIVE	plays to win, determined to beat others, poor loser
ACHIEVING	ambitious, sets sights high, career centred, results orientated
DECISIVE	quick at conclusions, weighs things up rapidly, may be hasty, takes risks

they lacked occupational relevance for many jobs. The scales 'Rule Following', 'Trusting' and 'Adaptable' were added, and minor item changes were made to produce what was known as OPQ32n (normative version) and OPQ32i (ipsative version).

Recent estimations have put the number of OPQ administrations globally at over 50 million.

Why was the OPQ a success?

The research project to develop the OPQ was probably the largest of its kind ever undertaken and was influenced, improved and adapted by the active involvement of the 50 sponsoring organisations, which gave us access to extremely large trialling groups. At the time, more modern computing capability was available, which would have made the analysis of such a large body of item data virtually impossible only a decade before.

In 1943, for example, Cattell distinguished the first 12 factors of the 16PF by two people inspecting ratings of 100 people on 171 adjectives and phrases from Allport's list, using the tetrachoric correlation coefficient. This would have given a total of 14,535 coefficients with a claimed inter-rater reliability of .70 to .80. When we replicated this work, we estimated it would take about one and a half years of work to compute such a large number of correlations by hand without a modern computer. Then one would need to hold and record 14,535 correlations in one's head to discover the 12 'true' factors of personality, with a potentially huge margin of error.

Undoubtedly the use of occupationally relevant items rather than the obscure or offensive made the questionnaire far more acceptable to managers and applicants alike. This was guided by dialogue over a number of years with HR practitioners in the course room, which helped define the kinds of variable which would be appropriate for the OPQ final form. I had also been fortunate in spending much time in my doctorate examining items which tended to work compared to those that failed statistical analysis. The better items tended to be behavioural, shorter, unambiguous and avoided idiomatic expressions. This resulted in relevant scales, with good reliability, which were shown to have validity in the workplace.

The OPQ recognised that personality was best conceived as a hierarchy, where the main 30 scales represented facets of personality that could be further reduced by factor analysis into a 14-variable solution (the Factor Model), an eight-factor model (the Octagon Model) and a five-factor solution (the Pentagon Model), which was published in 1984 and was essentially a measure of what is now known as the 'Big Five' or Five-Factor Model (FFM) of personality. This gave test users a choice of versions which varied in length from around one hour to 15 minutes. Subsequently, Saville and Sik produced Images, which added a six-factor solution with the extra variable of 'Drive'.

The choice of personality variables and items avoiding complex phrases and idioms also meant that the OPQ was capable of being translated from English into such diverse languages as Arabic, Chinese, Japanese and Russian.

The OPQ was possibly the first omnibus personality questionnaire which was comprised of both normative (rating) and ipsative (ranking) formats. This was to produce considerable controversy amongst academics, especially those who believed that the normative form could be used for inter-person comparison, but the ipsative could only be used for intra-person comparison. As it was to happen, the ipsative form became much more popular worldwide in the belief that it was more difficult to fake in selection, but, as things transpired, ipsative questionnaires were later shown to have good scale validity in measuring job performing criteria.

Whilst the psychometric characteristics of an instrument must be foremost in a user's mind, the OPQ gained traction because it had been professionally designed by my own brother John Saville, who was Director of Design at Her Majesty's Stationery Office. It was Alex Burnip who took on the enormous job of co-ordinating the proofing and printing of some 100 components, including wire-bound booklets, answer sheets, acetate scoring keys, technical manuals and practice materials, all within a six-month period.

Bill Mabey, who had extensive experience in market research surveys, organised large general population and graduate standardisation projects, with the help of the Office for National Statistics (ONS). He was also to produce specialised outputs of the OPQ which described the individuals' preferred occupational job team roles. In the same way, Lisa Cramp was responsible for co-ordination of the 'OPQ Development Project' throughout its four-year duration. She also contributed, as did Bill Mabey, to the generation of items for the various trials. It was very much a team effort.

Criticisms of the OPQ

With the impact which the OPQ had, it was not surprising that one would receive both plaudits and criticism. An initial point was that 30 scales of personality was too many and just five would do – openness to experience, conscientiousness, extraversion, agreeableness and neuroticism. However, these 'Big Five' typically explained only a little more than 50 per cent of the variance in personality. The authors' view was that although the Big Five is a very useful taxonomy in academic research, it lacks the detail which is required in applied psychology. For example, the variable of Conscientiousness is made up of at least two distinct characteristics; dependability and drive.

Similarly, Extraversion can be broken down into outgoingness and dominance. Matthews and Stanton (1994) found during the factor analysis of the Concept Model of the OPQ that although it was designed to be deductive in construction backed up by detailed item analysis, more than 20 factors were discernible in the instrument, not just five. The OPQ Concept Model, it must be re-affirmed, was deductively derived, with careful selection of items, and was not claimed to be factorially pure. If a practitioner wished to use the FFM, the Pentagon version of the OPQ was available for their use. It is now generally accepted that whilst the

Big Five is a good organising structure, it is not necessarily the best taxonomy for predicting success in the workplace.

Regarding the desire to reduce personality down to as few variables as possible, it has even been proposed by Digman (1997) that only two factors of personality may be required for its description. He refers to these as factors Alpha (the combination of agreeableness, conscientiousness and emotional stability) and Beta (the combination of extraversion and intellect/openness). And others have suggested that we can describe personality in terms of just a single factor – what is known as 'The Big One'.

In essence, different solutions for the structure of personality will evolve depending upon the assumptions made by the researcher and the particular form of factor analysis they use. There is unlikely to be an ultimate 'truth' in personality questionnaires. The answer must lie in considering carefully what objectives one has in measuring personality and guiding one's item writing accordingly.

On the question of seeking parsimony in the personality questionnaire, there is a danger of over-reduction. Consider the Challenger space shuttle disaster of 1986, when the rocket exploded 73 seconds after take-off, killing five astronauts and two support personnel. The tragedy was put down to the failure of the O-rings, seals which allowed hydrogen to escape, ignite and explode. What percentage of all the mechanical parts of the shuttle did the O-rings represent? Probably not one ten-thousandth. But their failure resulted not only in the postponement of the American space programme but also the tragic deaths of seven individuals.

When giving lectures on statistics in market research, Eric Willson, who was a protégé of distinguished British statistician Sir Maurice Kendall, would comment: 'In factor analysis, size does not matter.' Most organisations recognise and get the big factors right in marketing, but often the smaller factors are just as important. What appear as more minor factors can make a very big difference.

A further criticism was the ipsative nature of CM4 and CM4.2 published by Johnson et al. (1988), who claimed that ipsative questionnaires exaggerated reliabilities and validities, and could not be used for comparisons between people. These researchers neglected, however, to consider the many response sets in normative questionnaires such as extremity bias (the tendency for some candidates to continually use the extreme item options whilst others answer consistently with middle responses on a Likert-type scale), which also make comparisons between individuals difficult. Further research was to show that the normative and ipsative profiles on the same individual were usually very close and that the ranking (ipsative) presentation of items can produce even higher validities than the rating (normative).

Then personality underwent a 'near-death experience' in the 1990s, when it was claimed that behaviour was dominated by the environment, not the individual, and that personality questionnaires had no validity whatsoever. Blinkhorn and Johnson (1990), writing in *Nature* magazine, had made the point that many personality test authors went 'fishing' by presenting any statistically significant but small correlations between personality scales in job performance, without *a priori* hypotheses. They particularly attacked the SHL OPQ validation review, calculating that many of the correlation coefficients with job performance when considering sample size and number of variables reported in the publication were not above chance. Unfortunately, however, they had failed to read the introduction to the review that not all validity coefficients had been reported, but only those with reasonable effect size, which rendered their calculations and conclusions invalid.

The SHL validation review enabled an independent meta-analysis by Robertson and Kinder (1993), where they considered some 20 OPQ validation studies against *a priori* hypotheses. They wrote that:

> Some versions of the instrument are ipsative and in some of the validation studies included in the sample, ipsative versions of the questionnaire had been used. The ipsative versions of the OPQ used in this study required respondents to select a least and most preferred item from a set of four alternatives. Although there has been concern about the use of ipsative personality measures (Johnson, Wood and Blinkhorn, 1988), recent research (Saville and Willson, 1991) has shown that normative and ipsative versions of the OPQ display very similar psychometric properties.

They continued:

> Overall, the results of the analyses suggest that, particularly for some criterion areas, personality scales produce practically useful criterion-related validity. Coefficients of the magnitude obtained here, uncorrected for unreliability or range restriction, compare reasonably well with coefficients obtained from meta-analysis of highly regarded predictors such as assessment centres, cognitive ability tests and work samples.

Finally, they added: 'The work reported here provides clear support for the notion that personality scales can provide unique criterion-related validity – findings that are in line with other research.'

Jesus Salgado (1996) re-ran the meta-analysis on the OPQ and found some computational errors, which was acknowledged by Robertson and Kinder to show that they had actually underestimated the extent to which the validity estimates obtained generalised well across criterion areas, jobs and organisations. This reinforced the conclusion that the OPQ had shown good validity.

A further validity study was conducted by Saville et al. (1996), which showed that the OPQ validities transferred well in measuring job competencies across time and in separate organisations, whether using the normative or ipsative formats of the questionnaire.

There is, of course, no claim that the OPQ was perfect in its structure. It began to be realised that items expressed in the negative form using the word 'not' had lower reliability than those which were positively loaded on a given scale. It was also apparent that reliability could be achieved by using significantly fewer items per scale. There was also the point that the OPQ items were a mixture of what an individual considers themselves good at compared with which activities they enjoyed.

Nevertheless, if some progress had been made in measuring personality by questionnaire, the objective had been achieved.

Notes

1 In 2009, the British Psychological Society's review of the OPQ noted that: 'At the time of its original publication the OPQ was considered groundbreaking in its style and approach'. This review is available online at: https://ptc.bps.org.uk/test-registration-test-reviews/search-registered-tests/viewtestsummary/185.
2 This domain was earlier named 'Ideas'.

References

Blinkhorn, S. and Johnson, C. (1990). The insignificance of personality testing. *Nature*, 348, 671–2.

Burisch, M. (1984). Approaches to personality-inventory construction – A comparison of merits. *American Psychologist, 39*(3), 214–227.

Digman, J. M. (1997). Higher-order factors of the Big Five. *Journal of Personality and Social Psychology*, 73(6), 1246–56.

Edwards, A. L. (1959). *Edwards Personal Preference Schedule: Manual*. New York: Psychological Corporation.

Eysenck, H. J. and Eysenck, S. B. G. (1975). *Manual of the Eysenck Personality Questionnaire*. London: Hodder & Stoughton.

Flanagan, J. C. (1954). The Critical Incident Technique. *Psychological Bulletin*, 51(4), 327–58.

Gough, H. G. (1957). *California Psychological Inventory*. Mountain View, CA: Consulting Psychologists Press.

Guilford, J. P. and Zimmerman, W. S. (1949). *The Guilford-Zimmerman Temperament Survey: Manual*. Beverly Hills, CA: Sheridan Supply Co.

Hathaway, S. R. and McKinley, J. C. (1943). *Manual for the Minnesota Multiphasic Personality Inventory*. New York: Psychological Corporation.

Johnson, E., Wood, R. and Blinkhorn, S. (1988). Spuriouser and spuriouser: The use of ipsative personality tests. *Journal of Occupational Psychology*, 61, 153–62.

Kelly, G. A. (1955). *The Psychology of Personal Constructs (Vols 1–2)*. London: Routledge.

Matthews, G. and Stanton, N. (1994). Item and scale factor analyses of the occupational personality questionnaire. *Personality and Individual Differences*, 16(5), 733–43.

Murray, H. A. (1938). *Explorations in Personality*. New York: Oxford University Press.

Robertson, I. T. and Kinder, A. (1993). Personality and job competencies: The criterion related validity of some personality variables. *Journal of Occupational and Organisational Psychology*, 66, 225–44.

Salgado, J. (1996). Personality and job competences: A comment on the Robertson & Kinder (1993) study. *Journal of Occupational and Organisational Psychology*, 69, 373–5.

Saville, P. (1977). A critical analysis of the 16PF. PhD dissertation. London: Brunel University.

Saville, P., Holdsworth, R., Nyfield, G., Cramp, L. and Mabey, W. (1984). *The Occupational Personality Questionnaire (OPQ)*. London: SHL.

Saville, P., Sik, G., Nyfield, G., Hackston, J. and MacIver, R. (1996). A demonstration of the validity of the Occupational Personality Questionnaire (OPQ) in the measurement of job competencies across time and in separate organisations. *Applied Psychology: An International Review*, 45, 243–62.

Saville, P. and Willson, E. (1991). The reliability and validity of normative and ipsative approaches in the measurement of personality. *Journal of Occupational Psychology*, 64, 219–38.

SHL (1999). *OPQ32 Manual and User's Guide*. London: SHL.

5

VALIDATING PERSONALITY QUESTIONNAIRES

This chapter is based on a paper which I wrote with colleagues in 1996:

> Saville, P., Sik, G., Nyfield, G., Hackston, J. and Maclver, R. (1996). A demonstration of the validity of the Occupational Personality Questionnaire (OPQ) in the measurement of job competencies across time and in separate organisations. *Applied Psychology: An International Review*, 45, 243–62.

This paper has been reprinted in full below with permission of the publisher, John Wiley & Sons Ltd. The copyright for this paper is with the International Association of Applied Psychology (© 1996).

A demonstration of the validity of the Occupational Personality Questionnaire (OPQ) in the measurement of job competencies across time and in separate organisations

Abstract

This article presents the results of two separate validation studies of the Concept Model of the Occupational Personality Questionnaire (OPQ). The two studies were separated by a four-year interval and the organisations came from different industry sectors in the UK. The results from the first validation study were used to predict the results in the second study. This cross-validation procedure ensured that the results in the second study were based on clear *a priori* hypotheses and were not merely the result of chance. In each of the studies the managers were assessed against a separate set of job competencies which each organisation developed independently. Five job competencies were present in the earlier study which were directly comparable to five in the later study. The scales of the OPQ that predicted success on each of the competencies in the first study were used as hypotheses in the second study. The results confirm that the OPQ predicts job success (over and above measures of ability) in a consistent and predictable fashion across different organisations and over time, and demonstrates that this relationship is not merely a reflection of chance effects in the data.

Introduction

Interest in the use of personality questionnaires for occupational selection in Europe and worldwide has never been higher. Very few would now disagree that personality questionnaires can provide useful information about people's likely job performance, particularly through concurrent validation studies, although predictive ones are also coming increasingly to the fore – see Schneider and Hough (1995) for a thorough overview. Despite meta-analytic studies demonstrating the validities of personality instruments within a 'Big Five' framework (Barrick and Mount, 1991; Tett, Jackson and Rothstein, 1991), Blinkhorn and Johnson (1990) and Johnson and Blinkhorn (1994) have raised issues over the methodological rigours that are needed to demonstrate the validity of particular personality scales against particular competencies in particular jobs (or sometimes one overall index of job performance), stressing the importance of genuine *a priori* hypotheses in such studies. Simply looking at a mass of correlations between many personality scales and many measures of job performance has been likened by Schneider and Hough to a 'scatter-gun' and by Blinkhorn and Johnson to a 'fishing expedition'; an approach that is likely to lead to mere chance correlations being adopted as meaningful.

Saville and Holdsworth Ltd (SHL) develop personality questionnaires for use by practitioners, and also seek to support the validation of such instruments. The Occupational Personality Questionnaire (Saville et al., 1984) suite of questionnaires is widely used in the UK and has been translated into some 15 different languages for use around the world. This paper looks at validity evidence for the Occupational Personality Questionnaire (OPQ) and attempts to avoid the 'scatter-gun' approach by cross-validating the OPQ across two client organisations.

The development of the OPQ

The first development phase of the OPQ took place in the UK between 1981 and 1984, and was supported by 53 sponsoring organisations in the private and public sectors which provided financial sponsorship and access to trialling groups. These organisations covered a wide range of activities including local and national government, manufacturing, banking, retailing, transport, oil, insurance, accountancy, leisure and service sectors. More extensive material on the construction and structure of the OPQ can be found in the OPQ Concept Model manual (SHL, 1993).

The development of the OPQ progressed via literature surveys, repertory grid analysis and critical incident techniques to develop initial models of personality which were extensively trialled and progressively refined. No single theory of personality was followed, but rather an eclectic approach was adopted using personality traits and management style constructs proposed by Eysenck, Cattell, Murray, Hersey and Blanchard, and other psychologists or management theorists. New scales were proposed by studying assessment centre criteria, management competencies and appraisal documentation, and eliciting personality constructs from a cross-section of people in work.

These constructs were defined by a team of 10 psychologists and items written to represent each of their respective scales. The personality scales were then subjected to a number of trials and refined over four years using itemetric and factor analytic methods. The structure of the OPQ is shown in Table 5.1.

The OPQ measures personality at three levels. First are six factors, five of which describe the Big Five factors plus an achievement factor. At the next level is a 16-factor solution. Third is the deductively rather than factor analytically derived 'Concept Model' consisting of 30 scales. These were designed to provide a more in-depth analysis of personality at the specific trait level than that provided by more parsimonious, but less detailed, factor-analytic versions.

Whereas some suspicion can be attached to scales with narrow bandwidths, i.e. those measuring a very limited *range* of behaviours, in the development of the OPQ Concept Model, it was actually felt that this was an advantage. The problem in interpreting instruments like the Eysenck Personality Questionnaire, for example, is understanding the meaning of scales like Psychoticism which have a very *wide* bandwidth. This scale covers many different behaviours, including suspicion of others, a disregard for own safety and cruelty to animals, which lend it rather limited value to the practitioner either in staff recruitment or development (see Burisch (1984) for an excellent discussion of this issue).

The OPQ Concept Model attempts to avoid the problem of each scale trying to cover too much. Indeed, the skill in using the OPQ lies not just in the meaning of individual scales, but in understanding what they suggest in combination. Think of the analogy of a company balance sheet; although each set of figures should be clear and concise, the skill is in understanding what the total picture means.

The OPQ has already been validated in several previous studies (for a review, see the OPQ Concept Model Manual from SHL (1993)). Relationships between the self-report OPQ scales and peer ratings were demonstrated by Saville and Willson (1991), and Dulewicz (1992) found relationships between OPQ scales and managerial competency ratings. The incremental validity of OPQ over ability tests was demonstrated by Sevy (1992) and, in a meta-analytic exercise based on 21 separate studies, Robertson and Kinder (1993) showed that self-report OPQ scales were particularly strongly related to such competencies as Creativity.

One way round the problem of over-interpreting chance correlations is to carry out research utilising only a small number of scales with clear *a priori* hypotheses specifying which scale should predict which criterion, in the same manner as

TABLE 5.1 The structure of the OPQs

Level I	Level II (Factor)	Level III (Concept)	
Gregarious (Extrovert, Surgent)	Influential Outspoken Sociable	Persuasive Controlling	Enjoys selling, changes opinions of others, convincing with arguments, negotiates. Takes charge, directs, manages, organises, supervises others.
		Independent Critical	Has strong views on things, difficult to manage, speaks up, argues. Likes probing the facts, sees the disadvantages, challenges assumptions.
		Outgoing Affiliative	Fun loving, humorous, sociable, vibrant, talkative, jovial. Has many friends, enjoys being in groups, likes companionship, shares things with friends.
		Socially Confident Modest (-)	Comfortable with strangers, likes to put others at ease. Reserved about achievements, avoids talking about self.
Sympathetic (Agreeable)	Empathic	Caring Democratic Behavioural	Considerate to others, helps those in need, sympathetic, tolerant. Encourages others to contribute, consults, listens and refers to others. Analyses thoughts and behaviour, psychologically minded, likes to understand people.
Imaginative (Intellectual)	Data Rational Conceptual Traditional (-)	Data Rational Artistic Conceptual Traditional (-)	Likes to work with data, operates on facts, enjoys assessing and measuring. Appreciates culture, sensitive to visual arts and music. Theoretical, intellectually curious, enjoys the complex and abstract. Preserves well-proven methods, prefers the orthodox, disciplined, conventional.
		Change Orientated	Enjoys doing new things, seeks variety, prefers novelty to routine, accepts changes.
	Innovative	Innovative Practical	Generates ideas, shows ingenuity, thinks up solutions. Likes repairing and mending things, enjoys using hands.
Methodical (Conscientious)	Methodical	Forward Planning	Prepares well in advance, enjoys target selling, forecasts trends, plans projects.
		Detail Conscious Conscientious	Methodical, keeps things neat and tidy, precise, accurate. Sticks to deadlines, completes jobs, perseveres with routine, likes fixed schedules.
Emotional (Anxious)	Relaxed (-)	Relaxed (-) Worrying	Calm, relaxed, cool under pressure, free from anxiety, can switch off. Worries when things go wrong, keyed-up before important events, anxious to do well.
		Tough Minded (-)	Difficult to hurt or upset, can brush off insults, unaffected by unfair remarks.
	Emotionally Controlled (-) Optimistic	Emotionally Controlled (-) Optimistic	Restrained in showing emotions, keeps feelings back, avoids outbursts. Cheerful, happy, keeps spirits up despite setbacks.
Achieving (Competitive)	Active Competitive Achieving Decisive	Active Competitive Achieving Decisive	Has energy, moves quickly, enjoys physical exercise, doesn't sit still. Plays to win, determined to beat others, poor loser. Ambitious, sets sights high, career-centred, results-orientated. Quick at conclusions, weighs things up rapidly, may be hasty, take risks.

Missing data due to subjects refusing to provide some information, cause given columns not to total 100%

employed in the meta-analysis by Robertson and Kinder (1993) and the studies reported by Dulewicz (1992) and Sevy (1992).

The study reported in this paper is based on two separate validation studies involving some 700 managers across two different types of organisations with a gap of four years between the two studies. The analysis reported has been designed to make use of the two studies serially: to provide a test of hypotheses derived from the results of the first sample by examination of the results from the second sample. In the first study, the scales that predicted job success were identified and then used to see if they correlated against semantically similar criteria in the second study, i.e. the first study was used as an exploratory vehicle to construct specific *a priori* hypotheses for the second study.

The design of this study therefore aims to avoid the danger of capitalising on chance effects in the data. If the results of this study, involving different managers in different organisations, show substantial cross-validation for the predictive scales, then this finding would offer significant support for the criterion-related validity of personality questionnaires.

The overall study is based on two separate one-day assessments, in two different organisations which included the use of the OPQ Suite and two tests of cognitive ability.

Method: Study 1

Sample

A total of 440 senior and middle managers were sampled at a large UK national bank (now part of an international banking group) in 1984 as part of an audit of human resources, prior to restructuring.

Procedure

Participants' immediate managers independently rated them on job performance characteristics on a two-point scale (very simply, 'they display it' or 'they do not') on a range of job performance criteria. The 440 managers separately completed the ipsative CM4 version of the OPQ as part of a one-day assessment centre, which also involved aptitude tests, a group exercise, an in-tray and an interview.

Measures

The bank had identified its own criteria associated with successful performance (competencies). These include 'analytical ability', 'good leader', 'strong in personal relationships', 'commercial flair' and 'creative thinker'. Each of these five competencies could potentially correlate with any of the 30 scales of the OPQ Concept Model.

Method: Study 2

Sample

Two groups of senior managers at an electrical manufacturing company (270 in all) took part in a similar exercise in 1988.

Procedure

The managers were rated by their superiors against criteria similar to those in the first study. This time a three-point scale was used (high/average/low). In addition to completing versions of the OPQs (either the normative OPQ Concept

3 + 5 or the ipsative OPQ Concept 4.2), each manager completed two SHL ability tests, one of numerical critical reasoning (NA4) and one of verbal critical reasoning (VA3). Those who took the normative versions of the OPQ had a bias to sales and marketing jobs; those who completed the ipsative forms to engineering and technical jobs.

Measures

The company again identified its own competency measures, of which those semantically compatible with those of the first study are 'intellect', 'leadership', 'interpersonal skills', 'entrepreneurial' and 'creative'.

The samples were chosen because they represent two of the largest managerial validation samples ever conducted in the UK. Selection decisions did follow, although the criterion data was collected concurrently and based on managers' performance in their *current* jobs. The situations were realistic and non-trivial, and were based on their real work setting. The 30 personality scales that were found to be the major correlates against key criteria in the first study were checked to see if they correlated against similar criteria in a second study in a different company, in a different sector of industry, with a different management group, with different Concept Model versions and four years later. The criterion for selecting the major correlates in the first study was that they exceeded a correlation of 0.2 with the job performance criterion. Where more than three OPQ scales correlated above 0.2 with a particular criterion, only the top three correlates were selected.

Five job performance criteria were present in the earlier study which were directly comparable to five in the later study. Criteria in the second study that were not present in the first have not been included here, even if the scales loading on to them might seem logically related (e.g. Strategic Skills).

The five overlapping criteria are:

Managers in Banking (N= 440) *1984 Study*	*Managers in Electrical Engineering (N= 270)* *1988 Study*
Analytical Ability	Intellect
Good Leader	Leadership
Strong in Personal Relationships	Interpersonal Skills
Commercial Flair	Entrepreneurial
Creative Thinker	Creative

It is worth remembering that these criteria were identified by the organisations themselves, and for that reason correspondence is imperfect, although this would be likely to reduce the significance of results rather than inflate them in any way.

There is perhaps nothing surprising in the obtained correlations between personality scales and job performance criteria in the first study (shown below). That

'Creative' managers are likely to be Innovative and Conceptual is predictable and might have been foreseen rationally. In the method adopted now, however, rational hypotheses are replaced by predictions based on the first of the two studies. The top three OPQ scales predicted to correlate in the second study (based on major OPQ scales that correlated significantly and with $r >= 0.2$ with job performance criteria in 440 senior managers in 1984) were as follows:

Job Performance Criteria	OPQ Scales Proposed to Correlate Significantly (Based on 1984 Study)
Analytical Ability/Intellect	Data Rational, Conceptual, Critical
Good Leader/Leadership	Controlling
Strong in Personal Relationships/ Interpersonal Skills	Critical (-), Affiliative, Forward Planning (-)
Commercial Flair/Entrepreneurial	Persuasive
Creative Thinker/Creative	Conceptual

Where correlations are corrected for attenuation (unreliability) in the criterion, a reliability of 0.6 for the criterion has been assumed. Because this correction is only a 'good approximation', wholly uncorrected correlations are also quoted.

As ability tests were used in both organisations, it is also possible to look at the incremental validity of personality measures over cognitive variables. The intercorrelation matrix, means, and standard deviations of the performance criteria and OPQ scales for the 1984 sample are given in Table 5.2 and for the 1988 sample in Table 5.3.

Results

The main results of this study are shown in Tables 5.4–5.8, where each deals with a different job performance criterion (or 'competency'). The results for the senior managers in electrical engineering (the second study) are broken down under three headings. First, the coefficients are given for the total sample (N = 270) for the selected personality scales. Then they are broken down for a sample of respondents who completed a normative version of the OPQ (Concept 3+5) and a sample of managers who completed an ipsative version of the OPQ (Concept 4.2). The latter sample had a bias towards technical managers with a background in engineering.

Next follows the multiple correlation (i.e. combined effect) of the personality scales. Following this are the results for the ability tests. Next are the multiple correlations of the two ability measures, the chosen personality scales and a test for incremental validity of personality over ability.

Results for each of the criterion constructs used in this research (using the terms in the second study to label them) will now be discussed.

TABLE 5.2 Intercorrelation matrix for the 1984 sample

		Mean	Std Dev	R1	R2	R3	R4	R5	R6	R7	R8	R9	T1	T2	T3	T4	T5	T6	T7	T8
R1	Persuasive	30.71	6.71																	
R2	Controlling	38.16	6.77	0.30																
R3	Independent	34.05	5.80	0.07	0.11															
R4	Outgoing	27.78	7.17	0.20	0.15	0.02														
R5	Affiliative	31.89	7.72	0.02	-0.16	-0.20	0.47													
R6	Socially Confident	31.81	6.73	0.40	0.27	0.01	0.57	0.34												
R7	Modest	31.20	6.66	-0.32	-0.29	-0.11	-0.23	-0.03	-0.25											
R8	Democratic	38.98	6.48	-0.04	0.02	-0.30	-0.30	0.14	0.02	0.18										
R9	Caring	36.30	7.20	0.01	-0.07	-0.20	0.07	0.38	0.14	0.15	0.27									
T1	Practical	36.04	7.24	-0.24	-0.15	0.01	-0.21	-0.17	-0.28	0.06	0.01	-0.17								
T2	Data Rational	36.69	8.37	-0.18	-0.08	0.05	-0.31	-0.23	-0.35	-0.08	-0.13	-0.30	0.20							
T3	Artistic	24.08	7.57	-0.06	-0.13	0.05	-0.02	0.11	0.06	-0.01	-0.09	0.09	0.04	-0.09						
T4	Behavioural	38.96	6.91	-0.08	-0.10	-0.03	-0.07	0.01	0.00	0.07	0.10	0.30	-0.20	-0.08	0.09					
T5	Traditional	31.32	7.25	-0.24	-0.24	-0.20	-0.24	-0.02	-0.29	0.26	0.04	0.09	0.05	-0.04	-0.05	0.07				
T6	Change Orientated	37.76	7.10	-0.03	-0.14	-0.01	0.08	0.13	0.06	-0.13	-0.02	-0.11	0.14	-0.01	0.11	-0.04	-0.19			
T7	Conceptual	28.34	6.40	-0.05	-0.06	0.14	-0.12	-0.17	-0.06	-0.15	-0.09	-0.16	-0.04	0.41	0.15	0.16	-0.33	0.04		
T8	Innovative	30.38	7.27	0.21	0.15	0.11	0.05	-0.18	0.12	-0.29	-0.09	-0.16	0.14	0.06	0.04	0.01	-0.50	0.09	0.34	
T9	Forward Planning	39.17	5.33	-0.04	0.19	0.05	-0.34	-0.35	-0.14	-0.21	0.00	-0.27	0.02	0.32	-0.07	0.04	-0.18	0.03	0.37	0.25
T10	Detail Conscious	31.64	8.78	-0.37	-0.30	-0.09	-0.37	-0.29	-0.46	0.25	-0.04	-0.12	0.27	0.30	-0.08	-0.16	0.43	-0.22	-0.09	-0.33
T11	Conscientious	35.11	5.70	-0.32	-0.18	-0.14	-0.38	-0.24	-0.37	0.23	0.05	-0.11	0.16	0.10	-0.09	-0.10	0.40	-0.21	-0.21	-0.27
F1	Relaxed	36.35	7.55	-0.08	0.00	-0.09	0.01	-0.13	-0.04	-0.02	-0.03	-0.06	-0.11	-0.22	-0.20	-0.07	0.03	-0.09	-0.21	-0.23
F2	Worrying	28.01	6.97	-0.38	-0.35	-0.09	-0.15	0.09	-0.31	0.32	0.03	0.11	0.15	0.03	0.00	0.06	0.48	-0.07	-0.17	-0.35
F3	Tough Minded	30.19	6.25	-0.04	-0.11	0.14	-0.05	-0.19	-0.08	0.14	-0.08	-0.08	-0.13	-0.10	-0.19	-0.07	0.04	-0.24	-0.11	-0.21
F4	Emotional Control	34.48	7.86	-0.13	-0.16	-0.30	-0.22	-0.10	-0.13	0.29	0.13	0.17	-0.04	-0.25	-0.12	0.08	0.22	-0.14	-0.25	-0.25
F5	Optimistic	41.27	7.97	0.05	-0.05	-0.16	0.12	0.12	0.04	-0.04	0.07	0.02	-0.16	-0.25	-0.18	-0.16	-0.05	0.05	-0.23	-0.11
F6	Critical	38.13	6.85	-0.21	-0.01	0.26	-0.23	-0.31	-0.30	-0.02	0.07	-0.34	0.18	0.42	-0.06	-0.16	-0.10	-0.08	0.40	0.14
F7	Active	35.33	8.88	0.00	0.00	-0.12	0.06	0.14	0.00	-0.11	-0.09	-0.13	-0.12	-0.14	-0.09	-0.11	-0.10	0.13	-0.29	-0.03
F8	Competetive	26.92	6.14	0.33	0.20	0.17	0.13	0.02	0.04	-0.26	-0.31	-0.17	-.25	-0.09	-0.07	-0.15	-0.16	-0.07	-0.16	0.07
F9	Achieving	26.79	5.94	0.38	0.31	0.31	-0.01	-0.22	0.07	-0.34	-0.26	-0.29	-0.23	0.02	-0.14	-0.07	-0.21	-0.04	0.02	0.17
F10	Decisive	32.25	7.01	0.05	0.15	0.16	0.00	-0.22	0.03	-0.17	-0.29	-0.22	-0.06	0.04	-0.06	-0.10	-0.21	-0.13	0.13	0.23
VA3	Verbal Reasoning	34.51	7.56	-0.05	0.00	0.16	0.15	-0.03	0.00	-0.05	-0.01	-0.17	-0.06	0.18	-0.05	0.07	-0.23	0.14	0.35	0.04
NA4	Numerical Reasoning	19.66	7.22	-0.14	0.00	0.09	-0.01	-0.01	-0.11	0.01	0.05	-0.15	-0.07	0.33	-0.17	0.07	-0.24	0.11	0.29	-0.01
AA	Analytical Ability	0.43	0.50	-0.22	-0.06	0.09	-0.21	0.21	-0.26	0.95	-0.05	-0.14	0.05	0.37	-0.05	0.04	-0.15	0.04	0.37	0.10
GL	Good Leader	0.29	0.45	0.12	0.27	-0.09	0.16	0.04	0.12	-0.04	0.07	0.05	-0.02	-0.13	-0.11	0.08	-0.07	-0.05	-0.08	0.11
PR	Personal Relations	0.34	0.47	0.15	0.05	-0.14	0.15	0.21	0.18	0.04	0.05	0.16	-0.05	-0.15	-0.04	0.07	0.04	-0.03	-0.19	-0.03
CF	Commercial Flair	1.10	0.30	0.27	0.06	-0.04	0.05	0.04	0.09	-0.11	-0.07	-0.08	-0.02	0.08	0.00	-0.11	0.04	0.09	-0.02	0.14
CT	Creative Thinker	0.26	0.44	0.04	0.09	0.08	0.00	-0.04	0.06	-0.07	-0.04	-0.04	0.01	0.05	0.14	0.01	-0.19	0.07	0.25	0.38

TABLE 5.3 Intercorrelation matrix for the 1988 sample

	CM3+5	CM3 = 5	CM4.2	CM4.2																
	Mean	Std Dev	Mean	Std Dev	R1	R2	R3	R4	R5	R6	R7	R8	R9	T1	T2	T3	T4	T5	T6	T7
R1 Persuasive	46.01	5.01	12.41	4.18																
R2 Controlling	49.20	4.52	17.93	3.48	0.26															
R3 Independent	45.21	4.53	12.71	3.15	0.13	0.14														
R4 Outgoing	40.84	7.01	8.63	3.72	0.25	0.14	-0.02													
R5 Affiliative	44.87	5.94	11.13	3.82	0.10	-0.19	-0.17	0.42												
R6 Socially Confident	44.23	6.6	12.50	4.10	0.39	0.23	-0.07	0.61	0.23											
R7 Modest	41.63	6.47	12.63	3.48	-0.14	-0.23	-0.05	-0.24	-0.08	-0.18										
R8 Democratic	43.64	5.68	15.98	3.81	-0.06	-0.01	-0.25	-0.03	0.26	0.03	0.17									
R9 Caring	49.36	4.36	14.56	3.88	-0.11	-0.05	-0.23	-0.01	0.25	0.00	0.28	0.35								
T1 Practical	48.28	5.88	16.68	3.67	-0.13	0.06	-0.02	0.02	0.13	0.03	-0.02	0.07	0.09							
T2 Data Rational	46.98	6.42	12.59	4.26	0.00	-0.06	-0.06	-0.15	0.09	-0.07	0.06	0.04	0.01	0.01						
T3 Artistic	40.63	5.68	6.83	4.00	0.10	-0.11	-0.09	0.10	0.20	0.15	0.01	0.10	0.15	0.03	0.11					
T4 Behavioural	46.82	5.36	13.29	4.10	0.13	0.06	-0.01	0.07	0.16	0.10	0.06	0.22	0.35	-0.07	-0.15	0.18				
T5 Traditional	37.65	6.23	10.54	4.38	-0.18	-0.11	-0.16	-0.16	-0.03	-0.17	0.11	0.05	0.11	0.16	0.01	-0.16	-0.13			
T6 Change Orientated	49.75	4.62	15.64	3.98	0.04	-0.09	0.05	0.06	0.21	0.11	-0.06	0.14	0.04	-0.04	0.13	0.19	0.13	-0.38		
T7 Conceptual	42.53	6.85	10.50	3.67	0.11	-0.01	0.10	-0.01	-0.03	0.09	0.02	0.03	-0.03	-0.17	0.34	0.41	0.13	-0.47	0.23	
T8 Innovative	42.41	7.37	13.83	5.01	0.06	0.09	0.16	-0.11	-0.24	-0.06	-0.11	-0.20	-0.15	0.09	0.09	0.11	-0.06	-0.28	0.03	0.46
T9 Forward Planning	44.52	5.79	17.15	3.96	0.02	0.12	-0.03	-0.18	-0.04	-0.01	-0.01	-0.01	0.04	-0.04	0.22	0.06	0.07	0.10	-0.06	0.07
T10 Detail Conscious	42.94	7.02	11.13	4.29	-0.04	-0.10	-0.09	-0.14	-0.01	-0.08	0.15	0.02	0.13	0.11	0.02	0.02	0.00	0.20	-0.16	-0.10
T11 Conscientious	41.31	5.44	14.04	3.20	0.00	0.01	0.00	-0.08	0.03	-0.08	0.04	-0.05	0.03	0.06	0.09	-0.10	0.03	0.21	-0.19	-0.18
F1 Relaxed	45.72	6.35	14.14	4.31	0.02	0.07	-0.05	0.08	0.04	0.18	0.01	-0.08	0.03	-0.02	0.02	-0.10	-0.08	-0.11	-0.03	-0.01
F2 Worrying	44.29	5.90	11.05	3.71	-0.18	-0.25	-0.09	-0.12	-0.01	-0.31	0.18	0.21	0.12	0.08	-0.01	-0.05	-0.01	0.27	-0.01	-0.19
F3 Tough Minded	39.69	6.26	10.99	3.16	0.14	0.14	-0.03	0.09	0.12	0.12	0.08	0.00	-0.10	-0.04	0.08	-0.08	0.03	0.10	-0.03	0.06
F4 Emotional Control	43.19	6.67	13.66	4.21	-0.12	-0.25	-0.30	-0.27	-0.05	-0.16	0.31	0.11	0.14	0.00	0.07	0.05	-0.05	0.07	0.06	0.05
F5 Optimistic	49.16	4.28	16.50	4.60	0.15	0.05	0.00	0.30	0.25	0.21	-0.07	-0.04	0.08	-0.02	-0.02	0.00	0.06	-0.26	0.18	0.01
F6 Critical	45.42	4.90	18.50	3.82	0.01	0.08	0.23	-0.19	-0.35	-0.16	-0.02	-0.19	-0.17	0.04	0.15	-0.06	-0.06	-0.01	-0.19	0.12
F7 Active	45.91	5.28	15.07	4.37	0.11	0.14	0.09	0.23	0.23	0.12	-0.05	0.15	0.07	0.10	0.04	-0.04	0.08	-0.22	0.29	0.00
F8 Competetive	39.14	7.58	14.56	3.83	0.35	0.28	0.27	0.24	-0.01	0.12	-0.29	-0.19	-0.27	-0.13	-0.07	-0.12	0.03	-0.31	0.02	0.04
F9 Achieving	42.17	6.68	12.22	3.49	0.33	0.23	0.21	0.13	0.02	0.16	-0.29	-0.09	-0.27	-0.14	-0.01	-0.04	0.08	-0.42	0.26	0.19
F10 Decisive	39.71	7.30	12.74	4.62	0.11	0.22	0.16	0.29	-0.02	0.12	-0.28	-0.21	-0.21	-0.05	-0.18	-0.05	-0.08	-0.18	0.04	-0.04
VA3 Verbal Reasoning	36.06	7.26	34.56	7.14	-0.04	-0.10	0.17	0.01	-0.11	-0.02	-0.04	-0.10	-0.16	-0.20	0.09	0.09	-0.07	-0.28	0.15	0.33
NA4 Numerical Reasoning	21.13	7.16	19.01	6.19	-0.11	-0.10	0.12	-0.06	0.00	-0.13	-0.01	-0.10	-0.11	-0.20	0.19	-0.05	-0.03	-0.25	0.11	0.19
AA Analytical Ability	2.41	0.57	2.53	0.53	0.07	0.01	0.13	-0.09	-0.07	-0.08	0.03	-0.14	-0.18	0.07	0.17	0.03	0.00	-0.14	0.04	0.35
GL Good Leader	2.33	0.63	2.22	0.56	0.21	0.30	0.18	0.10	0.03	0.07	-0.02	0.08	-0.05	-0.10	-0.04	-0.13	-0.07	-0.07	0.08	0.01
PR Personal Relations	2.22	0.63	2.16	0.64	0.16	0.04	-0.02	0.30	0.28	0.22	0.03	0.22	0.12	-0.01	-0.20	-0.04	-0.01	0.02	0.11	-0.10
CF Commercial Flair	2.13	0.59	1.80	0.62	0.11	0.06	0.16	0.23	0.10	0.17	-0.03	-0.06	0.05	-0.02	-0.06	0.07	0.09	-0.29	0.25	0.23
CT Creative Thinker	2.18	0.68	2.19	0.63	-0.01	0.03	0.19	0.00	-0.12	0.04	-0.04	-0.08	-0.09	-0.07	0.09	0.11	-0.04	-0.27	0.06	0.39

TABLE 5.4 Validity for Intellect criteria

Personality Dimensions

Ipsative				Direction	Value
N = 440 Managers (1984)					
Data Rational				+	0.37**
Conceptual				+	0.37**
Critical				+	0.35**
Verbal Critical Reasoning				+	0.30**
Numerical Critical Reasoning				+	0.31**

Personality Dimensions	N = 270 Combined		N = 153 Normative (CM3+5)		N = 116 Ipsative (CM4.2)	
	Dir	Value	Dir	Value	Dir	Value
N = 270 Managers (1988)						
Data Rational	+	0.17**	+	0.25**	+	0.16*
Conceptual	+	0.35**	+	0.36**	+	0.44**
Critical	+	0.27**	+	0.20**	+	0.33**
Multiple R. (Above personality dimensions only)	+	0.42**	+	0.42**	+	0.49**
Multiple R. (Corrected for attenuation)	+	0.54**	+	0.54**	+	0.63**
Verbal Critical Reasoning	+	0.30**	+	0.15**	+	0.42**
Numerical Critical Reasoning	+	0.28**	+	0.24**	+	0.30**
Multiple Correlation Ability	+	0.33**	+	0.31**	+	0.40**
Multiple Correlation	+	0.48**	+	0.48**	+	0.55**
Personality & Ability Diff erence[1]	+	0.15**	+	0.17**	+	0.15**

**Signifi cant at 1% level
NS = Not signifi cant
*Signifi cant at 5% level
[1] Significant level or R^2 change (F test)

If we look at Table 5.4, we can see the results for the Intellect criterion, first for the banking study and second for the engineering managers. As expected, the verbal and numerical reasoning tests correlate significantly and as predicted (r is about 0.3). Allowing for unreliability of the criterion, the adjusted correlation is a little above 0.4, a sizeable and useful association. As predicted, the personality scales of Data Rational, Conceptual and Critical all correlate significantly with a combined value of about 0.4. When corrected for unreliability in the criterion their combined effect is approximately 0.5, with significant incremental validity over ability tests alone.

Only one scale (Controlling) was hypothesised to correlate with Leadership. As can be seen from Table 5.5, this does correlate significantly in the normative, ipsative and combined managerial replication sample with an adjusted validity of 0.4. It is interesting that, regardless of any other aspects of personality, those who 'enjoy being in charge' tend to be perceived by their bosses as being good

TABLE 5.5 Validity for Leadership criteria

Personality Dimensions						
Ipsative					**Direction**	**Value**
N = 440 Managers (1984)						
Controlling					+	0.27**
Verbal Critical Reasoning						NS
Numerical Critical Reasoning						NS

Personality Dimensions	N = 270 Combined		N = 153 Normative (CM3+5)		N = 116 Ipsative (CM4.2)	
	Dir	**Value**	**Dir**	**Value**	**Dir**	**Value**
N = 270 Managers (1988) Controlling	+	0.30**	+	0.40**	+	0.25**
Multiple R. (Above personality dimensions only)	+	0.30**	+	0.40**	+	0.25**
Multiple R. (Corrected for attenuation)	+	0.39**	+	0.52**	+	0.32**
Verbal Critical Reasoning		NS		NS		NS
Numerical Critical Reasoning		NS		NS		NS
Multiple Correlation Ability		NS		NS		NS
Multiple Correlation	+	0.31**	+	0.40**	+	0.26**
Personality & Ability Difference	+	0.26**	+	0.35**	+	0.21**

**Signifi cant at 1% level
NS= Not signifi cant
*Signifi cant at 5% level.
[1]Signifi cant level or R^2 change (F test)

leaders. The ability tests do less well against this criterion and clear evidence of the incremental validity of personality over ability is shown. One might have predicted that personality rather than intellect is a key component of this aspect of managerial success.

The position is a little more complicated with the Interpersonal Skills job performance criterion (see Table 5.6). The Critical scale shows significant negative correlations in the combined and normative sample; the Affiliative scale correlates significantly across all samples, whereas Forward Planning correlates negatively and significantly in the combined group. The personality variables give significant incremental validity over the ability tests for the normative and combined samples.

The results for the Entrepreneurial job performance criterion are given in Table 5.7. The personality variable of Persuasive correlates significantly in the total sample and in the normative group, but not significantly in the ipsative sample. Ability tests also show a moderate level of correlation here (combined value about 0.2).

OPQ scales correlating with 'Entrepreneurial', which were not hypothesised, include being less Traditional (i.e. more radical) and more Change

TABLE 5.6 Validity for Interpersonal Skills criteria

Personality Dimensions						
Ipsative					**Direction**	**Value**
N = 440 Managers (1984)						
Critical					-	24**
Affiliative					+	0.21**
Forward Planning					-	0.20**
Verbal Critical Reasoning						NS
Numerical Critical Reasoning						NS
	N = 270 Combined		**N = 153 Normative (CM3+5)**		**N = 116 Ipsative (CM4.2)**	
Personality Dimensions	**Dir**	**Value**	**Dir**	**Value**	**Dir**	**Value**
N = 270 Managers (1988)						
Critical	-	0.23**	-	0.33**		NS
Affiliative	+	0.28**	+	0.34**	+	0.16*
Forward Planning	-	0.18**		NS		NS
Multiple R. (Above personality dimensions only)	+	0.34**	+	0.37**		NS
Multiple R. (Corrected for attenuation)	+	0.44**	+	0.48**		NS
Verbal Critical Reasoning		NS		NS		NS
Numerical Critical Reasoning		NS		NS		NS
Multiple Correlation Ability	+	NS		NS		NS
Multiple Correlation	+	0.34**	+	0.47**		NS
Personality & Ability Diff erence[1]		0.32**	+	0.33**		NS

**Signifi cant at 1% level
NS= Not signifi cant
*Signifi cant at 5% level
[1]Signifi cant level or R^2 change (F test)

Orientated, Conceptual and Innovative. For the normative sample, but not the ipsative, significant correlations were also found for the scales Controlling, Independent, Outgoing, Competitive, Achieving, Decisive and less for Data Rational, Detail Conscious, Worrying and Emotional Control. The reasons for the differences between the two samples on this criterion may be due to the normative sample being primarily composed of sales and marketing managers and the ipsative sample comprising more engineering or technical executives. It might be that this was a more appropriate job performance dimension for the normative sample, in that more relevant behavioural data were available to rate the sales and marketing managers, and therefore the performance criterion is more valid.

If this is the case, it does build up an intriguing pen-picture of the more entre-preneurial managers as being more persuasive and controlling of others, more

TABLE 5.7 Validity for Entrepreneurial criteria

Personality Dimensions

Ipsative			Direction	Value
N = 440 Managers (1984)				
Persuasive			+	0.27**
Verbal Critical Reasoning				NS
Numerical Critical Reasoning				NS

	N = 270 Combined		N = 153 Normative (CM3+5)		N = 116 Ipsative (CM4.2)	
Personality Dimensions	Dir	Value	Dir	Value	Dir	Value
N = 270 Managers (1988)						
Persuasive	+	0.11**	+	0.25**	+	NS
Multiple R. (Above personality dimensions only)	+	0.11**	+	0.25**	+	NS
Multiple R. (Corrected for attenuation)	+	0.14**	+	0.32**	+	0.15*
Verbal Critical Reasoning	+	0.17**	+	0.12*	+	0.20**
Numerical Critical Reasoning	+	0.10*	+	NS	+	0.15*
Multiple Correlation Ability	+	0.17**	+	0.14*	+	0.21**
Multiple Correlation	+	0.21**	+	0.28**	+	0.22**
Personality & Ability Diff erence[1]	+	NS	+	0.14**	+	NS

**Significant at 1% level
NS= Not signifi cant
*Significant at 5% level
[1]Signifi cant level or R^2 change (F test)

difficult to manage, more inclined to make fast decisions by gut feeling, more radical in thinking, innovative and disliking bureaucracy, less worried about things going wrong, likely to express their feelings, optimistic and highly competitive, and career ambitious.

Finally for the 'Creative' criterion, Table 5.8 shows the Concept scales that are predicted to correlate significantly. The results for the selected two OPQ scales (Innovative and Conceptual) are persuasive; the raw multiple correlation is in excess of 0.4 and when adjusted for unreliability in the criterion it is in excess of 0.5. Again significant incremental validity is shown over ability (which nevertheless itself still has validity).

Discussion

On one of the largest ever UK studies on the validity of assessment techniques in managers (N = 710 overall), both ability tests and nominated OPQ self-report personality scales show predictable, significant and substantial correlations with criteria of management job success, the majority of the estimated validities being in the region of 0.3 to 0.5 – high coefficients by the standards of personality

TABLE 5.8 Validity for Creative criteria

Personality Dimensions

Ipsative					Direction	Value
N = 440 Managers (1984)						
Innovative					+	0.38**
Conceptual					+	0.25**
Verbal Critical Reasoning						NS
Numerical Critical Reasoning						NS

	N = 270 Combined		N = 153 Normative (CM3+5)		N = 116 Ipsative (CM4.2)	
Personality Dimensions	Dir	Value	Dir	Value	Dir	Value
N = 270 Managers (1988)						
Innovative	+	0.34**	+	0.36**	+	0.33**
Conceptual	+	0.39**	+	0.43**	+	0.41**
Multiple R. (Above personality dimensions only)	+	0.43**	+	0.46**	+	0.42**
Multiple R. (Corrected for attenuation)	+	0.56**	+	0.59**	+	0.54**
Verbal Critical Reasoning	+	0.21**	+	0.17*	+	0.27**
Numerical Critical Reasoning	+	0.13*	+	NS	+	0.23**
Multiple Correlation Ability	+	0,21**	+	NS	+	0.28**
Multiple Correlation	+	0.44**	+	0.47**	+	0.45**
Personality & Ability Diff erence[1]	+	0.23**	+	0.30**	+	0.17**

**Significant at 1% level
NS= Not significant
*Significant at 5% level
[1]Significant level or R^2 change (F test)

validation. Significant incremental validity of personality scales over ability was also demonstrated.

It is perhaps worth considering why this pair of studies was able to provide such valid predictions about successful job performance based on self-report questionnaires. One concern frequently expressed is the possibility of respondents 'overselling' themselves, presenting themselves more favourably than they really are, particularly in selection. It is certainly the case that intuitively one would expect more distortion if selection decisions were based on the questionnaire's responses. However, here valid predictions have been made despite the fact that decisions about promotion were based on the findings. It is important not to exaggerate the problem of social desirability in responding; not every respondent is out to deceive. Recent research (Hough et al., 1990) has shown that response distortion due to social desirability does not appear to significantly affect validity coefficients. Another point is that because data were shared with respondents during a feedback interview, not only were they probably less likely to be deliberately dishonest, but they could well have been more motivated to respond thoughtfully.

Another possible reason for the success of this validation study is that the criteria against which individual scales were validated were specific (e.g. Interpersonal Skill) rather than a more global and general overall performance criterion. As this study suggests, higher scores on some personality scales might predict success against certain criteria, yet failure against others. The Critical scale, for example, is positively correlated with ratings of Intellect, but negatively with Interpersonal Skill. Evidently fault-finding, cynical managers are perceived less favourably in the interpersonal domain.

Both ipsative and normative questionnaires were used in the study, and it seems that both can effectively predict performance against external criteria. In terms of the information that can be obtained from them, they are fairly interchangeable.

Overall, this pair of studies shows substantial criterion-related validity for personality scales as predictors of specific independent measures of job competency or performance. The importance of personality as a major factor in performance, and the incremental validity of personality questionnaires over ability tests, is supported by these findings.

References

Barrick, M.R. and Mount, M.K. (1991). The Big Five personality dimensions and job performance: A meta-analysis. *Personnel Psychology*, 44, 1–25.

Blinkhorn, S. and Johnson, C. (1990). The insignificance of personality testing. *Nature*, 348, 671–2.

Burisch, M. (1984). Approaches to Personality-Inventory Construction – A comparison of merits. *American Psychologist*, 39(3), 214–27.

Costa, P.T. (1996). Work and personality: Use of the NEO-PI-R in industrial/organisational psychology. *Applied Psychology: An International Review*, 45, 225–41.

Dulewicz, V. (1992). Assessment of management competencies by personality questionnaires. *Selection & Development Review*, 8(1), 1–4.

Hough, L., Eaton, N. K., Dunnette, M. D., Kemp, J. D. and McCloy, R. A. (1990). Criterion-related validities of personality constructs and the effect of response distortion on those validities. *Journal of Applied Psychology*, 75(5), 581–95.

Hunter, J. E. and Schmidt, F. L. (1990). *Methods of Meta-analysis*. Newbury Park, CA: Sage.

Johnson, C. and Blinkhorn, S. (1994). Desperate measures: Job performance and personality test validities. *The Psychologist*, 7(4), 167–70.

Johnson, E., Wood, R. and Blinkhorn, S. (1988). Spuriouser and spuriouser: The use of ipsative personality tests. *Journal of Occupational Psychology*, 61, 153–62.

Robertson, I. T. and Kinder, A. (1993). Personality and job competencies: The criterion related validity of some personality variables. *Journal of Occupational and Organisational Psychology*, 66, 225–44.

Saville, P., Holdsworth, R., Nyfield, G., Cramp, L. and Mabey, W. (1984). *The Occupational Personality Questionnaire (OPQ)*. London: SHL.

Saville, P. and Willson, E. (1991). The reliability and validity of normative and ipsative approaches in the measurement of personality. *Journal of Occupational Psychology*, 64, 219–38.

Schneider, R. J. and Hough, L. M. (1995). Personality and industrial/organizational psychology. In C. L. Cooper and I. T. Robertson (eds), *International Review of Industrial and Organizational Psychology*, vol. 10 . Chichester: Wiley, pp. 75–139.

Sevy, B. A. (1992). The incremental validity and efficiency of personality tests in selection. Paper presented at the Seventh Annual conference of the Society for Industrial and Organisational Psychology, Inc. Montreal.

SHL (1993). *OPQ Concept Model Manual*. London: SHL.

Tett, R. P., Jackson, D. N. and Rothstein, M. (1991). Personality measures as predictors of job performance: A meta-analytic review. *Personnel Psychology*, 44, 703–42.

6

DEVELOPMENT OF A VALIDITY-CENTRIC WORK-BASED QUESTIONNAIRE

Saville consulting wave®

This chapter is based on an article published in the British Psychological Society's *Selection and Development Review* in 2006:

> MacIver, R., Saville, P., Kurz, R., Mitchener, A., Mariscal, K., Parry, G., Becker, S., Saville, W., O'Connor, K., Patterson, R. and Oxley, H. (2006). Making Waves: Saville Consulting Wave Styles questionnaires. *Selection and Development Review*, 22(2), 17–23.

The article has been reprinted here with the permission of the British Psychological Society.

Between 2004 and 2006, Rab MacIver and I headed up a team, which included those individuals named above as co-authors, who developed the groundbreaking Wave questionnaires.

This article was our first external and official publication of our work and, unveiled the new Wave approach to measuring workplace behaviours. This was noted in an issue of the *Selection and Development Review* by the Editor of the time, John Boddy:

> Peter Saville has played a leading role in the development of psychometric assessments for occupational settings in this country but, for various reasons, has been quiet for some time. Now we know why. He has been gestating a new, highly innovative suite of assessment tools in the new organisation that he has set up. The SDR Editorial Team has to tread a fine line in keeping the academic and practitioner community informed of new developments in psychometrics, whilst not providing a blatant marketing vehicle for test publishes. We felt that the Saville Consulting Wave tools represent important developments and that it was, therefore, right to publish an invited article by

Rab MacIver and the Development Team, giving key technical information and particularly outlining innovative features and their rationale, such as the integration of normative and ipsative measures, making it 'validation-centric' and indexing the match between talent and motivation. We believe that the instruments involve a number of new concepts that are worth debating and we welcome discussion of them.

Nearly a decade later, we believe that this article still provides one of the best syntheses of our work during the early years of Saville Consulting.

Making waves: Saville Consulting Wave Styles questionnaires

The Saville Consulting (SC) Wave Styles questionnaires have been developed by Saville Consulting, an entirely new business founded by Professor Peter Saville. The vision of the company is to transform assessment and the first tranche of new products have now been launched, including a range of aptitude tests and culture assessment tools.

The SC Wave Styles questionnaires are central to the integrated development strategy. The individual measures (the styles questionnaires) of the SC Wave suite and the organisational measures (culture and climate) have been developed from one integrated model.

This article discusses the concepts and development that formed the backbone of the individual measures: the SC Wave Styles questionnaires.

SC Wave Styles: an overview

SC Wave Styles presents a uniquely integrated model of personality, competency, culture and motivation. The concepts of motive and talent are integral to the structure and have real implications for individual development, career planning and performance management as well as selection.

Rather than taking a paper questionnaire and putting it on the internet, SC Wave Styles questionnaires are an innovative suite of self-report measures developed with the opportunities and challenges of the internet at the heart of their design. They operate as both trait and type instruments and rely on a new hierarchical model of work performance that we have developed. Our model is aligned to the Big Five personality factors and the Great Eight competencies, but provides more information than either model.

The development of the questionnaires has benefited from a performance-driven or validation-centric methodology to maximise the validity of the questionnaires by selecting the most valid items from our item pools.

A new dynamic online format integrates rating and ranking responses, and results in a combined profile that highlights differences between the ipsative and normative scores on the profile. This new scaling technology also allows unprecedented levels of detail to be tapped, yet with radically reduced completion times.

The research matching the questionnaire to the preferred culture, environment and job demands allows individuals (and their managers) to gain new perspectives on what they can take from their job and what will motivate them.

SC Wave Styles questionnaires are different in several respects from established psychometric questionnaires. Below we provide an overview of the new features and approach before taking a brief look at the reliability, validity and applications of the questionnaires.

The motive-talent concept

SC Wave Styles questionnaires have been developed to separate out talents from underlying predispositions or motives. For every work construct measured there is one motive item and one talent item.

The Expert Report profile indicates where 'motive-talent splits' occur. This allows the user to identify whether the individual is motivated to develop in a particular area or needs their talent in an area supported or encouraged because there is a lack of underlying motivation or interest.

The approach has profound implications for the development of individuals. Because the model matches every talent item with an underlying motive item, it is much simpler to understand the impact of motivation on work performance.

Performance-driven content

SC Wave Styles questionnaires have been developed (and continue to be developed) using a variety of development strategies, but at the core is a validation-centric strategy.

As Burisch (1984) points out, mixed approaches, which include validity data as part of scale development, are surprisingly rare in questionnaire development:

> Actually this is rarely done, particularly the combination of deductive scale writing and external information for item analysis.

For the initial development of the Professional Styles questionnaires, 214 work constructs were written (each with separate motive and talent components; 428 work constructs in total). A total of 108 of these constructs (facets) made it into the final questionnaire with item selection based first and foremost on criterion validity. Items were correlated with external ratings on relevant work behaviour competencies as well as overall job proficiency and potential for promotion.

The SC Wave Styles questionnaires are therefore based on the work constructs which are the best indicators of performance (i.e. performance-driven).

The facet approach to measurement ensures that each item in the questionnaires measures a different work construct to help avoid the feeling of 'needless repetition' that respondents can experience when completing questionnaires.

Clearer interpretation

One of the criticisms that can be fairly levelled at self-report questionnaires is that despite their reliability and validity, there is a degree of subjectivity in their interpretation.

Despite users being trained prior to questionnaire use, subject matter experts in assessment believe that poor interpretation is a significant source of error in the use of personality questionnaires (Smith and Foley, 2006). A lack of consistency between interpreters is much more likely where an aspect of work performance is predicted by a complex combination of predictor scales, which is the situation with many multi-scale self-report personality instruments.

Is inconsistency a given? Can we do anything about it? With the performance-driven approach, the work constructs that best predict a work competency are brought together to form a scale. This largely removes the need to look around the profile for what scales relate to a particular competency (i.e. we move from predictor-centric models to criterion-centric models of work performance and have to work less hard to join the dots).

The feedback provider also no longer has to guess what an average score overlooks; where there are differences in scores underpinning a dimension, these are highlighted in the profile.

Better interpretation inevitably leads to improved validity in decision making based on questionnaire data (i.e. better decision making, fewer selection errors and better identification of development needs).

Dynamic normative-ipsative format

There are advantages and disadvantages to both normative and ipsative response formats. At the practitioner level, it is useful to have both sources of information. The online SC Wave Styles questionnaires first present a group of six normative statements. The system then calculates their ipsative rankings based on the order in which the statements have been rated (this saves the individual time by calculating the majority of rankings for an individual). Where an individual ties their ratings, the system immediately represents the tied items to be placed in rank order.

Where there are differences between normative and ipsative scores, these are highlighted on the profile to allow the user to explore the reasons for the difference (which of the two scores is most representative of the true score and which is more distorted). The user can then focus on specific areas where socially desirable responding (or overly self-critical responding) may have occurred.

New levels: new lessons

SC Wave is a model with several levels in its hierarchy. The new scaling technology allows much more to be assessed in less time.

At the top of the Professional Styles model are four clusters which also provide the basis of the Saville Consulting Types model, which profiles People Type and Task Type.

Each cluster breaks down into three sections, giving a total of 12 sections. Each of the Big Five and Great Eight constructs has a counterpart with one of these sections and four further areas are covered.

Each of the 12 sections covers three themes giving 36 dimensions, which is the fidelity level of many occupational personality measures.

The newly developed scaling allows SC Wave to go down one more level with each of the 36 dimensions being composed of three facets, giving a total of 108 facets.

The 216 questions are usually answered in around 40 minutes. The ultra-compact Wave Focus questionnaires measure 36 facets, selected for their strong validity, in just 15 minutes.

The new dynamic 'Ra-Ra' (Rate-Rank) format combining ipsative and normative scores has profound implications for measurement – it is simply not necessary to have six or eight items in a scale when two items can do as well or better (strong validity, strong reliability, good spread of scores, etc.). More items are required to achieve this with conventional five-point Likert items or ipsative-only questionnaires (MacIver, 1997).

The profile highlights within any of the 36 dimensions where there is a significant 'facet range', i.e. one or more of the three underlying facets having markedly different scores from the others.

As well as many more individual scales being measured, this provides the user with much more detailed insight into the 'uniqueness' of the individual.

Configurable competency reporting

The level of detail that SC Wave Styles achieves also enables a more detailed match with client competency models, allowing for fast configuration of output reports to predict client competencies and even their competency indicators.

This detailed configuration has also enabled the Entrecode® model of successful entrepreneurs developed by Professor David Hall and his associates to be available as a separate report.

Enhanced security

The internet offers great convenience in allowing individuals to respond at great geographical distance (without an administrator present) by sending a link to the questionnaire directly to an email address. This so-called 'controlled' mode does present security concerns. For example, not being sure the questionnaire is completed honestly by who you have sent it to (and not, say, by a group of the candidate's friends one evening).

We believe strongly that as well as 'controlled' or 'Invited Access' forms, a self-report questionnaire (particularly questionnaires that can be used for selection or

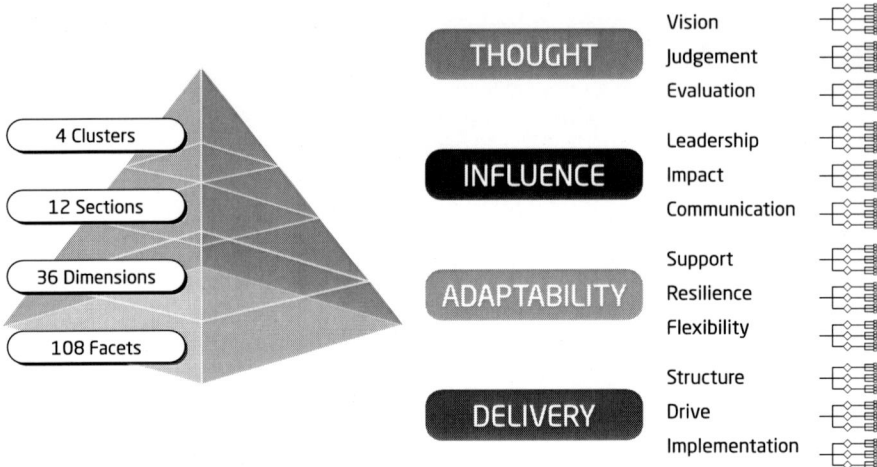

THOUGHT — Vision, Judgement, Evaluation

INFLUENCE — Leadership, Impact, Communication

ADAPTABILITY — Support, Resilience, Flexibility

DELIVERY — Structure, Drive, Implementation

4 Clusters

12 Sections

36 Dimensions

108 Facets

FIGURE 6.1 The Saville Consulting Wave work hierarchy

other decision-making processes) should have a separate supervised secure form. Therefore, two parallel forms of SC Wave are available for 'Invited Access' and more secure 'Supervised Access' administrations.

Culture match

The SC Wave development programme has also developed measures of work culture that are parallel to the SC Wave Styles model. This empirical research allows us to indicate the preferred culture/environment and job demands that would suit an individual based on the completion of SC Wave Styles questionnaires.

From the perspective of Positive Psychology, Seligman (2003) has argued that work can be changed to suit the employee (rather than just finding an employee that fits the job or trying to develop the individual to better match/meet job demands). Assessment can be constructed to support this approach.

With our unique model (see Figure 6.2) which ties together motive, talent, competency and culture, we can help individuals understand what work demands (culture, job and environment) they are most likely to favour.

Armed with this understanding, it becomes easier to discuss what enhances or inhibits individuals' performance at work and therefore facilitate constructive discussions about how a job could better reflect a person's motives and talents.

This approach can also help managers think about how to tailor work to suit individual employees to keep them satisfied and motivated.

Reliability

A development goal of the SC Wave Styles questionnaires was to have alternate form and test-retest reliability estimates as high as possible. In contrast, the SC

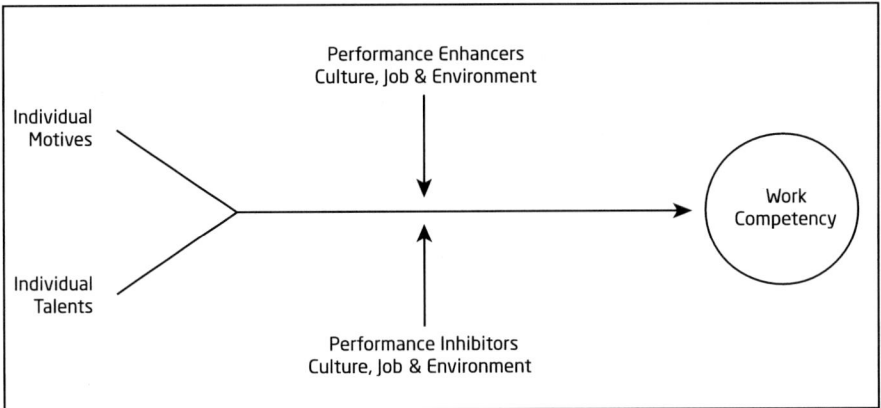

FIGURE 6.2   The Saville Consulting model of work performance effectiveness

Wave Styles questionnaires were designed to have moderate (0.6 to 0.8) rather than high internal consistencies at the dimension level (as they are made up of six different work constructs).

The alternate form reliability average across the two forms of the Professional Styles questionnaires is 0.86, with the lowest reliability 0.78 and the highest 0.93 ($N = 1153$).

The highest correlation with a scale in one form was with its respective twin in the other form (e.g. Inventive in Invited Access form correlates most highly with Inventive in Supervised Access form, not with any other scale).

The internal consistencies of the dimensions of the two Professional Styles questionnaires range from 0.58 to 0.87 with an average of 0.76 ($N = 1153$).

Test-retest average is 0.79 across the dimensions of the two normative Professional Styles questionnaires with an interval of one month. The lowest reliability was 0.71 and the highest ranged up to 0.91 ($N = 112$).

Validity

SC Wave has already been validated on over 1,500 people globally during its development, standardisation and initial use. Gathering validity on every item continues on an ongoing international basis.

The validation results from the development trial were cross-validated in the standardisation trials of the questionnaire. As each dimension has been designed in the development trial to predict one of 36 work competencies, there were clear a priori hypotheses for the standardisation trial of which SC Wave Style dimension will correlate with which work competency.

In the standardisation, 34 out of the 36 dimensions had significant correlations ($p < 0.05$, one-tailed) with their matched criteria across the two forms. The combined ipsative and normative dimensions predict external ratings (manager or colleague) of effectiveness on the work competency that each was designed to predict with an average of 0.39 for the Invited Access form and 0.39 for Supervised Access. These figures are corrected for criterion unreliability, but no other corrections have been applied, e.g. restriction of range, predictor unreliability, etc. ($N = 556 - 658$).

Validity figures based on multiple regression equations cannot be used as an unbiased estimate of the validity of the questionnaire when they are not cross-validated. The mean validity of the composite equation of SC Wave Styles dimensions in relation to the 36 work competencies is an average of 0.46 for both forms. This was based on developing the equation on one half of the standardisation data and cross-validating the equation to the second half of the standardisation sample. These figures are corrected for criterion unreliability, but no other corrections have been applied, e.g. restriction of range, predictor unreliability, etc. (Hold out Sample $N = 252 - 316$).

Reporting

The profiles are not simply static text describing the content of a scale. Instead, the text in the profile feeds back the individual facets (giving different verbal descriptions for the different score (Sten) positions). This reduces the thinking time for the person giving feedback as they do not have to think how to explain the score. It also means that the recipient of the feedback understands the content of the profile much faster with less need for explanation.

Two of the main reports provided from SC Wave Styles are the Expert and the Types Reports. Each report comes with a free personal report for the respondent.

The Expert Report: Summary of Individual's Response Styles; Full Wave Psychometric Profile (with Motive Talent Splits, Ipsative-Normative Splits and Facet Ranges); Culture/Environment Prediction Report; Competency Potential Report.

Types Report: The Types report brings together perspectives on teams, leadership and management in one straightforward 'individual differences' model of performance at work. These are performance-driven types that predict external work performance as they are based on our performance-driven methodology.

First, individuals are classified by their People Type, which can be one of four: Individualist, Influencer, Adaptor or Transformer. Second, they are classified as having a Task Type, again one of four: Preserver, Thinker, Doer or Transactor.

This leads to their overall Saville Consulting Type which is made up of an individual's People and Task type combined, e.g. Influencer Doer. This is followed by a bulletpoint summary of how they will tend to lead, work in teams and manage change.

Applications of Saville Consulting Wave

Saville Consulting Wave Styles are designed to be applied throughout the employee's lifecycle. Below are some of the applications of SC Wave Styles with an insight into where they make a difference.

Selection: SC Wave Styles are designed to create a platform for much better decision making from a self-report questionnaire, leading to increases in the calibre of employees. As a feed into interview or as a source of data to cross-reference with other data and pull together a more coherent picture of an individual, SC Wave gives more valid data in less time. The detail in SC Wave also allows bespoke reports to be created with a better content match to client competency models.

Career planning: In thinking about how to manage the future of an individual's career, it is useful for the individual to understand what areas they are interested in developing (insight from motive-talent splits) and what type of culture will enhance or inhibit their success and motivation (culture prediction report). By giving this unique perspective, SC Wave allows an individual a perspective on what they want from their work in the future.

Coaching and development: SC Wave Styles provide insights which are useful to the person being coached and provide a clear link to understanding the impact of their personal style (motive and talent) on their performance at work. Facet splits provide more detail and interesting contrasts that lead to a precise understanding of the individual's approach to work. In development it is also extremely useful to know where an individual has an internal incentive or motive to develop, or has little internal incentive or motive to improve performance (which is provided by motive-talent splits).

Self-selection: Self-selection can be aided by highlighting to individuals where they have more or less fit with job demands and culture. It may be that self-selection happens before a formal application is made by candidates or as part of the selection process itself. By supplying each candidate with a culture prediction report, we can enable individuals to have their own perspective on whether they feel they are suited to the role in question.

Individualised induction: SC Wave Styles can be used in induction to give an individual a view of what they would like to get out of their work. Despite new starters tending to be satisfied in general, their satisfaction ratings are relatively weak when they are asked about the feedback, or lack of feedback, assessment data collected during their selection (Miles, 2006). The culture prediction report provides new starters with a picture of what is most likely to enhance their performance at work and can help them consider how best to make the most of their talents.

Team development: The Saville Consulting Types Model helps members of teams see how they complement each other (e.g. Thinker Influencers are complemented by Adaptor Doers). Group profile reporting is available for team building to explore how two or more people are likely to interact. And the detail provided on the full SC Wave Expert reports can also provide deeper insight into how people interact with each other.

Organisational talent audit/benchmark: SC Wave provides a vehicle for benchmarking groups in terms of their perceived motives and talents. This information can be combined with our organisational surveys of preferred and actual culture to give a unique insight into how the motives and talents of employees are aligned to the organisational culture which can help inform future organisational development strategy.

Conclusion

Saville Consulting Wave Styles provide a different approach to assessment. The new methods of scaling have led to super-short and valid scales. The presence of ipsative and normative responses helps to make faking more difficult and allows the user to focus in on potential areas of distortion (socially desirable over-rating and self-critical under-rating).

The SC Wave matched model of performance aids better interpretation and decision making. It brings together motives, talents, competency and culture in one integrated model, providing the 'Expert User' with clearer links between an individual's motivation, work environment and performance at work.

The culture prediction component helps the individual being assessed (and their manager or colleagues) have a perspective on how the job could alter to enhance their performance and satisfaction at work.

References

Baron, H. (1996). Strengths and limitations of ipsative measurement. *Journal of Occupational and Organisational Psychology*, 69, 49–56.

Burisch, M. (1984). Approaches to Personality Inventory Construction: A comparison of merits. *American Psychologist*, 39(3), 214–27.

Kurz, R. and Bartram, D. (2002). Competency and individual performance: Modelling the world of work. *Organisational Effectiveness: The Role of Psychology*, 10, 227–55.

MacIver, R. (1997). A shorter OPQ? *Selection & Development Review*, 13(1), 13.

Miles, A. (2006). Issues surrounding the engagement of new starters. *Proceedings of the British Psychological Society Division of Occupational Psychology Conference*, 11–13 January, Glasgow.

Seligman, M. (2003). *Authentic Happiness: Using the New Positive Psychology to Realise Your Potential for Lasting Fulfilment*. London: Nicholas Brealey Publishing.

Saville, P. and Willson, E. (1991). The reliability and validity of normative and ipsative approaches to the measurement of personality. *Journal of Occupational Psychology*, 64, 219–38.

Smith, M. and Foley, M. (2006). The specific nature of error variance in selection. *Proceedings of the British Psychological Society Division of Occupational Psychology Conference*, 11–13 January, Glasgow.

7

LONG VERSUS SHORT SCALES

In 2012, we presented a symposium at the British Psychological Society's annual Division of Occupational Psychology conference. One of the papers in this symposium tackled the issue of long versus short scales within psychometric assessments. It is my belief, backed up by our evidence and research by others (e.g. Burisch, 1997), that this is at the heart of quality assessment construction.

Indeed, we argued in this paper that short scales can be just as effective (and sometimes even more so) than longer ones. The implications of this are far-reaching, particularly in an age where assessments need to be completed as efficiently as possible. Saving just a few minutes per candidate can result in huge time and cost savings, especially where large volumes of individuals are being tested.

The paper below, which forms the core of this chapter, therefore adds to the body of work which overturns the conventional wisdom that long, laborious and 'thorough' scales are required to measure something reliably and validly:

> Hopton, T., Kurz, R., MacIver, R. and Saville, P. (2012). Which aspects of work performance do we endeavour to measure and Predict? Convergence of four overall performance scales. Symposium presented at the British Psychological Society Division of Occupational Psychology Annual Conference, Chester, January.

Our findings presented in this paper support the work of Burisch (1997), who noted that shortening a measurement scale in a questionnaire to just a few questions can actually improve its validity. Hitting the core of a concept with good items is arguably one of the most important components of questionnaire construction. Three well-written and direct items can achieve the same (if not a greater) level of validity when compared to a large number of poorer items (Burisch, 1997).

Of course, in order to be able to achieve shorter, more efficient scales, one needs to make sure the items within the scale are especially well-written. As noted by Michael Eysenck (2010): 'Good questionnaire items are short and unambiguous.' He quotes the example of an 84-word item from a questionnaire devised with Grossarth-Maticek, which I would argue is neither short nor unambiguous:

> Do you change your behaviour according to consequences of previous behaviour, i.e., do you repeat ways of acting which have in the past led to positive results, such as contentment, well-being, self-reliance, etc., and to stop acting in ways which lead to negative consequences, i.e., to feelings of anxiety, hopelessness, depression, excitement, annoyance, etc.? In other words, have you learned to give up ways of acting which have negative consequences, and to rely more and more on ways of acting which have positive consequences?

One might argue that this question is measuring multiple different constructs, has multiple components, can only be given a yes/no response and, at its heart, is complex to understand – all of which combine to reduce its value.

The 'keep it simple' approach was also demonstrated by other researchers such as Lie (2008), who showed that one item can screen for excessive daytime sleepiness as effectively as a full day of physiological and psychological tests. That one item was: 'Measure your sleepiness on a typical day, where 0 = none and 10 = highest.' Looking at the completion experience from the respondent's perspective, we would argue that it is no surprise that people can become bored and inconsistent in their responses if they are asked the same question a dozen times.

As a coda to this introduction, after the paper central to this chapter was presented, we made contact with Matthias Burisch. The three other authors from this paper were subsequently delighted to co-present with Burisch in a related symposium given at the International Testing Commission conference later that year (MacIver et al., 2012).

Which aspects of work performance do we endeavour to measure and predict? Convergence of four overall performance scales

Abstract

The measurement of overall effectiveness at work can be accomplished by different methods. A top-down approach is to gather rating(s) of overall effectiveness, whereas a bottom-up approach can be created by summing or averaging behavioural criterion measures. These approaches are compared on a mixed occupational group (N = 308) and a high degree of convergence is found between the behavioural criterion composite and the overall measures (r>=.68). The correlation between these measures and style composites supports the construct validity of all four scales. Validities are highest with the three item overall (global) effectiveness measure which forms a promising alternative to single-item criterion measures in academic and practitioner research.

Introduction

The measurement of performance is clearly central to Work and Organizational Psychology, but the degree of effort in researching the performance domain is a small fraction of the effort placed into the research and development of predictor instruments. The performance domain needs to be better understood (Rojon, McDowall and Saunders, 2011). Yet validation studies rely on criterion data selected or developed in the absence of this clarity. This paper expands the understanding of the structure of work effectiveness across different models of work performance.

There are arguments in favour of individual outcome measures which are sometimes considered hard, 'objective' data. In practice, such hard data often suffers from large proportions of construct irrelevant variance (e.g. sales income being heavily influenced by sales region) which renders such criteria far from 'objective'. Specific outcomes, by their nature, also tend to differ across jobs.

The measurement of overall performance is a contentious issue. We can distinguish between two types of overall performance measure:

1. The sum of behavioural ratings.
2. An overall evaluation or rating.

The first approach is to create a sum (or average) across all the criteria. As criteria tend to correlate positively with each other, they form an overall scale which has a degree of internal consistency.

The second approach is to have an independent rating (or ratings) of overall effectiveness. The International Validation Study (Nyfield et al., 1995) measured two components of overall effectiveness related to job proficiency and promotability. The Saville Consulting Performance Culture Framework breaks down overall effectiveness into three components (or sections), which are Applying Expertise, Accomplishing Objectives and Demonstrating Potential. These are averaged to give an overall Global Effectiveness scale.

Clearly, using the overall evaluation is faster than creating a composite. If overall effectiveness criterion is a poorer relation for the sum of behavioural ratings criterion, we would expect it to be more poorly predicted by a composite of behavioural predictors.

Design and methodology

In the development of Saville Consulting Wave®, criterion-centric, inductive and deductive approaches were combined, resulting in a hierarchal model of four

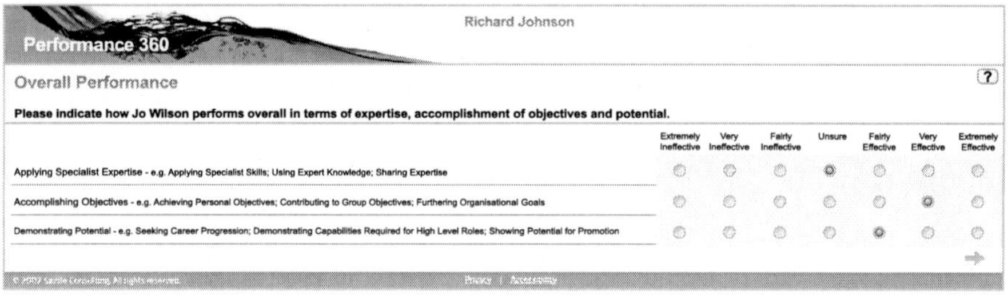

FIGURE 7.1 Wave Performance 360 external rating of performance on the three global dimensions

Clusters, 12 Sections, 36 Dimensions and 108 Facets, where measures of stylistic inclinations have been aligned to key behaviours that have been shown to underpin work performance.

The Wave Performance 360 tool assesses these and gathers Self, Boss, Peer and Report perspectives on performance across 36 Behaviour, six Ability and three Global Dimensions. Activity-oriented items are rated on a seven-point Likert scale ranging from Extremely Ineffective through Unsure to Extremely Effective (see Figure 7.1).

A special research version was designed where single items representing the 'Great Eight' competencies (Kurz and Bartram, 2002) were added, based on definitions in the article of Bartram (2005) as well as four items representing the four Wave clusters defined through three Wave sections each. In the Project Epsom large scale co-validation study (as reported by Saville et al., 2009), the performance of N = 308 participants in a mixed occupational group was assessed by a self-nominated external rater.

Four different kinds of external rater data were collected:

1. Global Effectiveness (three items).
2. Wave Behavioural Clusters (four items).
3. Great Eight Behavioural Competencies (eight items).
4. Full Behavioural Competency Profile (36 Behavioural items).

A high degree of convergence exceeding .70 was expected between the four Overall Effectiveness measures.

Results

All higher-order results are computed as averages to retain the semantic link to the seven-point effectiveness ratings given, resulting in descriptive statistics for external ratings as shown in Table 7.1. The means for the four scales are all about halfway between the 'Fairly' and 'Very Effective' rating.

Internal Consistency (Cronbach's Alpha) reliability increases with scale lengths while standard deviations tend to decrease.

TABLE 7.1 Descriptive statistics and internal consistency reliability of effectiveness scales (numbers of each item are given in brackets)

External Rating Scale (No. Items)	Mean	Standard Deviation	Reliability Alpha
Global Effectiveness (3)	5.69	.77	.67
Wave 4 Behavioural Clusters (4)	5.55	.69	.71
Great 8 Behavioural Competencies (8)	5.53	.72	.83
Full Behavioural Competency Profile (36)	5.53	.60	.93

TABLE 7.2 Correlations between the effectiveness scales

	Global Effectiveness	Wave 4 Behavioural Clusters	Great 8 Behavioural Competencies	Full Behavioural Competency Profile
Global Effectiveness (3)	1	.67**	.74**	.68**
Wave 4 Behavioural Clusters (4)	.67**	1	.84**	.79**
Great 8 Behavioural Competencies (8)	.74**	.84**	1	.82**
Full Behavioural Competency Profile (36)	.68**	.79**	.82**	1

Significant correlations at the .05 level are highlighted by asterisks

Table 7.2 shows the correlation of the various effectiveness scales. The effectiveness scales form a strong positive manifold with the overall and composite behavioural scales being highly correlated. Significant correlations at the .05 level are highlighted by asterisks.

To judge the validity of the various criterion scales, they need to be correlated with other relevant constructs. Saville et al. (2009) reported that the Saville Consulting Wave® Professional Styles questionnaire was the highest-performing personality predictor in Project Epsom at .32 (uncorrected). Table 7.3 illustrates how this validity value changes against the various measures of Overall Effectiveness.

All the overall and behavioural scales show a clear relationship with the a priori styles predictor. Somewhat surprisingly, scale length is inversely associated with this indicator of validity.

In a joint Principle Components Analysis of the 51 effectiveness constructs in Table 7.3, plus six additional ability items, a total of 12 components with an

TABLE 7.3 Correlation of Saville Consulting Wave® Professional Styles

External Rating Scale (No. Items)	Wave Styles Prediction (a priori composite predictor)
Global Effectiveness (3)	.32**
Wave 4 Behavioural Clusters (4)	.27**
Great 8 Behavioural Competencies (8)	.28**
Full Behavioural Competency Profile (36)	.25**

Significant correlations at the .05 level are highlighted by asterisks

eigenvalue >1 emerged. A scree-plot suggested extraction of three components accounting for 30%, 7% and 6% of the variance.

Following Varimax rotation they represent what we have termed Promoting Change, Demonstrating Capability and Working Together, respectively. The Great Eight competencies Leading & Deciding, Interacting & Communicating, Creating & Conceptualising and Enterprising & Performing load highest on Promoting Change. Analysing & Interpreting, together with Organising & Executing, load highest on Demonstrating Capability. Supporting & Co-operating loads exclusively on Working Together, while Adapting & Coping has considerable cross-loadings on the other two components.

Of particular interest are the component loadings for the three items in the Global Effectiveness scale: Applying Specialist Expertise loads highest on Demonstrating Capability as expected, but also cross-loads on both of the other components. Accomplishing Objectives interestingly loads most highly on Working Together, but cross-loads substantially on the other two. Demonstrating Potential loads highly on Promoting Change with a lower loading on Demonstrating Capability.

Discussion

The various effectiveness scales correlate highly. The global overall effectiveness evaluation correlates strongly with the averaged behavioural measures, suggesting that the overall workplace effectiveness construct can be captured in a variety of ways. The results showing that all behavioural and overall measures align with a priori styles prediction lend support to the construct validity of the global (overall) performance measures, as well as the behavioural measures. The Great Eight items seem particularly suitable for academic research as they can be reproduced free of charge, and can be combined with the seven-point effectiveness scale or other rating scales. The global overall measure carries certain advantages as a short measure and does not rely on an assumption of differentially weighting behaviours, as these may be of different levels of importance in different roles. The global overall measure provides a metric across roles and captures the 'Demonstrating Potential' aspect missed by the other methods.

Having said this, there are differences between the weighting of Applying Expertise, Accomplishing Objectives and Demonstrating Potential between different roles. Profiling the importance of these three components to a job role and profiling individuals on these three components can help inform which of the three factors of effectiveness is likely to be instrumental in an individual's effectiveness at work. Factor analysis of our data elaborates the distinction between Task vs. Contextual performance (Borman and Motowidlo, 1993), by adding what may be thought of as a Leadership performance component (Promoting Growth). In higher-level roles where Demonstrating Potential becomes more important, for example, behaviours associated with Promoting Growth are more likely to be instrumental in effective overall performance. On the other hand, Accomplishing Objectives is likely to be a major determinant in entry-level roles, which are more likely to be focused on behaviours related to Demonstrating Capability and the Working Together factor.

Conclusions

The high degree of convergence between various measures of Overall Effectiveness is encouraging. It provides support for the use of behavioural composites and overall measures of effectiveness. Breaking down performance into behavioural competencies and breaking down overall global measures of effectiveness can provide helpful information to the user of what is contributing to effectiveness within ratings (and both can be regarded as useful for 360 assessment in general). In research contexts, understanding the links between overall measurement and effectiveness is useful in clarifying the nomological net that links different performance measures together. Further studies are needed to replicate the structure and trends found in this study.

References

Bartram, D. (2005). The Great Eight Competencies: A criterion-centric approach to validation. *Journal of Applied Psychology*, 90, 1185–203.

Borman, W. C. and Motowidlo, S. J. (1993). Expanding the criterion domain to include elements of contextual performance. In N. Schmitt and W. C. Borman (eds), *Personnel Selection in Organizations*. San Francisco, CA: Jossey Bass, pp. 71–98.

Burisch, M. (1997). Test length and validity revisited. *European Journal of Personality*, 11, 303–15.

Eysenck, M. (2010). Book review of "Playing with Fire: The Controversial Career of Hans J. Eysenck". *The Psychologist*, 23(9), 736.

Kurz, R. and Bartram, D. (2002). Competency and individual performance: Modelling the world of work. In I. T. Robertson, M. Callinen and D. Bartram (eds), *Organizational Effectiveness: The Role of Psychology*. Chichester: Wiley, pp. 227–55.

Kurz, R., Saville, P., MacIver, R. and Hopton, T. (2010). Stakeholder perspectives on behaviour, ability and global performance: Evidence for a three-factor model. Paper at the BPS DOP Conference, Brighton.

Lie, D. (2008). A single subjective question may help screen for excessive daytime sleepiness. *Journal of Clinical Sleep Medicine*, 4, 143–8.

MacIver, R., Kurz, R., Burisch, M., Hopton, T. et al. (2012). So short? That valid! Symposium presented at the International Test Commission Conference, Amsterdam, July.

Nyfield, G., Gibbons, P. J., Baron H. and Robertson, I. (1995). The cross-cultural validity of management assessment methods. Paper presented at the 10th Annual SIOP Conference Orlando, Florida, May.

Rojon, C., McDowall, A. and Saunders, M. (2011). Individual workplace performance revisited: A systematic review of the criterion-space. Paper at the BPS DOP Conference, Stratford-upon-Avon.

Saville, P., MacIver, R., Kurz, R., Hopton, T., Staddon, H., Mitchener, A., Tonks, K., Schmidt, G., Schmidt, S. and Saville, J. (2009). A step towards validity generalisation across self-report personality questionnaires: A co-validation of Saville Consulting Wave Professional Styles, Wave Focus Styles, Saville PQ, OPQ32i, NEO-PI-R, Hogan Personality Inventory and 16PF5. Paper presented at the BPS Division of Occupational Psychology (DOP) Conference, Blackpool.

8

NORMATIVE AND FORCED-CHOICE SCALES

One of the biggest debates in psychometrics which has occurred during my time in the field has been about the relative merits of free-choice and forced-choice response and scoring methods. Although it may initially seem like a fairly dry or academic consideration, it actually has far-reaching implications.

Two categories of response format which are very commonly used in psychometric assessments are the 'normative' (often involving 'free-choice' ratings) and the 'ipsative' (often involving 'forced-choice' rankings).

Normative response formats are designed to minimise the relationship between the items in an assessment. The response to any normative item is, theoretically, independent of the responses to all other items. The score on any normative item should, in theory, only impact the score on the one thing which that particular item is measuring. The respondent has true 'free choice' when responding to each statement and, in theory at least, the response to any one statement shouldn't have influenced the response given to any other statement. Agreement rating scales, where one can decide how much one agrees with a series of statements individually, are a common example of a normative format.

Ipsative questionnaires, on the other hand, have scores with a clearer degree of dependency on each other. The response to one item will have an impact on the possible responses to other items and so will have an impact on more than one thing that the assessment is trying to measure. In essence, by giving a score on an item to one scale, you take it away from another (or others). For example, if you are asked to rank how effective you are in terms of three workplace behaviours, 'Evaluating Problems', 'Building Relationships' and 'Processing Details', this is an ipsative response format. Every person would always have a first choice, a second choice and a third choice. Once you have indicated your first choice, you cannot give another first choice. So your second and third choices are limited to just two options. By the time you have indicated your second choice, your third choice has already been determined because there is only one option left. Your responses are therefore said to be dependent on each other. It would be impossible with this response format for anybody to have a higher or lower total score than anybody else. All that would vary between people is the order of their rankings.

As part of the 'normative versus ipsative' debate, some people have raised objections about comparing ipsative responses between individuals. A common-sense view is that ipsative scores present a comparison within an individual, not between individuals. Hence, it is argued that a comparison of *within*-individual scores *across* individuals is not meaningful and makes standardising against a comparison group inappropriate.

I carried out some research with Eric Willson in the early 1990s which forms the basis of this chapter. Our paper, referenced below, provided our response to such criticisms:

> Saville, P. and Willson, E. (1991). The reliability and validity of normative and ipsative approaches in the measurement of personality. *Journal of Occupational Psychology*, 64, 219–38.

Conclusions from this paper, which is reprinted in full below with permission of the publisher, John Wiley & Son Ltd. and the British Psychological Society (copyright with the British Psychological Society, 1991), have been supported by others, including the much-respected Lee Cronbach and researchers Salgado and Tauriz (2014).

The reliability and validity of normative and ipsative approaches in the measurement of personality

Ipsative questionnaires of personality have been attacked as necessarily inferior to normative approaches. Some even go so far as to accuse the authors of ipsative scales of reporting spurious statistics and of 'cheating at patience'. Despite previous papers which claim to demonstrate that ipsative scales overestimate reliabilities, cannot be factored soundly and yield uninterpretable validity coefficients, this investigation shows with synthetic data that these generalisations are ill-advised. The results demonstrate with simulated data that ipsative scores can be factored soundly, that reliability data are not overestimated, and that under moderate conditions of central tendency bias in normative items, ipsative scores actually correlate better with hypothetical 'true' scores than the normative form. When replicated on real data from a sample of 243 subjects, a high correlation was found between ipsative and normative scale scores, ipsative scaling did not produce spuriously high reliabilities, and both normative and ipsative data showed sensible and significant correlations with external rating criteria.

Personality assessment by questionnaire is currently very widespread. Despite the attacks, particularly of Mischel (1968), there now seems to be good evidence that people do show behavioural consistency across situations (Block, 1977;

Gifford, 1982; Moskowitz, 1982), that these consistencies are not just illusory by-products of the language system (Borkenau and Angleitner, 1985; Rowe, 1982) and that self-report measures correlate significantly with external ratings of personality attributes (e.g. McCrae, 1982; Norman and Goldberg, 1966).

One issue of current controversy concerns the scaling procedure to be employed – normative or ipsative? Ipsative scaling methods, used in questionnaires like the Edwards Personal Preference Schedule, the Gordon Personal Profile and Inventory and one version of the SHL Occupational Personality Questionnaire (OPQ – Saville et al., 1984), have been criticised (Johnson, Wood and Blinkhorn, 1988). Johnson, Wood and Blinkhorn (1988) state that 'manipulating ipsative measures as if they were normative measures is an exercise in futility, like cheating at patience'. For this reason, they conclude that ipsative tests should not be used in personnel selection, and that conventional statistics and reliability data calculated on ipsative scores are uninterpretable. The latter is apparently also the view of the British Psychological Society's Test Standards Committee (1989).

Hicks (1970) made similar points some 20 years before Johnson, Wood and Blinkhorn, stating that ipsative scales are inherently subject to critical statistical bias, whereas normative measurement avoids such statistical limitations. He concluded that ipsative scores may legitimately be employed only for purposes of intra-individual comparisons and that normative scores are the preferred measurement technique for purposes of inter-individual comparisons. Despite these criticisms, there is little evidence that normative questionnaires are more valid than ipsative forms. Indeed, data have rarely been gathered which permit direct comparisons between the two methods, and there is some evidence (Gordon, 1953; Perry, 1955) that certain ipsative questionnaires produce rather good test criterion correlations.

The two approaches

A personality, motivation or interest questionnaire is said to be ipsative when the sum of the scores obtained over the attributes or scales measured for each respondent is a constant (Clemens, 1966).

	Ipsative		Normative		
	Most True	**Least True**	**False**	**Unsure**	**True**
(a) I am sympathetic to other people's problems	0	0	0	0	0
(b) I win at most things I do	0	0	0	0	0
(c) I have lots of friends	0	0	0	0	0
(d) I produce many imaginative ideas	0	0	0	0	0

FIGURE 8.1 Example item(s) scored as an ipsative quad and normatively

In the ipsative case a respondent is asked to indicate which of the four options are most and least true. Clearly the choice of 'I win at most things I do' as most true (score +1) produces a positive score on one scale (say 'competitive'), but also causes lower scores to be obtained on the scales represented by the other three options (score either 0 or, if the least true is chosen, -1). Because a respondent assigns two 0 responses, a + 1 and a − 1 in each quad, the total score which that respondent receives overall will be the same (i.e. zero), but the scores will be distributed differently across the scales, depending on the choices which that individual has made. It is this which causes mathematical dependence between scales and has given rise to the generalisation that ipsative scoring cannot be used for comparing between individuals.

With normative scaling the respondent selects one option from a range of graded responses to each item. Response alternatives may be false/unsure/true, like/indifferent/dislike, or a four-, five- or even seven-point rating scale from, say, 'strongly agree' to 'strongly disagree'. As each item is endorsed separately, the assumption is made that the normative format does not produce mathematically interdependent scores and is therefore superior to the ipsative.

Why use ipsative scaling?

Ipsative scaling is used for two main reasons: the better control of response sets and to reflect the position that life is about choices.

The better control of response sets. For a full explanation of different types of response sets in self-report questionnaires and rating scales, see Guilford (1954). Here we consider acquiescence, social desirability and central tendency.

Acquiescence, as with most response sets, may be a personality variable in its own right; those who more usually respond 'yes' to items are often more optimistic and better adjusted than those who respond 'no' (Rundquist, 1966). Nevertheless, Closs (1975) in the manual to the APU Interest Guide talks of respondents who give over 200 likes out of 224 interest items and others who give over 200 dislikes. As he states: 'Confronted with scripts like these it is difficult for an adviser to know what to do with them!' Accordingly, Closs advocates both normative and ipsative scaling for assessing occupational interests.

Social desirability response sets seem to take two forms (Paulhus, 1984): self-deception (factor alpha) and impression management (factor gamma). It has been found that people often believe themselves to be less heavy than they really are and claim to consume less alcohol than they really do (Robertson and Heather, 1986). Interestingly, it is a characteristic of the better adjusted to show exaggerated alpha responses, despite the implication that this shows less valid self-insight (Roth and Ingram, 1985; Sackeim, 1983).

Impression management is the deliberate distortion of information and is more likely when questionnaires are used as part of the selection procedure. As Wiggins (1986) has pointed out, the view that every respondent is out to deceive us, even in selection, is certainly false. Using occupationally relevant questionnaires with non-contentious item content, giving feedback on results and using inventories alongside group activities may do much to reduce deliberate distortion. Moreover, impression management by candidates can rest on wrong assumptions. For example, the belief that sales and managerial personnel should show high scores on scales of modesty, emotional control and detail consciousness has been contradicted by empirical validity studies in which these scales have correlated negatively with measures of job success (Saville & Holdsworth Ltd, 1989). Whilst ipsative questionnaires can be faked when subjects are *expressly* instructed to do so (Saltz, Reece and Ager, 1962), it may be that the ipsative questionnaire, using items matched in terms of social desirability, will help in controlling deliberate distortion in the selection context (Paulhus, 1986).

A third response set, known to beset normative items, is that of central tendency responding. With normative item formats, some subjects plump consistently for options near to the middle, whilst others predominantly use extreme options. It is not unknown in five-point Likert-type rating scales for some respondents to use the extreme options over 50 per cent of the time, whilst others are loath to use them at all. Simpson (1944) showed with a seven-point scale that the term 'frequently' meant over 80 per cent of the time to some students and under 40 per cent to others. The normative item 'I have lots of friends', whilst not devoid of all meaning, might beg the question: what is 'lots' (five, ten, 15, 20 or more?) and what is 'a friend' (acquaintance, spouse, relative, work colleague)? Thus, when candidates are faced with normative items, their choice of option is, to some extent, unstandardised and arguably inter-individual comparisons are as difficult with normative as with ipsative scales.

Ipsative scales, because of their mathematical interdependence, tend to force negative correlations in the data, whilst normative scales, because of various response sets such as central tendency bias, force up correlations between scales, thus flattening profiles. Essentially the question is whether one might prefer scale estimates *plus* response sets like central tendency and social desirability (normative) or scale estimates *minus* response sets like central tendency and social desirability (ipsative).

Life is about choices. A second line of argument is that behaviour requires us continuously to choose between options: in that sense, life itself is ipsative. In market research data, one frequently finds respondents equally liking (on normative scales) a number of products such as shampoos or quality cars. The ipsative choice of 'which do you prefer?' or a rank ordering of the products will often reveal as much about purchasing habits as rating data alone. Green and Tull (1978) state:

> In many kinds of market research studies it is difficult for respondents to make numerical judgements about the degree of relative dissimilarity among pairs of objects. However they frequently experience no difficulty in making ranking type judgements.

As Broverman (1962) has pointed out, many models in psychology are ipsative in nature. For example, in the area of learning theory, Spence (1956) maintains that when different response tendencies are aroused in an individual, the one possessing the strongest habit strength will occur. Many theories of personality, like those of Murray (1938), Lewin (1935), Rogers (1947) and Cattell (1965), stress the importance of ipsative relationships between different personality and motivational structures. Consider also the classic conflict between id, ego and superego in psychoanalytic theory (Freud, 1943) and in Jung's (1933) theory of types.

Provided that a sufficient number of paired comparisons are made, may ipsative or rank order scales take on the properties of interval measures? Shephard (1966) shows with the use of non-metric multidimensional scaling how a series of paired comparisons and rankings between cities gives a good representation of the true interval distances between them. Moreover, Green and Tull (1978) confirm that it is not unusual in applied studies to find a high degree of correspondence between true ratio and ordinal solutions even when the inputs are 'merely' rankings. And the work of Miner (1988) demonstrates that, although ranking as a method of job evaluation has been out of favour over the last 30 years, a dual response method of rating and ranking did not in fact emerge as superior to simple ranking data.

Johnson, Wood and Blinkhorn (1988) state five 'uncontroversial' facts regarding ipsative tests:

1. They cannot be used for comparing individuals on a scale-by-scale basis.
2. Correlation between scales cannot be legitimately factor-analysed in the usual way.
3. Reliabilities of ipsative tests overestimate the actual reliabilities of the scales.
4. Validities overestimate their utility – indeed, correlations between ipsative scales and external criteria are uninterpretable.
5. Basic statistics such as means, standard deviations and correlation coefficients are not independent and cannot be interpreted in the usual way.

In view of the different types of bias inherent in normative and ipsative scaling, is there any way to test the relative efficiency of the two methods for measuring attributes of personality and motivation? Because it is difficult to do this with data obtained in everyday use, we decided to construct data sets of known characteristics.

We will take up the points made by Johnson, Wood and Blinkhorn first by using a computer simulation basis on synthetic data and second by considering real data on the concept and factor versions of the Occupational Personality Questionnaire.

A computer simulation

We created a set of hypothetical or 'true' scores on a range of personality scales for a sample of pseudo-respondents. Normative item versions of the scores were generated by transforming the original, hypothetical scores. Items were also assembled into groups of four to form quads and scored ipsatively on a most/least true basis. Thus, there were three types of item scores: (1) the original item scores, ranged 1 to 100; (2) normative item scores, by transforming these original scores; and (3) ipsative item scores, by applying quads to original scores.

Original normative and ipsative versions of items were factor-analysed separately to look at the similarity of factor structures. Alpha reliability coefficients were calculated for all versions. Scale scores calculated by simple item score addition from the normative versions were correlated back to scale scores from the normative versions with just one response bias, that of central tendency, introduced. Finally, scale scores from the ipsative versions of items were also correlated with scale scores derived from the original item scores.

First, a set of original scores was established on 32 scales for a sample of 1,000 pseudo-respondents. The number of 32 scales was chosen because it closely represents the OPQ Concept Model which has 30 scales. Using the ipsative quad design mentioned above, it gives a perfectly balanced solution by contrasting every scale once and only once with every other scale.

The 1,000 pseudo-respondents were assigned uniformly distributed scores on the 32 dimensions, with scores ranging from 1 to 100. This was achieved by employing a random number generator (VAX/VMS Fortran function RAN [iseed]). The process used to generate data was similar for all 1,000 respondents, except that the data for each successive respondent was independent of previous respondents. For any one respondent, the random number generator was used to create 32 initial or 'core' item scores for each of the 32 scales, ranged from 1 to 100. Since each core item score was generated independently of others, the 32 scores were not correlated.

In addition to the core item scores for each scale, a number of additional, similar items were generated to simulate the method used in the OPQ design. In this simulation a total of 13 items (core plus 12 others) were generated to represent each scale. Each set of additional items was constrained to be similar to its respective core item value by limiting the range of the random number generator to be close to the core item. For example, if the core item had a value of, say, 30, then each additional item might be constrained to fall in the range 20 to 40. The actual range about each core item was varied in several experiments. In the main body of analyses reported below, the actual maximum permitted about the core item score was plus/minus 12.5. The resulting random values within that range would only rarely have reached the maximum limit. This range limit gave high correlations, around .9 for all related items. The method and limits set were the same for all core items, but the achieved range would depend on the outcome of the random numbers generated.

Thus, each pseudo-respondent has 416 original item scores, being 32 scales each represented by 13 item scores. This data structure ensured that this set of scores would yield a very clear 32-factor solution. Having constructed this synthetic data structure, the main objectives of the subsequent computer analyses were:

a.   to test the effect of both normative and ipsative transformations of the item scores on the factor structure;

b.   to examine the correlations between scales scores (simple linear combinations of item scores) for the original scores compared with both the normative and ipsative variants.

To appreciate fully the results noted later, a brief description of the transformation methods follows.

In the case of normative scores, each original score was simply ranged into a number of equal intervals. For example, if the original score ranged 1–100 and a five-point transformation was required, then original scores of 1–20 would become 1, scores of 21–40 become 2, 41–60 become 3, 61–80 become 4 and 81–100 become 5. A similar process was applied for a number of points in the normative version. In the experiments preceding the main five-point analyses presented below, all options between 3 and 10 inclusive were tried. The five-point versions were analysed in the most detail and reported below because they were typical of many normative scoring systems used commercially.

In the case of ipsative scores, the process was more complex. In order to maintain the similarity with the OPQ methodology, the items were first assembled into a quad design. In this quad design each of the underlying 32 scales is contrasted with all 31 others. For a perfect design (all contrasts made but none repeated) this requires that each scale occurs exactly 13 times (hence the 13 items per scale described earlier). No scale is represented twice in any one quad, but as each scale is repeated in subsequent quads, it is represented by the next, unused, related item in the set of 13.

In any one quad, four scales are represented by four particular items. The ipsative scoring requires that the most preferred or appropriate item is scored +1, the least is scored –1 and the other (unselected) two each score 0. In this simulation it was assumed that the item with the highest original (1–100) score was most preferred and the item with the lowest original score was least. It must be noted that each of the 13 items which represented any one scale was a similar but random variate of the core item value. Hence, due to this random element, it was possible for a Scale A item to have a score of, say, 25 against a Scale B item of, say, 29. In another quad a different Scale A item might have a score of, say, 31 against a Scale C of, say, 29. Thus, if two or three underlying scales were valued similarly (by chance) for a few respondents (in the original random generation of core item values), the 'winner' and 'loser' would vary from respondent to respondent according to that random effect. This effect can occasionally cause quite widely separate scales to 'swap' positions if the higher one happens to have a low item variant representing it and the lower scale happens to have a high variant. This random noise was primarily introduced to avoid 32 identical blocks of 13 items for each respondent, but clearly it also has the advantage of simulating the real-life effects of item semantics and respondent imprecision which cause inconsistencies in data.

TABLE 8.1 Factor loadings in normative and ipsative scoring regimes

	Original (0–100) factor solution	5–point normative factor solution	Ipsative factor solution
Lowest loadings	.00–.01	.00–.04	.00–.30
Highest loadings	.96–1.00	.94–.98	.86–.94

Original, normative and ipsative versions of the items were then separately factor-analysed using a Varimax-Promax rotated principal components analysis. The more options in the normative items, the better they replicated the underlying 32-factor solution. This was observed as the eigenvalues became more equal and the loadings tended more towards 1.0 and 0.0. There was little difference, however, between, say, five and seven options. Factor congruence coefficients were not calculated, but the following range of loadings was noted.

The ipsative items when analysed gave only 31 clear factors. As one would expect, because of the interdependence of the ipsative scoring, one factor, with the weakest alpha, did not emerge.

Scale scores were formed by the addition of items (13 items per scale). These scale scores were formed for all types, namely original, normative and ipsative forms. These sets of scale scores were then correlated with each other for each of the corresponding 32 scales. In all cases, when the normative and ipsative versions were correlated, the correlations exceeded .9. As an example (using five options in the normative version), the mean correlation was .96 varying between .95 and .96 over the 32 scales. When the normative (five options) versions were correlated back to the original, basic versions, the mean correlation was over .99, varying only in the third decimal place. When the ipsative versions were correlated back to the original versions, the mean correlation was over .95, varying between .954 and .962 over the 32 scales. These means, together with other data noted below, are summarised in Table 8.2.

However, as we have already discussed, normative items are known to suffer from central tendency as well as other types of response bias. Let us consider what happens, for example, when a true 1 response to an item (say, strongly disagree) is more cautiously rated as a 2 response (disagree), which we will call type A distortion. Or, what if a 2 or 4 response replies with a cautious 3; this we have called type B distortion. Table 8.2 sets out the results.

In type A distortion, if a response would have been either extreme value of 1 or 5, then the score is translated to 2 and 4 respectively, thus avoiding the extreme values only. This distortion only applies to the proportion reported in each case below. Respondents who are not in the selected proportion are not affected, except in the special case where all respondents distort.

Type B distortion includes type A, but, in addition, if a response would have been either 2 or 4, then the score is translated to the central response, 3. This does not mean that a 5 becomes a 4 which then becomes a 3 – only one move is made. Thus, type B distortion 'squeezes' all affected responses towards the centre by one

TABLE 8.2 Correlations of normative and ipsative scoring with 'true' or original scores

	Mean correlations	
	Original with normative without distortion	**Original with ipsative**
	.9975	.9572
	Original with normative Type A distortion	**Original with normative Type B distortion**
Proportion of sample distorting *(percentages in parentheses)*		
1 in 7 distort (14)	not tested	.9613
1 in 6 distort (16)	not tested	.9557
1 in 5 distort (20)	not tested	.9468
1 in 4 distort (25)	.9824	.9335
1 in 3 distort (33)	.9784	.9132
1 in 2 distort (50)	.9707	.8733
All distort (100)	.9666	.8666

point. When distortion is of type A, the normative form shows slightly higher correlations, but the differences are marginal. When the distortion is of type B and when more than one person in six distorts, then the correlation between the ipsative and the original version is actually higher than normative with original.

Discussion of the computer simulation

The most obvious (and perhaps predictable) difference between the original, normative and ipsative factor solutions was the absence of a final, 32nd factor in the ipsative case. There were only 31 'real' factors detected; the 32nd having a very small eigenvalue and being 'random' in character with no coherent items loaded on it. The 'missing' factor is, of course, caused by the linear dependence in the ipsative data forms. Within a quad, any item can be determined by the value of others and is therefore linearly dependent on them. Given the particular nature of the design of the quads (based on factor replicates), this further translates to factors. Any one factor can be well-estimated (given the deliberate random noise present) by the values of the remainder.

It is clear that one should be cautious in using ipsative forms of data to develop a factor structure. The linear dependence must eliminate at least one factor – perhaps more in the case of unbalanced quad designs.[1] Nevertheless, in all other respects the factor structures were essentially the same. The argument that factor analysis of ipsative items produces spurious results is not supported here. Nor could evidence be found that the ipsative scoring produced unrealistically high alpha statistics. The analyses based on the original (untransformed) data gave the highest alpha values, whilst the alphas for the normative data (three-, five- and seven-point forms) were

TABLE 8.3 Mean item intercorrelations and the alphas for the original, normative and ipsative data

	Original	Normative (5 options)	Ipsative
Mean item intercorrelation	.93–.98	.89–.93	.49–.62
Alpha values for 13-item factors	.98–.99	.96–.98	.93–.94

only slightly lower. The ipsative form alpha values were slightly lower again than the normative values.

Since all factors involved 13 items each and the level of intercorrelation was .9 or more, all alpha values were high (see Table 8.3) compared to other experiments (not detailed here) involving fewer items per factor. This is a characteristic of the coefficient alpha as displayed in Table 1 in McKennel (1970).

The average correlation of normative scales with the original scores of .99 is of course unrealistically high, because we are dealing with relatively unbiased normative items. Even so, the average ipsative scale correlations with original scores are not far behind at .96. When central tendency responding is simulated in the data and more than 16 per cent of respondents show a moderate degree of central bias, then the ipsative form actually correlates higher than the normative with the original scores. It may be that the use of a uniform rather than normal distribution has increased the effect of simulating central tendency bias in this data. However, we have only collapsed responses into the middle of the normative options and have not introduced the type of bias where some respondents exaggerate their response out from a middle to an extreme option.

Since the original work which was done on 32 factors of 13 items each, the authors have also been able to complete similar exercises for both 16 factors of five items each and seven factors of four items each. These runs were used to test for expected rate of decline in the performance of ipsative scoring as a means of 'predicting' original scores. As the number of scales declines, it was expected that the ipsative scores would correlate less with original scores, especially as fewer items were used to create factor or scale scores. A brief summary of results follows in Table 8.4 – clearly, the ipsative versions weaken, but not dramatically.

TABLE 8.4 Mean correlations of normative and ipsative with original scores for 16 and seven scales

	Original with normative (5 options)	Original with ipsative
32 scales of 13 items each	.99	.96
16 scales of 5 items each	.99	.92 (range .91–.93)
7 scales of 4 items each	.99	.89 (range .87–.91)

From these and many other runs employing different numbers of pseudo-respondents, different numbers of options in the normative versions and different methods of ranging original scores into normative options, the authors are satisfied that ipsative scores do not exhibit many of the failings others have attributed to them.

One final note of caution must be made with respect to these simulations. It must be emphasised that these simulations were *not* an attempt to emulate 'real life' responses, but merely to apply specific forms of data treatment to an artificial data set in order to isolate the effects of those treatments and nothing else. It may well be true that different results can be discovered from 'real' data, especially since, in real life, all scales are correlated to a greater or lesser extent. The remainder of this paper therefore concentrates on data collected from human – not electronic – respondents.

Reliability and correlational data for ipsative and normative personality questionnaires

The synthetic data runs show that three 32-scale ipsative data do produce sensible results when factored, that alpha reliabilities appear not to be overestimated, that the correlations with normative equivalents are high and that with a moderate degree of central tendency bias in normative items, the ipsative scores actually correlate higher with hypothetical 'true' scores than the normative form.

But is the study in any way tautologous? Obviously the best test of this is to use real rather than synthetic data. Accordingly, a sample of 146 adults from management courses completed a questionnaire which requires both normative and ipsative item responses, known as the CM7 version of the OPQ (Saville & Holdsworth Ltd, 1988). The OPQs were first published in 1984 as a result of a four-year development programme. They were a response to a demand from industry and commerce for a self-description questionnaire with occupationally relevant scales and non-contentious item content. The OPQ is a suite of tests consisting of five-, eight- and 15-scale versions based upon factor-analytic principles of construction, and a 30-scale version based on a deductive approach to describing personality at work. Versions of the OPQ have been translated and applied in most European languages (Spanish, Italian, Swedish, Danish, Norwegian, French, Dutch and German) and also into Chinese and Japanese.

The CM7 version of the OPQ assesses 30 dimensions of personality with approximately 13 items per scale. Unlike our synthetic (orthogonal) data, these scales are correlated. The 146 subjects completed CM7 prior to attendance at courses on personality assessment. The majority were personnel and training managers, with a degree background. About half of the sample was female and the ages ranged from 24 to 55 years.

In CM7, subjects evaluate groups of four statements (quads) on a five-point normative Likert-type scale from 'strongly agree' to 'strongly disagree' and then they indicate which of four statements in a group is the most true and which the least true. In this way, we gain both a normative and ipsative profile of results. In our analysis, no editing was done on the data. If there were inconsistencies from the item responses (e.g. a normative response of four being chosen as 'most true' in preference to a response of five), then these were allowed to stand.

The intercorrelations for this sample on the 30 OPQ dimensions are given in Table 8.5. The first line of each row gives the correlation for the normative and the second the corresponding intercorrelation for the ipsative format.

As is to be expected, the correlations between scales are generally lower in the ipsative form with more tendency to negative intercorrelation. Of course, it would be naive to assume that the normative intercorrelations are the real or 'true' position, forced up as they are by response sets like central tendency responding. The result of correlating all the pairs of ipsative and normative correlations in Table 8.5 is nevertheless relatively high at .77.

The Cronbach alpha coefficients of internal consistency reliability for the normative and ipsative scaling on the 30 personality dimensions of OPQ CM7 are given in Table 8.6. We can see that the alpha reliabilities for the normative scales vary from .94 to .77 with a mean of .79. The ipsative alphas in fact tend to be slightly lower than the normative; there is no evidence for spuriously high reliabilities in the ipsative form.

Table 8.6 also presents the correlation between normative and ipsative scaling, and we can see that these 'alternate form' figures are again relatively high, ranging from .65 to .86 with a mean of .78. These values are considerably higher than those quoted as alternate form reliabilities for identical normative item formats of the 16PF (Cattell, Eber and Tatsuoka, 1970), for example, and higher even than those for cognitive tests such as the Graduate and Manager Battery (Blinkhorn, 1985). Moreover, the correlation of the ipsative with the normative scores is about the same as the ipsative alpha statistics.

Lack of space prohibits reporting of a complete item analysis, but Table 8.7 gives the item scale and item partial scale (i.e. with the item removed from the scale score of which it is part) correlations for the first 12 items of the Affiliative, Innovative and Critical scales of the OPQ. These were chosen at random, each one representing one of the three principal domains of OPQ, i.e. relationships with people, thinking style, and feelings and emotions respectively. Coefficients are given for the same item endorsed both normatively and ipsatively. As would be anticipated from the alpha figures given in Table 8.6, the item scale correlations are in general higher when the items are expressed normatively than when they are ipsative in form (note what has been said about certain response sets when using normative scales). When an item has a higher item scale correlation in the normative format, it also tends to have a higher coefficient in the ipsative form. When an item is less strong normatively (e.g. item one on critical), it is less strong ipsatively.

The validity of ipsative and normative versions of the OPQ

So the correlation between ipsative and normative data on a 30-scale model of personality on average approaches .8 with no evidence that the alpha statistics are

TABLE 8.5 Intercorrelations of the 30 OPQ scales for the normative (first row) and the ipsative (second row) formats (N = 146)

Note: Each cell contains the normative correlation (upper value) and the ipsative correlation (lower value), reported as correlations ×100. The matrix is lower-triangular; only the diagonal (=1) and cells below it are populated.

	R1	R2	R3	R4	R5	R6	R7	R8	R9	T1	T2	T3	T4	T5	T6	T7	T8	T9	T10	T11	F1	F2	F3	F4	F5	F6	F7	F8	F9	F10
R1	1																													
R2	51/26	1																												
R3	43/26	38/19	1																											
R4	51/21	37/-03	19/01	1																										
R5	14/-20	06/-40	-03/17	38/17	1																									
R6	59/41	41/37	37/16	-40/06	39/29	1																								
R7	-16/-28	-14/-19	-19/-12	-19/-26	-12/39	10/-18	1																							
R8	07/-13	21/-10	-10/-27	-43/-03	-18/06	23/53	19/-07	1																						
R9	16/-19	14/-20	14/-24	-20/-24	20/-05	21/10	21/-18	28/28	1																					
T1	03/-23	15/-18	15/06	-18/01	-32/-09	-07/-18	-07/-27	19/05	40/-07	1																				
T2	15/01	13/17	-11/-10	17/-11	-18/-24	07/-09	-18/-27	28/28	52/20	07/-07	1																			
T3	07/-13	-12/-31	19/11	19/01	05/-23	22/19	09/...	04/...	40/01	19/-07	11/12	1																		
T4	31/13	22/-04	13/01	01/13	14/...	37/15	17/-07	23/14	66/01	27/16	14/-02	11/04	1																	
T5	-23/-37	-05/-14	-28/-24	-24/-31	-34/-02	-10/-34	15/19	07/09	10/24	-00/01	01/04	04/27	-09/16	1																
T6	43/03	27/-02	27/32	27/32	17/14	37/...	21/-06	15/01	20/17	34/15	37/32	15/24	30/21	37/-26	1															
T7	23/09	20/-06	37/13	13/-06	32/...	27/17	15/20	01/15	15/04	20/23	24/21	20/09	30/23	13/-29	29/37	1														
T8	51/32	34/36	36/15	15/01	15/...	36/28	23/23	28/18	14/-08	16/01	25/16	18/-16	15/-26	31/06	-37/02	38/07	1													
T9	27/-10	38/21	21/-01	-01/-10	16/...	04/28	13/-09	05/18	07/05	21/16	24/12	16/09	17/-20	17/-29	02/29	25/-06	27/27	1												
T10	-10/-32	01/-36	01/-13	-13/-23	11/24	28/26	29/06	-03/06	-15/-33	43/41	-07/29	29/17	-23/04	-06/-06	-18/-06	04/-06	18/25	31/25	1											
T11	-02/-39	15/-21	15/-23	-21/-23	24/25	28/26	29/-08	17/-47	09/15	41/21	-22/05	-21/-20	32/-05	-37/-22	-37/-07	09/-03	-18/-21	-05/-23	68/63	1										
F1	18/-05	22/13	13/-13	13/-13	20/14	23/08	14/-07	19/05	23/07	12/07	07/22	05/-22	07/-22	-01/-00	-22/-21	-03/00	09/27	06/-06	18/41	35/01	1									
F2	-22/-40	-21/-38	18/22	-24/-18	29/31	04/44	-04/-00	-35/32	44/21	25/05	24/13	21/-20	18/14	-26/04	31/31	35/-18	44/-03	18/04	04/-06	50/19	35/01	1								
F3	20/-14	27/-10	-06/-08	-12/20	-28/-28	-08/-08	-05/-05	-08/04	-20/-00	-21/20	-05/-26	-20/-24	-14/14	-20/07	-14/-13	-02/17	23/35	-01/-06	-06/00	21/00	29/41	31/-22	1							
F4	07/-16	-16/-10	-10/-35	-35/-10	-04/37	09/47	-04/18	-12/-06	-16/...	-24/-14	-21/-14	-24/04	-21/16	-28/-21	-16/29	16/-02	16/-00	15/04	-18/25	-18/07	48/53	38/44	26/-20	1						
F5	24/-10	26/03	03/-04	-04/37	06/08	08/18	07/...	33/05	12/04	04/-17	04/00	09/-20	28/-25	21/-21	-03/-18	21/00	29/-01	23/-06	-06/04	37/-23	32/44	31/60	26/00	44/28	1					
F6	40/11	11/04	04/20	04/20	08/06	06/06	02/-29	09/-03	00/...	-08/07	07/38	09/17	35/31	28/14	13/21	35/23	29/15	21/10	35/17	21/28	28/-07	14/-00	09/03	-26/03	03/09	45/-04	1			
F7	28/-14	20/-06	17/28	17/-06	20/17	04/-04	06/-05	06/-05	14/-10	39/-06	05/-20	01/-01	23/18	16/-18	-02/-02	11/11	04/-04	01/-13	11/-09	11/04	02/-09	14/10	24/-24	1						
F8	56/61	54/62	22/36	13/45	45/05	20/30	17/-11	35/02	28/31	04/06	15/07	35/02	35/31	35/05	23/29	15/39	13/29	13/29	26/25	04/12	22/10	22/43	29/03	45/31	1					
F9	41/19	33/30	62/30	36/37	13/07	42/03	30/07	28/-16	54/27	17/43	42/30	08/00	39/12	09/32	28/-05	39/-28	12/-21	-12/39	13/05	-06/-26	03/18	21/-28	26/30	14/05	13/-17	00/05	10/71	41/07	1	
F10	41/19	19/27	46/27	27/41	05/03	27/20	10/32	19/17	-16/-06	03/19	19/10	07/-09	43/-27	-26/20	20/...	26/30	30/10	17/...	10/32	03/-17	05/13	34/30	05/-17	26/05	39/11	14/-13	07/41	39/07	1	

TABLE 8.6 Alpha reliability coefficients and form correlations for normative and ipsative response formats on the OPQ CM4.2

Scale	Normative alpha	Ipsative alpha	Correlation of normative with ipsative
Persuasive	.88	.76	.76
Controlling	.94	.86	.82
Independent	.86	.74	.83
Outgoing	.88	.81	.80
Affiliative	.90	.86	.81
Socially confident	.89	.80	.81
Modest	.77	.68	.75
Democratic	.86	.78	.73
Caring	.87	.75	.76
Practical	.90	.79	.83
Data rational	.92	.84	.86
Artistic	.94	.88	.85
Behavioural	.89	.83	.79
Traditional	.90	.80	.78
Change oriented	.88	.76	.72
Conceptual	.89	.77	.80
Innovative	.92	.84	.84
Forward planning	.85	.75	.65
Detail conscious	.90	.81	.81
Conscientious	.85	.76	.77
Relaxed	.91	.80	.76
Worrying	.79	.73	.78
Tough minded	.88	.80	.68
Emotional control	.92	.85	.82
Optimistic	.91	.86	.78
Critical	.86	.80	.68
Active	.90	.83	.85
Competitive	.88	.72	.80
Achieving	.80	.68	.75
Decisive	.89	.76	.75

Note: first published in Saville and Sik (1991)

inflated for ipsative scores. But what about validity? With such high intercorrelation, it is unlikely that one form (ipsative or normative) will drastically differ from the other, but validity still remains an essential issue.

Now with real data, we cannot correlate back to 'true' scores as these are clearly unknown, but we can correlate with rather more fallible external ratings of the personality attributes which the OPQ was designed to measure. Accordingly, a further sample of 243 personnel and training managers on management courses completed an ipsative version of the OPQ (CM4.2) and up to four independent ratings were collected for the same attributes. These ratings were completed by the subject's

TABLE 8.7 Analysis of the Affiliative, Innovative and Critical OPQ scale items scored normatively and ipsatively (N = 243)

	Affiliative				Innovative				Critical			
	Normative		Ipsative		Normative		Ipsative		Normative		Ipsative	
	a	*b*	*a*	*b*	*a*	*b*	*a*	*b*	*a*	*b*	*a*	*b*
1	.648	.596	.602	.531	.815	.772	.648	.564	.185	.068	.234	.119
2	.683	.609	.584	.492	.585	.505	.477	.390	.546	.484	.598	.523
3	.627	.562	.656	.581	.751	.702	.549	.456	.645	.574	.531	.426
4	.645	.566	.590	.508	.718	.661	.541	.453	.642	.580	.519	.414
5	.750	.705	.671	.605	.871	.840	.671	.600	.626	.550	.606	.515
6	.713	.632	.591	.499	.800	.759	.632	.551	.657	.593	.531	.441
7	.742	.701	.647	.585	.647	.608	.582	.512	.558	.465	.613	.517
8	.503	.455	.438	.353	.724	.671	.617	.527	.612	.545	.415	.298
9	.780	.739	.616	.540	.627	.566	.592	.498	.520	.451	.569	.478
10	.727	.676	.646	.577	.834	.801	.619	.534	.646	.586	.442	.340
11	.729	.687	.646	.578	.515	.430	.530	.435	.674	.628	.524	.439
12	.668	.577	.610	.521	.860	.829	.692	.610	.442	.366	.459	.385

Key: *a* = Item scale r   *b*= Item partial r

superior at work, a subordinate or colleague, a friend and his/her partner on four-item Likert–type rating scales. The four items representing each OPQ dimension in the rating scale, which acted as the criterion in this study, were chosen on a purely content-based approach. Subsequent item analysis has meant the amendment of 23 of these items. The 243 subjects nominated those to complete the rating scale, but were asked not to collude on its completion. No scoring keys in the self-completion questionnaire or the rating scale were available to respondents.

Of course, friends, partners, bosses and subordinates see individuals in varying behavioural contexts and situations, and interpret them differently, so they do not completely agree. Also, it is well known that such ratings contain a degree of unreliability and subjectivity. The coefficient alphas for these independent ratings where each rater's rating was treated separately are given in Table 8.8. We can see that the majority are in the range .5 to .6.

Clearly, if comparisons between individuals cannot be validly made with ipsative scores, we would expect non-significant correlations of the ipsative self-report scale scores with the external ratings. Fiske (1986) informs us that the correlation of (normative?) self-report with external ratings tends to be around .35. The correlations of the ipsative self-report scales with the mean of the four raters' judgements are also given in Table 8.8. They range from .26 to .58 with an average of .4. Had we allowed for the unreliability (attenuation) of the four-item rating scale (final column in Table 8.8), the corrected coefficients would range from .33 to .75. All these coefficients are significant at beyond the one per cent level. On average, they slightly exceed the figure provided by Fiske.

But might a normative questionnaire have done better than these correlations between ipsative self-reports and normative external ratings? To test this possibility, 75 of the subjects cooperated by completing the CM7 version of the OPQ

TABLE 8.8 Alpha of external ratings and correlations of ratings with ipsative self-report (N = 243)

	Alpha of ratings	Ipsative with ratings	Ipsative corrected for attenuation in ratings
Persuasive	.61	.26	.33
Controlling	.64	.39	.49
Independent	.53	.35	.48
Outgoing	.71	.54	.64
Affiliative	.61	.37	.48
Socially confident	.61	.44	.57
Modest	.51	.32	.45
Democratic	.36	.30	.50
Caring	.62	.37	.46
Practical	.50	.48	.67
Data rational	.63	.58	.72
Artistic	.83	.59	.62
Behavioural	.52	.29	.40
Traditional	.69	.44	.52
Change oriented	.51	.24	.34
Conceptual	.51	.54	.75
Innovative	.79	.39	.43
Forward planning	.71	.40	.47
Detail conscious	.80	.51	.57
Conscientious	.80	.47	.52
Relaxed	.65	.41	.51
Worrying	.63	.30	.37
Tough minded	.68	.32	.38
Emotional control	.69	.45	.54
Optimistic	.46	.32	.48
Critical	.51	.32	.45
Active	.52	.35	.48
Competitive	.62	.32	.40
Achieving	.52	.45	.63
Decisive	.67	.42	.52

Note: first published in Saville and Sik (1991)

(Saville & Holdsworth Ltd, 1988). For these respondents, it was possible to correlate not only the ipsative but also the normative scale scores with the external ratings. These coefficients, uncorrected and corrected for attenuation in the ratings, are given in Table 8.9. In Table 8.9, the alpha figures from Table 8.8 have been used to give the best reliability estimates available for the internal consistency of the ratings in this smaller sample. The smaller sample can be expected to show greater sampling error and greater restriction of range than the sample in Table 8.8. For this reason, there is little to be gained by correlating one table's set of corrected coefficients with that of another.

The results in Table 8.9 show for both forms of measurement, ipsative and normative, the uncorrected coefficients with external (normative) ratings to be about .40 with no significant difference on any scale. After correction for attenuation, these values are on average a little above .50 for both normative and ipsative forms.

Normative and ipsative scoring using four personality scales

Based on a relatively large number of personality scales, these data suggest that the normative and ipsative approaches correlate relatively well with each other and

TABLE 8.9 Correlations of normative and ipsative scale scores with external (normative) ratings (N = 75)

	Normative with ratings	Ipsative with ratings	Normative corrected for attenuation in ratings	Ipsative corrected for attenuation in ratings
Persuasive	.22	.20	.28	.26
Controlling	.41	.47	.51	.59
Independent	.45	.51	.62	.70
Outgoing	.51	.35	.61	.42
Affiliative	.35	.33	.45	.42
Socially confident	.39	.37	.50	.47
Modest	.35	.37	.49	.52
Democratic	.30	.19	.50	.32
Caring	.22	.30	.28	.38
Practical	.58	.54	.82	.76
Data rational	.56	.48	.70	.60
Artistic	.74	.74	.81	.81
Behavioural	.25	.37	.35	.51
Traditional	.41	.51	.49	.61
Change oriented	.48	.43	.67	.60
Conceptual	.56	.55	.78	.77
Innovative	.44	.41	.50	.46
Forward planning	.33	.52	.39	.62
Detail conscious	.55	.56	.61	.63
Conscientious	.42	.44	.47	.49
Relaxed	.40	.24	.50	.30
Worrying	.43	.31	.54	.39
Tough minded	.37	.27	.49	.33
Emotional control	.46	.42	.55	.51
Optimistic	.29	.29	.43	.43
Critical	.22	.26	.31	.36
Active	.47	.43	.65	.60
Competitive	.19	.13	.24	.17
Achieving	.52	.62	.72	.86
Decisive	.43	.36	.53	.44

Note: first published in Saville and Sik (1991)

about equally well with external criteria. But what might be the correspondence with considerably fewer, say, four, personality scales?

To investigate the correspondence between normative and ipsative scores with four personality scales, a separate study was set up using the following procedure. A sample of 415 applicants for foundation courses in computer programming in Colleges of Further Education which had been given the OPQ Factor Model (FM5) was taken as the data set.

The OPQ Factor Model is a 15-scale questionnaire with six (normative) items per scale on a Likert-type format.

For each subject, four of the normative scales were taken and raw scores found from the six Likert-type items. The items representing these scales were put into six quads; the highest rated response was used to represent 'most true' and the lowest 'least true' in each quad. Where two or more items tied, the winner/loser was chosen at random. Responses were then summed across the quads to form ipsative responses for each subject. The scales were then intercorrelated for the normative and ipsative scoring methods. Table 8.10 gives the results for four scales (each of six-item length) of relatively high intercorrelation in the normative form and Table 8.11 the results for four scales of lower intercorrelation.

Tables 8.10 and 8.11 suggest that when scale intercorrelations are relatively high, the correlations are moderate (from .45 to .71), but with just four scales

TABLE 8.10 Ipsative and normative form correlation for four personality scales of higher intercorrelation (N = 415)

	Normative intercorrelations				Ipsative intercorrelations				'Alternate form' r (ipsative with normative)
	P21	P22	V22	P24	P21	P22	V22	P24	
P21 (Influence)	1	.56	.31	.48	.1	-.11	-.21	-.24	.45
P22 (Social confidence)		1	.36	.64		1	-.31	.10	.71
V22 (Active)			1	.32			1	-.21	.66
P24 (Gregarious)				1				1	.71

TABLE 8.11 Ipsative and normative form correlating for four personality scales of low intercorrelation (N = 415)

	Normative intercorrelations				Ipsative intercorrelations				'Alternate form' r (ipsative with normative)
	C24	E22	V22	P24	C24	E22	V22	P24	
C24 (Detail Conscious)	1	.30	.23	.08	1	00	-.19	-.36	.74
E22 (Phlegmatic)		1	.12	.05		1	-.33	-.34	.77
V22 (Active)			1	.32			1	-.06	.79
P24 (Gregarious)				1				1	.81

of lower intercorrelation, the correlations of normative and ipsative scoring are relatively strong (from .74 to .81). It is interesting that whereas the ipsative scales intercorrelate negatively and the normative scales intercorrelate positively (as is to be expected given the response sets they encourage), the correlation of normative with corresponding ipsative scales is in the .70s. Differing scaling methods yield very similar final outcomes.

Conclusions

Ipsative scaling has often been criticised as an intrinsically inferior form of measurement. In commenting on one of the papers challenging ipsative scoring, Cronbach (personal correspondence) writes:

> This overstates the complaints. Ipsative scales can be used for comparing individuals scale by scale. The intercorrelations can be factored soundly. Reliabilities are entirely sound when properly interpreted; there is no overestimation that I know of. I see no reason for regarding validity coefficients as overestimates.

Using a relatively large number of personality scales, our data support Cronbach's view by showing with synthetic data:

1. a high degree of correspondence between the factor analysis of ipsative and normative scores;
2. high correlations between ipsative and normative scaling;
3. comparable alpha reliabilities with no evidence for the ipsative form to produce overestimates – in fact, ipsative alphas are somewhat lower than those of normative scales;
4. both the ipsative and normative forms produce good estimates and hypothetical original (or 'true') scores;
5. that with a moderate degree of central tendency response bias introduced into normative items, ipsative scoring actually correlates better with hypothetical true scores than does the normative scoring.

When these results are examined in real data:

1. high correlations were found between ipsative and normative scores;
2. the ipsative scale internal consistency reliability data did not appear to be overestimated compared with the normative internal consistency reliability data on the same subjects – in fact, they were slightly lower than the normative alphas and of about the same magnitude as the ipsative-normative 'alternate' form correlations;
3. both ipsative and normative data showed sensible and significant correlations with external (normative) ratings;
4. the correspondence between ipsative and normative scoring was high even with as few as four personality scales.

Clearly we must be cautious about generalising too widely, but from these studies on synthetic and real data, we would conclude that individuals can be as validly compared on a scale-by-scale basis on ipsative scales as normative, that ipsative data can be factor-analysed legitimately and that neither reliabilities nor validities appear to be overestimated. It is unlikely that conclusions with ipsative data, based at least on a relatively large number of scales, are any less valid than those based on the normative. It is true that the interpretation of ipsative questionnaires needs to recognise the interdependence which exists between scales, but response sets cause problems of inter-individual comparison with normative scales too. Ipsative scores do have their limitations, but so do the normative; it is a matter of trading one type of bias for another. Indeed, there is a lot to be said for using ipsative *and* normative scaling methods for measuring models in psychology. Both have their pros and cons. The development of inadequate constructs or the use of poor items are far greater sources of bias in personality questionnaires than issues of normative versus ipsative presentation of items.

If it is the case that normative items are more prone to impression management on the part of candidates (a view held by many practitioners), then ipsative scales may sometimes be preferable to the normative scales in the selection context. Finally, we would still be wise to remember that ipsative scores are not absolutes – but for that matter nor are the normative scores!

Acknowledgements

The authors would like to thank Professor Lee Cronbach, Professor Peter Warr, Roger Holdsworth and Helen Baron for their valuable comments; George Sik for his work on the final draft; the SHL and Digitab staff who handled the data analyses; and Jane Saville for tolerating the interruptions to the family holiday caused by drafting this paper.

Note

1 As Lee Cronbach (1984) points out in personal correspondence, one scale can be dropped in the factor analysis and the loadings of the withheld variable can be determined algebraically, in which case the factor analysis tells the whole story.

References

Blinkhorn, S. (1985). *Graduate and Managerial Assessment*. Windsor: NFER-NELSON.
Block, J. (1977). Advancing the psychology of personality: Paradigmatic shift or improving the quality of research. In D. Magnusson and N. S. Endler (eds), *Personality at the Crossroads: Current Issues in International Psychology*. Hillsdale, NJ: Erlbaum, pp. 37–63.
Borkenau, P. and Angleitner, A. (1985). *Systematische Verzerrungen in der Beurteilung von Personen: Faktum oderFiktion?* In D. Albert (ed.), *Bericht über den 34.* Kongreb der Deutschen Gesellschaft fur Psychologie in Wien, vol. II. Gottingen: Hogrefe, pp. 327–30.
British Psychological Society (1989). *Psychological Testing: Guidance for the User*. Leicester: British Psychological Society.

Broverman, C. (1962). Normative and ipsative measurement in psychology. *Psychological Review*, 69(4), 295–305.

Cattell, R. B. (1965). *The Motivational Analysis Test*. Illinois: IPAT.

Cattell, R. B., Eber, H. W. and Tatsuoka, M. M. (1970). *Handbook for the 16 PF*. Champaign, IL: IPAT.

Clemens, W. V. (1966). An analytical and empirical examination of some properties of ipsative measures. *Psychometric Monographs*, 14.

Closs, J. (1975). *Manual of the APU Occupational Interest Guide (Standard & Advanced Forms)*. London: Hodder & Stoughton.

Cronbach, L. (1984). *Essentials of Psychological Testing*. New York: Harper & Row.

Fiske, D. (1986). The trait concept and personality questionnaire. In A. Angleitner and J. S. Wiggins (eds), *Personality Assessment via Questionnaire*. Berlin: Springer-Verlag, pp. 35–48.

Freud, S. (1943). *A General Introduction to Psychoanalysis*. Garden City, NY: Garden City Publishing Co.

Gifford, R. (1982). Affiliativeness: A trait measure in relation to single-act and multi-act behaviour criteria. *Journal of Research in Psychology*, 16, 128–34.

Gordon, L. V. (1951). Validities of the forced-choice and questionnaire methods of personality measurement. *Journal of Applied Psychology*, 35, 407–12.

——. (1953). *Gordon Personal Profile Inventory*. Sidcup: Harcourt Brace Jovanovich.

Green, E. and Tull, D. (1978). *Research for Marketing Decisions*. Englewood Cliffs, NJ: Prentice Hall.

Guilford, J. P. (1954). *Psychometric Methods*. New York: McGraw-Hill.

Hicks, L. E. (1970). Some properties of ipsative, normative and forced choice normative measures. *Psychological Bulletin*, 74, 167–84.

Johnson, C. E., Wood, R. and Blinkhorn, S. F. (1988). Spuriouser and spuriouser: The use of ipsative personality tests. *Journal of Occupational Psychology*, 61, 153–62.

Jung, C. (1933). *Psychological Types*. New York: Harcourt.

Lewin, K. (1935). *A Dynamic Theory of Personality*. New York: McGraw-Hill.

McCrae, R. R. (1982). Consensual validation of personality traits: Evidence from self-reports and ratings. *Journal of Personality and Social Psychology*, 43, 293–303.

McKennel, A. (1970). Attitude measurement. *Sociology*, 4(2), 227–45.

Miner, J. B. (1988). Development and application of the rated ranking technique in performance appraisal. *Journal of Occupational Psychology*, 61, 291–305.

Mischel, W. (1968). *Personality and Assessment*. New York: Wiley.

Moskowitz, D. S. (1982). Coherence and cross-situational generality in personality: A new analysis of old problems. *Journal of Personality and Social Psychology*, 43, 385–99.

Murray, H. A. (1938). *Explorations in Personality*. New York: Oxford University Press.

Norman, W. T. and Goldberg, L. R. (1966). Raters, ratees and randomness in personality structure. *Journal of Personality and Social Psychology*, 4, 681–91.

Paulhus, D. L. (1984). Two component models of socially desirable responding. *Journal of Personality and Social Psychology*, 46, 598–609.

——. (1986). Self-deception and impression management in test responses. In A. Angleitner and J. S. Wiggins (eds), *Personality Assessment via Questionnaire*. Berlin: Springer-Verlag, pp. 143–65.

Perry, D. K. (1955). Forced-choice vs. L.I.D. response items in vocational interest measurement. *Journal of Applied Psychology*, 39, 2–262.

Robertson, I. and Heather, N. (1986). *Let's Drink to Your Health!* Leicester: British Psychological Society.

Rogers, C. R. (1947). Some observations on the organisation of personality. *American Psychologist*, 2, 358–68.

Roth, D. L. and Ingram, R. E. (1985). Factors in the Self-Deception Questionnaire: Associations with depression. *Journal of Personality and Social Psychology*, 48, 243–51.

Rowe, D. C. (1982). Monozygotic twin cross-correlations as a validation of personality structure: A test of the semantic bias hypothesis. *Journal of Personality and Social Psychology*, 43, 1072–9.

Rundquist, E. A. (1966). Item and response characteristics in attitude and personality measurement. *Psychological Bulletin*, 66, 166–77.

Sackeim, H. A. (1983). Self-deception, self-esteem and depression: The adaptive value of lying to oneself. In D. Masling (ed.), *Empirical Studies of Psycho-analytic Theories*. Hillsdale, NJ: Erlbaum, pp. 101–58.

Salgado, J. F. and Tauriz, G. (2014). The Five-Factor Model, forced-choice personality inventories and performance: A comprehensive meta-analysis of academic and occupational validity studies. *European Journal of Work and Organizational Psychology*, 23(1), 3–30.

Saltz, E. Reece, M. and Ager, J. (1982). Studies of forced-choice methodology: Individual differences in social desirability. *Educational and Psychological Measurement*, 22, 365–70.

Saville, P., Holdsworth, R., Nyfield, G., Cramp, L. and Mabey, W. (1984). *The Occupational Personality Questionnaires*. London: SHL.

Saville & Holdsworth Ltd (1988). *OPQ Update No. 3, CM7*. London: SHL.

——. (1989). *SHL Validation Review*. London: SHL.

Saville, P. and Sik, G. (1991). Ipsative scaling: A comedy of measures, as you Likert or much ado about nothing. *Guidance and Assessment Review*, 7(5), 1–3.

Shephard, D. (1966). Metric structures in ordinal data. *Journal of Mathematical Psychology*, 3, 287–315.

Simpson, R. H. (1944). The specific meanings of certain terms indicating different degrees of frequency. *Quarterly Journal of Speech*, 1944(30), 328–30.

Spence, K. W. (1956). *Behaviour Therapy and Conditioning*. New Haven, CT: Yale University Press.

Wiggins, J. S. (1986). Epilog. In A. Angleitner and J. S. Wiggins (eds), *Personality Assessment via Questionnaire*. Berlin: Springer-Verlag, pp. 225–34.

PART III

Practicalities of psychometrics

9

DO ASSESSMENTS WORK?

This chapter is based on a paper we wrote in 2009:

> Saville, P., MacIver, R., Kurz, R. and Hopton, T. (2009). Project Epsom: How valid is your questionnaire? (Phase 1). Saville Consulting Group, Jersey.

It is worth noting that this was at a particularly interesting time for workplace personality assessment. A group of eminent psychologists (Morgeson et al., 2007) had recently released a paper which contained a number of criticisms of the use of personality tests in personnel selection contexts. Our 2007–8 research, which is discussed in the paper in this chapter, offered a counter-narrative to some of the criticisms that had been levelled.

Project Epsom: how valid is your questionnaire?

Abstract

A major research initiative, Project Epsom, compared the validities of a range of the most popular personality questionnaires using the same sample and the same work performance measures. In this study the Saville Consulting Wave® Professional Styles was the most valid questionnaire in terms of measuring job performance. The questionnaires compared were validated against the externally developed Saville & Holdsworth Limited (SHL) Great Eight competency framework (Kurz and Bartram, 2002) and a global performance measure in order to ensure fairness of comparison and to avoid bias towards the Saville Consulting questionnaires. Great care was taken in the use of these work performance criteria and the equations for predicting work performance published by Bartram (2005) were utilised for the Occupational Personality Questionnaire (OPQ®).

The questionnaires were also compared to other models of work performance, including the extensive Saville Consulting model of work effectiveness (Kurz et al., 2009). Against this model, the Saville Consulting questionnaires performed better still, but for the purposes of this paper, these results are not presented here. The Saville Consulting Wave Professional Styles questionnaire therefore outperformed the OPQ against its own model of work effectiveness.

The newly developed Saville Personality Questionnaire (Saville PQ™; Saville et al., 2008a) also performed as well, if not better than the OPQ and many other established questionnaires. The Saville PQ was developed using the same approach as the OPQ, takes under 15 minutes to gather both normative and ipsative responses, and makes a crucial distinction between a person's talents and motivations. Many of the other questionnaires compared in Project Epsom did show at least a moderate level of validity in measuring job performance.

In considering the results from this research, the present paper also provides an initial orientation in the key concepts surrounding personality questionnaires and offers readers guidance on how to select the most appropriate questionnaire for measuring work performance. This paper finally considers why the Saville Consulting questionnaires were found to be the most valid measures of work performance.

Background

Nelson Mandela once asked: 'Does anybody really think that they didn't get what they had because they didn't have the talent or the strength or the endurance or the commitment?' In this statement, Mandela recognises the importance that personality plays in driving success in life. For example, a representative reported that in one major office technology company, some 80% of their sales consistently came from just 20% of their best salespeople.

What, then, is personality? There has been no shortage of answers to this question. In developing the OPQ, Saville et al. (1984) defined personality as 'an individual's typical or preferred ways of behaving, thinking and feeling'. A similar definition has been proposed by Costa and McCrae (1992) with their Big Five model of personality. More recently, Digman (1997) distinguished between Alpha personality characteristics and Beta personality characteristics, a distinction which is similar to that between people who 'get along' and those who 'get ahead'.

Cronbach (1970) saw personality as a 'behavioral posture' and, as with other researchers, Cattell (1965) emphasised the criticality of validity when he stated that personality is 'that which enables us to predict what a person will do in real-life situations'. In our application, validity represents job success.

It is increasingly acknowledged in the contemporary world that job-relevant and well-constructed personality questionnaires can be used successfully to measure what a person will do in real-life situations, and in particular to improve decisions in the selection and development of people at work. There is a proliferation of personality questionnaires available purporting to offer the means to achieve this. In the field of personality assessment, there are a number of reasons why it can be difficult to choose between the different questionnaires available and to select that which is most suitable.

Some test publishers use complicated jargon which may confuse many test users, while others refrain from publishing negative findings. Statistical techniques can be misapplied in an attempt to overestimate the effectiveness or usefulness of a test. For example, statistical procedures might only be carried out on the top and/or bottom 10% of people in the sample, ignoring the majority of the sample and vastly inflating the apparent relevance of the test. Additionally, some tests are merely compared with other tests to assess the degree to which they agree in their measurement. Such correlation techniques, however, do not ensure that the test necessarily demonstrates job-relevance or will measure performance at work. As Wiggins (1973) succinctly puts it:

> Regardless of the theoretical considerations which guide scale construction or the mathematical elegance of item-analytic procedures, the practical utility of a test must be assessed in terms of the number and magnitude of its correlations with non-test criterion measures.

The *validity* of a test in this context is the degree of relevance the test has in assessing effectiveness at work. A valid test must be able to measure how the test-taker is likely to perform in a given job. Data must be presented to back this up. If no evidence is presented to show that a test works, it should not, quite simply, be used to make decisions which could impact on people's careers and well-being at work. Choosing valid tests with established links to performance drives superior selection methods and in turn makes an organisation more effective by driving improved individual performance. Needless to say, validity is the single most important characteristic of any test and concerns whether a test actually works.

Other important concepts in testing include *norms*, *reliability* and *return on investment (utility)*. Test *norms* such as 'percentiles' and 'stens' show how an individual compares to a relevant sample of people. Norms are of course useful for such comparisons, but do not in themselves 'prove' that a test works: they are not the *sine qua non* of testing. Indeed, there are occasions where one does not even need to have norms. For example, filling job vacancies by selecting the highest performers on a valid and job-relevant test can result in improved productivity, without necessarily comparing these scores against an external norm group. In this instance, the test could be highly valuable to the organisation despite not having norms.

Some tests are published with multiple norm groups, creating a bewildering choice with meaningless practical implications. The Saville Consulting Wave Focus questionnaire, which takes just 13 minutes to complete, has over 40,000 people in its norm groups, but this does not in itself guarantee validity. One could theoretically flip a coin 40,000 times as a basis for selecting people, but it is unlikely to predict their work performance effectively. Once a norm group reaches above 500 people in size, the additional insights offered are actually marginal. At this size of sample, adding further people is likely to change a sten score, a standardised scale which has a range from one to ten, by as little as 0.1 of a sten. That said, under most circumstances, norms are useful in assessing people against an appropriate benchmark group, but the need for norms is very much secondary to the need for validity.

Reliability is a measure of accuracy or consistency of a test. This is usually calculated by comparing the test against itself at a different time (test-retest method); by comparing the test against another similar (parallel) version of itself (alternate form method); or by comparing some of the questions that make up the test with the other questions (internal consistency method). Ensuring high reliability is important as it improves validity, yet there remains no point in using a test that has been completed by many people and that measures each person consistently if it is completely irrelevant to their performance at work (and hence has no validity). *In essence, reliability can be thought of as 'getting the test right', whereas validity is 'getting the right test'.*

Return on investment (or *utility*) is achieved by using a valid test in conjunction with other methods, such as a good structured interview, to select the appropriate candidates. There are different methods for calculating return on investment, but one must know the validity of the test (the correlation with job performance) and how productivity at output varies between workers. The relationship between return on investment and validity is *linear* (and not based on the square of the validity, as is sometimes reported). That is, as the validity of the measurement method goes up, so does the return on investment.

While all of these concepts are important in testing, validity is central. Possession of reliability makes a questionnaire more likely to have validity, but it is not a guarantee. Where a questionnaire can show, through a process of hypothesis testing, that it has superior validity this will impact on fairness and legal defensibility. Valid questionnaires lead to better decisions, fewer selection errors, more accurate identification of development needs and hence better performance of organisations and a higher return on initial investment. The first consideration for an individual deciding to use an assessment is: 'What is the validity, and how does this compare to the validity of other assessments?'

Because test authors tend to use very different and often ad hoc samples to demonstrate validities, it becomes virtually impossible to directly compare validity data reported from different questionnaire manuals. Because of this and incumbent financial and resource costs, few studies have attempted to directly compare a large number of different questionnaires on the same sample, and to assess them against independent measures of performance at work. So, a study on a single sample and against the same work performance criteria was critically needed to advance knowledge in the field of personality measurement and to improve selection and development practices in the world of work.

Project Epsom

Project Epsom compared a range of the better-known personality questionnaires to determine which among them are the more valid measures of work performance. This project compared the major personality questionnaires in one study against the same job performance criteria to create a level playing field for a direct and fair comparison. The extent to which each could measure the performance of the test-taker in a work context, as defined by both an overall measure of global performance and by the Great Eight competency framework (Kurz and Bartram, 2002), was assessed. The Great Eight framework is an independent model of work performance skill, personality, motivation and intelligence, which was not developed by Saville Consulting. The content of the global performance measure originates with the work of Nyfield et al. (1995) and covers three key areas: applying specialist knowledge, accomplishing objectives and demonstrating potential.

Method

A total of 308 participants completed a range of different questionnaires. In this phase one report, we consider the better-known of these, including the Professional Styles and Focus Styles versions of the Saville Consulting Wave® questionnaire, Saville PQ™, OPQ, Hogan Personality Inventory, 16PF5 and NEO-PI-R. The majority of these participants also completed a larger range of questionnaires (29 in total), including the Hogan Development Survey, Thomas International DISC, DISCUS, and MBTI assessments. The presentation order of these questionnaires was counterbalanced across participants in order to prevent fatigue effects. Each participant was asked to nominate two other people who would act as independent raters and who evaluated their performance at work.

The performance rating questionnaire

The Performance 360 assessment is a separate instrument from the Saville Consulting Wave questionnaires, which was designed specifically to measure work performance. It provides work performance criteria against which the different personality questionnaires used in Project Epsom can be compared. It helps to bring the field of competency measurement up to date and into the age of online business and assessment. It assesses performance completely independently of personality measurement, considering a range of different behavioural, ability and global areas of work performance. Figure 9.1 below illustrates the three items of global performance as presented in the Performance 360 questionnaire.

When completing the Performance 360 assessment, the independent raters were asked to indicate how effective the main participant is in these and other areas on a seven-point rating scale from Extremely Ineffective to Extremely Effective. In addition to the global performance assessment, raters also provided an external rating of the performance of participants in terms of Saville and Holdsworth Limited's (SHL) Great Eight work competencies. Crucially, the Performance 360 assessment provided independent measures of the effectiveness of the individual in their job.

Raters were also asked to complete a personality questionnaire on themselves (Wave Focus Styles). This forms the basis of further study, looking at how the

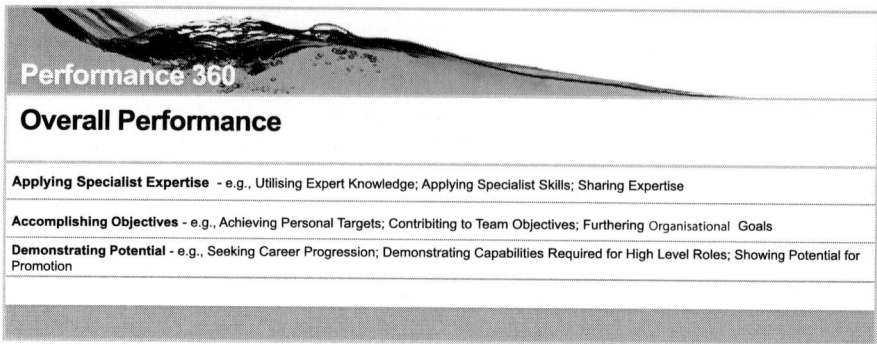

FIGURE 9.1   Measuring global performance using the Performance 360 questionnaire

personality of the raters might influence their judgement of the work performance of others.

Initial data in Project Epsom were collected from October 2007 to February 2008 and a number of follow-up studies were run after six months to establish questionnaire predictive validities over time. Participants were paid for their involvement in this project and were invited to cooperate across a wide range of organisations in the UK and the USA, with fewer numbers of participants from Bulgaria, Canada, Germany, France, Ireland, the Caribbean, India, South Africa, Australia and New Zealand.

Analyses

All questionnaires were compared using an identical approach against the Great Eight model and the global performance measures from the Performance 360 questionnaire. There has been some misinterpretation of the methods used in this study. *This study did not correlate the various self-report questionnaires with the Wave questionnaires.* Rather, the self-report questionnaires were correlated with independently gathered work performance ratings from participants' managers and work colleagues using the Great Eight competency model developed by SHL (Bartram, 2005), as well as a global job performance rating. We used the Great Eight framework as this is a relatively well-known model of job competencies. These ratings of work performance were collected from managers, work colleagues, family members, partners and friends who were required to have a knowledge of the participant's behaviours at work.

It was then possible to evaluate independently which self-report questionnaires correlated best with a third party's ratings of job performance in terms of overall job performance and performance of core workplace competencies. The use of an external independent model provided the fairest possible means of assessing the performance of each of the questionnaires competing in Project Epsom. We compared questionnaires against the Great Eight criteria using exactly the wording of Bartram (2005) and for the OPQ32i, we used the exact Great Eight equations published by SHL in Bartram (2005). Statistical approaches such as multiple or canonical regression, which can lead to overestimates of validity, were not used. Prior to analysis, the aspects of work performance in the Great Eight model that each questionnaire should measure were hypothesised. This was based on statistical modelling and content review. Approaches such as multiple or canonical regression, which can lead to overestimates of validity, were not used.

The Saville Personality Questionnaire

Psychometric test users sometimes become attached to a favourite test, convinced that certain scales cannot possibly be measured by other questionnaires. To challenge this orthodoxy, a completely new questionnaire, the Saville Personality Questionnaire (Saville PQ™), was developed. This combines modern Wave measurement technology with the same 'deductive' development approach that was employed with the OPQ nearly 25 years ago (Saville et al., 1984). The Saville PQ was developed to demonstrate the recent advances in knowledge and to see if the same level of validity as is possessed by the OPQ could be produced in a questionnaire that takes less than a quarter of the time (13 minutes) to complete.

Like the Saville Consulting Wave Professional Styles and Focus Styles questionnaires, the Saville PQ also has the added advantage of providing separate measures of people's talents and motives in a given area, as Saville Consulting research indicates that these measures need to be clearly separated. For example, our research has revealed a distinct difference between being good at and enjoying an activity, though many questionnaires confuse the two. Questions asking about motives and talents are not identified in the OPQ as separate measures and this can cause confusion in interpretation. For example, in the normative version of the OPQ32®, the 'Forward Thinking' scale has three questions asking about whether the respondent likes to forward plan and three questions asking about whether they are good at forward planning. About 60% of the OPQ items refer to being good at an activity and 40% refer to liking an activity. Having separate measures of motivations and talents, as in the Saville Consulting questionnaires, also helps to identify the specific development needs of individuals at work. The Saville PQ also gathers normative (free-rating) ipsative (forced-choice ranking) responses within its sub-15-minute completion time. This dynamic nipsative format, also pioneered in the Saville Consulting Wave questionnaires, helps a questionnaire counteract the natural tendency of respondents to agree with the majority of statements presented to them. A respondent can agree with as many statements as they like in the free-rating normative task, even repeatedly giving the highest rating possible to many questions if they so choose, but they are then required to further clarify equally rated questions by ranking these questions in terms of how much they agree with them (ipsative ranking task).

It is noteworthy that in order to generate both a normative and an ipsative measure using the OPQ portfolio, the respondent would be required to complete two much longer questionnaires, which take nearly two hours in total. The Saville

Questionnaire	Number of Questions	Typical Completion Time
OPQ32i	416	60 mins
NEO-PI-R	240	40 mins
Wave Professional Styles	216	40 mins
Hogan Personality Inventory	206	30 mins
16PF5	185	30 mins
Wave Focus Styles	72	13 mins
Saville PQ	72	13 mins

FIGURE 9.2 A summary of seven questionnaires compared in Project Epsom

PQ also avoids negative questions, as research has found that such questions were significantly less reliable than positively phrased questions (e.g. Angleitner and Lö, 1986). The Saville PQ was used for the first time in Project Epsom.

Seven key questionnaires: a summary

Figure 9.2 below provides a summary of seven key questionnaires that are compared in this paper.

What level of validity should we expect?

Validity, the degree of relevance a test has to work performance, is normally expressed as a value between -1 and +1. This correlation coefficient indicates the extent of the relationship between the questionnaire and job performance. A validity of zero indicates a chance measurement. This is as effective as flipping a coin to predict how an individual is likely to perform at work.

A validity of 1 would be a perfect measurement of how an individual is likely to perform at work. Of course, a perfect measurement of performance is impossible as no single assessment method can account for all of the factors that constantly impact on people's performance at work. Validities in the range of +0.8–0.9 are also unlikely in the extreme to be obtained using any single method.

Studies using huge databases of information suggest that a good personality questionnaire can be expected to show validities of about +0.3, which is a very useful degree of validity. To put this into context, ability tests may have validities around +0.5, a standard job interview is likely to have validity of around +0.2 and references or educational qualifications are likely to be as low as +0.1 (Schmidt and Hunter, 1998).

These validity figures come from a statistical procedure known as meta-analysis which takes into account such factors as the degree of unreliability inherent in obtaining various subjective ratings of job performance. Such factors had previously led to underestimates of the 'true' validity of a selection method. In Project

Epsom, the unreliability in the ratings of job performance obtained was statistically taken into account, but crucially we report on a complete data set where we did not exclude any data. This was done in order to ensure a standardised method across all questionnaires and to keep the playing field as even as possible.

Results summary

Total job performance was measured through a three-item Global Performance scale (Kurz et al., 2009). Figure 9.3 shows the validities of seven key questionnaires in measuring global work performance, as assessed by the raters through the Performance 360 questionnaire. This global measure was chosen to ensure a standardised assessment across all of the questionnaires and represents a view of performance at work in terms of applying specialist knowledge, accomplishing objectives and demonstrating potential.

The Global Performance measure used is particularly useful as it is a general criterion which does not favour any particular personality questionnaire over the others. The more accurately we can use the responses on a given personality questionnaire to predict what an independent rater has said about the work performance of the test-taker, the more valid this personality questionnaire can be considered to be.

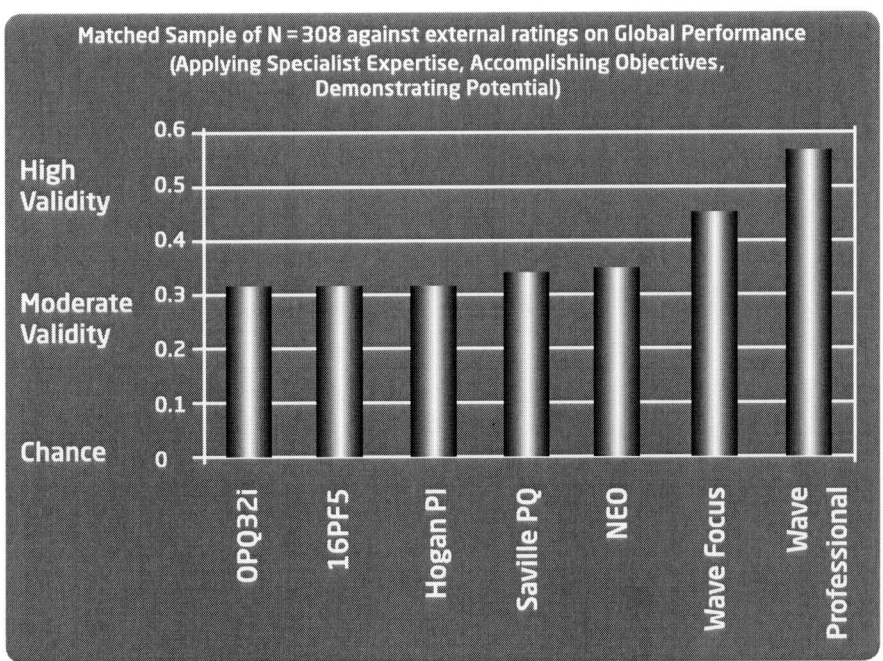

FIGURE 9.3   The validity of seven key questionnaires in measuring total job performance

All of the seven questionnaires here showed at least a moderate level of validity in predicting work performance, considerably higher than the values considered by many studies of personality testing (e.g. Schmitt et al., 1984; Barrick and Mount, 1991; Morgeson et al., 2007). The Wave Professional Styles questionnaire eclipses all other questionnaires. The Saville PQ compares favourably to the OPQ32i despite taking just 25% of the completion time and is also comparable in validity to the Hogan Personality Inventory and 16PF5, which take approximately twice as long.

These seven key questionnaires were also compared against external ratings of the Great Eight work performance competencies in turn. Validities were calculated for measuring each of the Great Eight competencies and these scores were then averaged together. These average validities in measuring work performance are shown below in Figure 9.4.

In terms of the Saville Consulting questionnaires, the results for the individual Great Eight competencies are thus consistent with the result for global performance.

'Power' relates to measuring effectiveness or output in a given unit of time – in terms of personality questionnaires, that which provides the greatest validity per unit of time. Figure 9.5 (below) compares the power of the questionnaires in terms of how much validity can be achieved by each in 15 minutes.

As can be seen, the Wave Focus Styles and Saville PQ questionnaires are the most powerful, offering good levels of validity in the shortest completion times.

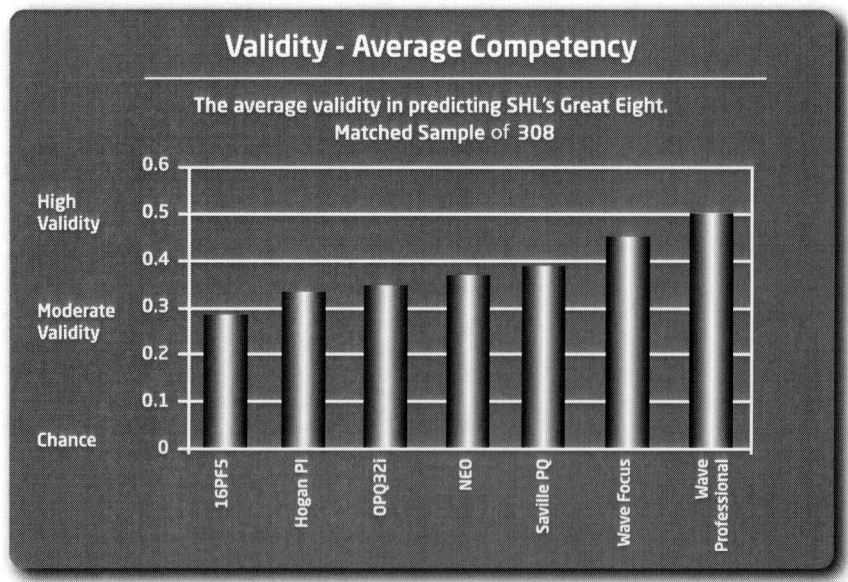

FIGURE 9.4 The average validity of seven key questionnaires in measuring the Great Eight competencies

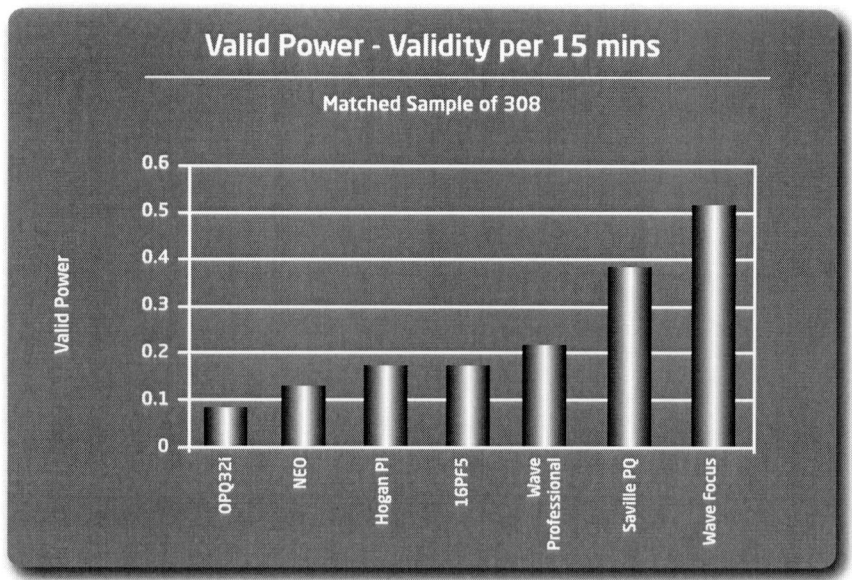

FIGURE 9.5 The power of seven key questionnaires in terms of their delivery of validity in 15 minutes

Further results from this large research project will be presented in a number of future papers to further complement the existing range of international validation studies on specific occupational groups. Saville Consulting Wave validation studies have been carried out in countries such as the UK, the USA, Mexico, Brazil, France, Denmark and Spain, and have looked specifically at occupational groups including managers, engineers, consultants and civil servants. For the Saville PQ, we are pleased to report that it is showing impressive levels of test-retest and alternate-form reliability over a period of six months, despite its short length. A number of other popular assessments were also included in Project Epsom and their performances are discussed in other papers. To give a flavour of these results, below we provide a brief summary of some of the key findings.

Thomas International DISC/DISCUS

The DISC model was first described in 1928 by William Marston, a 'psychologist and inventor' whose greatest achievement was perhaps his creation of the cartoon character Wonder Woman. The Thomas International website stated that their version of the DISC questionnaire 'measures work behaviours and is +0.75–0.95 valid'. No validity was found of this magnitude, either for Thomas International DISC or the DISCUS variation. Indeed, no questionnaire or performance measurement method has been shown, to the authors' knowledge, to have validity at this high level.

The results for the DISC questionnaire were in line with the Buros review of DISC, but curiously discrepant from the more positive British Psychological Society Psychological Testing Centre review. To quote part of the Buros review of the DISC model (Plake and Impara, 2001):

> There appears no research that finds DISC to measure the traits measured in Marston's model. The evidence does not meet the criteria established in the APA (American Psychological Association) Standards for Educational and Psychological Testing as of 1999. There are no studies that specify what the DISC predicts. The test suffers from questionable reliability and unknown validity. The use of DISC is not recommended.

The Myers-Briggs Type Indicator (MBTI)

There was limited support for validity of two of the MBTI scales. There was some degree of support for responses to MBTI questions about 'Extraversion' accurately measuring a person's ability to influence people at work. Similarly, there was some evidence that people who were high on 'Judging' in the MBTI were seen as being better at delivering results at work.

The Hogan Development Survey (HDS)

It was difficult to relate the HDS to job performance. In the HDS, if an individual scores beyond the 84th percentile in certain areas (e.g. Sceptical), they go into the 'Dark Side', an area of extreme strength identified as being potentially problematic.

When 180 participants re-completed the HDS questionnaire one week later, only 8% kept exactly the same 'Dark Side' profiles. The well-established problem of having arbitrary cut-off scores in psychometric assessments is highlighted here and the situation is resonant of the 11+ assessment which was a feature of British education some years ago. Every child at the age of 11 took an IQ test, which served as a selection test to enter more or less academic senior schools. When retested two years later at the age of 13, some 35% of children fell the other side of the cut-off from where they were at 11.

Implications of Project Epsom

As has been discussed, return on investment is linearly related to validity. Moving from recruiting using a test with a validity of +0.2 to using a test with a validity of +0.4 can double the cost benefit because tests with a higher validity are more likely to ensure the candidates who are going to perform better are selected. Small increases in validity can also have a large effect. For example, going from using a test with a validity of +0.3 to +0.4 is a 25% increase, which can have a huge impact on the organisation's productivity and hence on return on investment.

	Validity	By selecting based on top 20% of questionnaire completers...
No Validity	0	4 out of the 20 will prove to be in the top 20% of job performers
Moderate Validity	.3	7 out of the 20 will prove to be in the top 20% of job performers
High Validity	.6	10 out of the 20 will prove to be in the top 20% of job performers*

*17 out of 20 will prove to be above average performers

	Validity	By selecting based on top 20% of questionnaire completers...
No Validity	0	1 person in 5 selected will prove to be bottom 20%
Moderate Validity	.3	1 person in 10 selected will prove to be bottom 20%
High Validity	.6	1 person in 50 selected will prove to be bottom 20%

FIGURE 9.6   The effect of validity on probability of selection errors

A key organisational requirement may be to identify your top 20% of performers (those with high potential). Figure 9.6 below illustrates the decrease in selection errors which will be incurred as validity is increased. The figure may vary of course from situation to situation, but this offers a general guideline.

Particularly serious errors occur when someone from the bottom 20% is identified as demonstrating top 20% potential. Once the validity of your assessment method is as high as +0.6, only one in every 50 of the bottom 20% performers will be incorrectly selected as demonstrating top 20% potential. In other words, tools with a higher validity dramatically reduce the frequency of serious selection errors. This simple example shows the importance of using tests which are valid and suitable for predicting actual performance at work, such as the Saville Consulting Wave Styles questionnaires. These were designed specifically to maximise prediction of performance and potential at work. It is not sufficient for test publishers merely to cite the degree of agreement between their test and another as the validity of the test. Tests must be designed to actually relate to real-life performance measures: with the study reported here, this is job performance.

Why are the Saville Consulting Wave questionnaires more valid?

Up until very recently, the academic consensus was that the highest obtained validities in measuring job performance for personality tests were low relative to those obtained by other tools (e.g. Hurtz and Donovan, 2000). This belief pervades the field of psychometrics and academics implore test publishers to 'provide a theoretical validation of their measures' (Ferguson, Payne and Anderson, 1994).

The recently developed Saville Consulting Wave Styles range (see MacIver et al., 2006a) is a modern job-relevant measure of personality which provides just such a theoretical validation of its measures and obtains validities in measuring job performance in excess of other popular questionnaires. There are two Wave questionnaires: the Wave Professional Styles questionnaire, which is most commonly completed by respondents in about 40 minutes to complete, and the 13-minute Wave Focus Styles questionnaire, which covers the most valid questions from the Professional Styles questionnaire and thus maintains about 80% of the validity of the fuller assessment. Both are built on the same Wave Styles framework. Below is a summary of the key reasons why the Saville Consulting Wave Styles questionnaires are revealed to be the most valid personality questionnaires.

1. The Wave questionnaires are modern and are written in the language of contemporary business

In taking into account recent advances in computerisation and the internet, they measure personal characteristics and competencies which are relevant for business today. For example, the Wave questionnaires measure inclination to use information technology, which has become a huge part of many people's daily work. Questionnaires developed in previous decades, naturally, have not taken into account the changing nature of job roles and work culture, and so may be measuring out-of-date aspects of work performance. A radical rethinking of the measurement base was warranted. Many other questionnaires are not related to industry at all, so it is little surprise that they are shown to be less valid than work-relevant assessment methods in measuring work performance (Robertson and Smith, 2001).

2. The Wave questionnaires were developed through an extensive understanding of the field of personality assessment and work performance

The Wave questionnaires were continuously validated during their construction, combining different development strategies (Saville et al., 2008b; Saville et al., 2008c). Individual items were validated against work performance criteria from conception and external ratings of work performance were obtained, so it was known which questions would measure which competency from the outset. Older questionnaires tend to focus on validity only at the more general scale level, whereas validity was written into the individual items of the Wave questionnaires from the very beginning (see MacIver et al., 2006b). This ensured that when the individual questions were combined to form scales, the scale validities were greatly enhanced too.

Professor Peter Saville, author of the OPQ, built on his extensive knowledge of the domain and combined this with online trialling of the questionnaires to select the most valid questions while his development team produced an overarching Wave framework considering personality, competencies, aptitudes and the impact of culture in the workplace. Kurz et al. (2008) showed how the Big Five personality factors and Great Eight competencies align with the Saville Consulting four

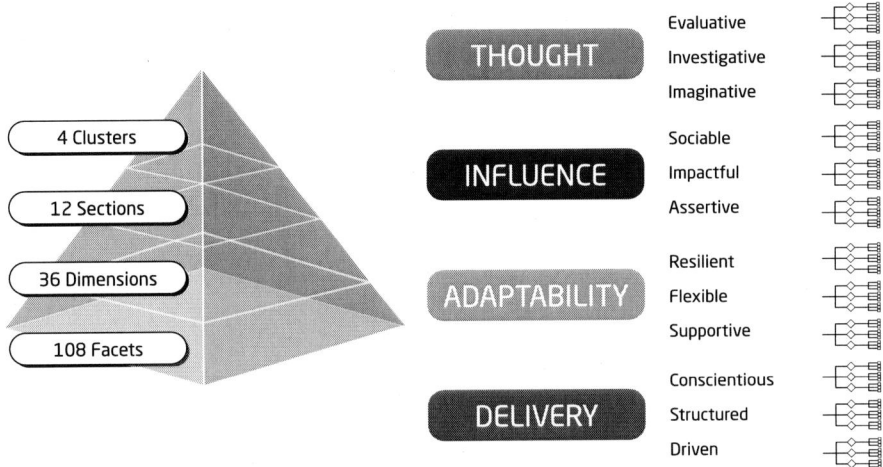

FIGURE 9.7 The Saville Consulting Wave Professional Styles model

Behavioral Performance Clusters and 12 Behavioural Performance Sections in the Wave model. Figure 9.7 below provides a graphical summary of the hierarchical nature of the Wave Professional Styles framework, moving from four overall clusters down to 108 facets. Each one of these facets is measured through a motive and talent question, meaning that the questionnaire has a total of 216 items.

Extensive research on personality questionnaires has indicated that certain strategies are key to successful questionnaire design and these were capitalised upon in the development of the Wave framework. For example, it is known that many questionnaires are full of badly worded, ambiguous and/or negatively phrased questions (Angleitner and Lö, 1986) which can reduce a questionnaire's validity. It is often the smallest words that can cause the biggest problems. 'Ifs', 'buts' and 'ands' complicate questions by allowing ambiguities in interpretation. Similarly, shortening a measurement scale in a questionnaire to just a few questions can actually improve its validity (Burisch, 1997).

Hitting the core of a concept with good items is more productive in questionnaire construction. Three well-written and direct items can achieve the same (if not a greater) level of validity when compared to a large number of poorer items (Burisch, 1997). This 'keep it simple' approach was demonstrated recently by Lie (2008), who showed that one item can screen for excessive daytime sleepiness as effectively as a full day of physiological and psychological tests. That one item was 'Measure your sleepiness on a typical day, where 0 = none and 10 = highest'. Looking at the completion experience from the respondent's perspective, it is no surprise that people can become bored and inconsistent in their responses if they are asked the same question a dozen times. The Wave questionnaires are built around extensively validated items from concise scales which provide clear, discerning links to work performance (Saville et al., 2008b, 2008c).

3. The Wave model introduces a number of groundbreaking features which provide breadth of information and sophisticated distortion detection

The dynamic rate-rank format combines ipsative and normative assessment in one interactive online measure and helps to identify how consistently people have answered the questionnaire. This format also counteracts the natural tendency of people to agree with most statements presented to them. It therefore offers a more judicious means to discriminate people's preferences and styles of behaviour (Saville et al., 2008b, 2008c). It is also a useful tool for assisting in identifying situations where respondents are attempting to manage the impression they are making in the questionnaire. For example, where the ipsative score is very much lower than the normative score, our experience indicates that the candidate may have exaggerated in the free-rating (normative) task. This provides a much more sophisticated measure than an overall social desirability scale as we can pinpoint specific areas to discuss in the report, rather than being left unsure where or why people are responding in a socially desirable way.

There is the problem with normative-only questionnaires that many people use the middle of the scale, while others continually use the extremes. This is known as a 'central tendency response set'. This makes the comparison between people, for example, in different nationality groups, problematic. As quoted by Saville and Willson (1991), Simpson, for example, found that the word 'frequently' meant over 80% of the time to some participants and under 40% of the time to others. It is also not unknown for some people to use extremes on a five-point scale over 50% of the time, while others never do. Ipsative questionnaires force a degree of negative correlations between scales, but it has been shown that with more than about 16 scales, this effect is minimal (Baron, 1996). There is also some evidence that ipsative scales can help to control distortion better than the normative format. Both normative and ipsative scales have inherent response biases and it is to counteract these limitations that the two methods were combined in the Saville Consulting questionnaires, improving validities by some 10%.

The Wave questionnaires (and Saville PQ) also exist in parallel forms, so there are two alternate and reliable versions of the questionnaire available for use. Thus, if there is some concern that a candidate is distorting their responses when completing an unsupervised questionnaire online, they can later complete a parallel version of the same questionnaire in a supervised format, affording comparison of their responses across the two completions. Nevertheless, it is interesting (and encouraging) that several meta-analyses have shown that candidate distortion in personality assessment is far less prevalent and affects the validity of responses less than has previously been assumed (e.g. Hough et al., 1990; Ones et al. 1996; Ellingson and Sackett, 2001; Schmitt and Oswald, 2006).

Separate motive and talent measures in the Wave questionnaires help identify specific areas where people are motivated to improve (where their responses to questions about their motivations are discernibly higher than their responses to

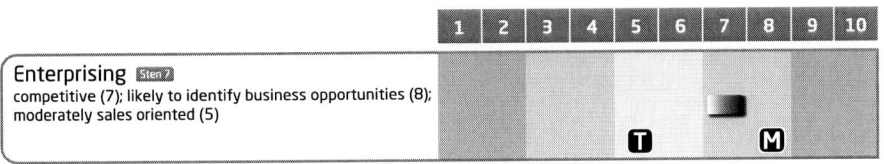

FIGURE 9.8   A motive–talent split

questions about their talents in the same area). Similarly, they allow us to see areas where a person may be less motivated, even if their talent (and hence outward behaviour) is not demonstrably low (where their responses to questions about their talents are discernibly higher than their responses to questions about their motivation in the same area).

Figure 9.8 below illustrates motive-talent splits in a Wave report. In this case, the M (motive) marker is somewhat higher than the T (talent) marker, indicating that the respondent is more motivated to act in an enterprising manner than they feel they are currently showing. This might well be an area that their manager could focus on developing with them, for example, by identifying which elements of their work environment may be impacting on their performance.

The Wave questionnaires show facet ranges where the respondent has answered closely related questions somewhat differently. This aspect of the response style is shown in the report as hatching marks. Below, in Figure 9.9, is an example of a facet range from the Wave Focus Styles profile of Ian Woosnam OBE, the captain of the European Ryder Cup 2006 team and formerly the number one-ranked golfer in the world.

While Ian is driven to achieve results and is likely to identify the means to do this, it is interesting to see that he reports less need to make things happen. This has resulted in a facet split in the Wave profile, where Ian has rated the questions that relate to business opportunities and achievement of results significantly higher than he has rated the questions about making things happen. Consequently, the facet split is a means to highlight a unique aspect of a given individual's preferred behavioural style. It is possible that for Ian, his success throughout his career has meant that he's never explicitly felt a need to consciously make things happen; instead, his inherent talents have meant that things simply do happen for him. More generally, facet splits add further richness of information and guide discussion about the unique responses of an individual.

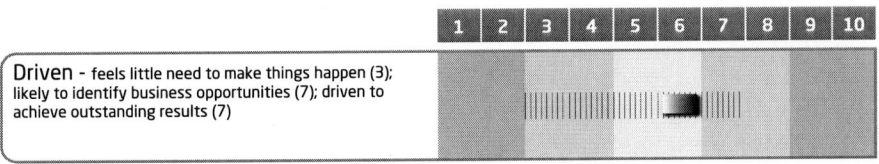

FIGURE 9.9   A facet range

4. The Wave questionnaires make their validities readily available to users and are easy to understand

The Wave questionnaires are administered and scored online to maximise ease of use for both the candidate and the practitioner. They also make their improved validities easily available to users. Being able to examine the validity of a questionnaire with statistical techniques does not necessarily make the validity meaningful to the user. Valid scores must be presented simply in a report or profile which can be easily interpreted and used as a direct measure of work performance (MacIver et al., 2008). Through the sophisticated yet user-friendly Wave reports, practitioners are provided with an even better understanding of people's behaviours and performance at work than has previously been available to test-users and even industrial psychologists.

Discussion

Project Epsom is one of the first studies to compare the criterion-related validities of a range of popular personality questionnaires in a single database. It also confirms existing research carried out on personality questionnaires. For example, the validities demonstrated here for the Hogan Personality Inventory are consistent with the meta-analysis by Hogan et al. (2008) and a study by Foster et al. (2008). The OPQ32i validities for the individual Great Eight competencies are similar to those reported by Bartram (2005), but the Great Eight total validities are considerably lower. Possible reasons for this are explored below.

In Project Epsom, we report on a full data set and did not employ multiple regression or somewhat dated statistical techniques such as canonical analysis (as used by Bartram, 2005), which can produce serious overestimates of validity. Canonical analysis can be thought of as juggling both the predictor (e.g. personality questionnaire scales) and the work performance criteria until some optimum equation is found which maximises the correlation between the predictor and criteria. The danger is that canonical analysis could lead us into a situation rather like the theory suggesting that an infinite number of monkeys using typewriters would ultimately produce the complete works of Shakespeare by chance. That is, the procedure keeps juggling the data until a best-fit solution is reached by chance. When conducted on ipsative (forced-ranking) personality scales, canonical analysis, with its enormous tendency to capitalise on chance effects, is a particularly deadly cocktail. No research is known to the authors where unreplicated canonical analysis on ipsative personality scales (as in Bartram, 2005) has produced a statistically legitimate outcome.

For example, based on canonical analysis, SHL has suggested that 'the true overall combined validities of the OPQ32 (ipsative version) . . . actually achieves +0.55'. What has possibly happened here, with respect, is the classic 'Popcorn Effect', where the method has selected the popcorn thrown up highest by the popcorn machine on a chance basis. Without replication in further samples, the serious danger of 'Blunderbuss- Empiricism' or 'Shotgun-Empiricism' exists, where the target is indiscriminately blasted until any hit is registered.

The deep-seated problem of using canonical analysis and related multivariate techniques with ipsative data may help explain the counter-intuitive formula by Bartram (2005) which *negatively* weighted emotional stability in order to measure job success. This completely conflicts with the worldwide research literature which shows that it is the emotionally stable people who tend to be more successful in jobs, and not the seriously neurotic and disagreeable. In the words of Cronbach (1970): 'The investigator should be particularly sceptical of weights that make little psychological sense, since they are likely to have come from sampling errors.' In this case, it is possible that the ipsative nature of Bartram's data, combined with the way multivariate statistical techniques capitalise on chance, has led to this counterintuitive finding. Cronbach is quick to point out that 'simply assigning equal weight to all relevant tests . . . often works just as well in the next sample'. Without replication in a new (cross-validation) sample, it is very difficult to ensure that such a counterintuitive finding is a valid one. In Project Epsom, as has been found in many other studies, results revealed that emotional stability was positively related to overall work success.

This is not to say that ipsative questionnaires with sufficient scales cannot be treated statistically. However, much more care and caution is advised (Saville and Willson, 1991), with replication in separate samples. Canonical analysis and multiple regression are post-hoc (after the event) techniques, where the known results are further investigated in order to maximise validity. Predicting what stocks and shares were worth yesterday is rather easier than predicting what they will be worth tomorrow! Improperly used, canonical analysis can therefore be the ultimate 'fishing trip', where results are simply fished out as suited. Canonical analysis is now considered by many to be a rather outmoded practice, superseded by superior methods. A more discerning practice is to designate a priori (before the event) which questionnaire scales should correlate with which measures of job performance and then test these specific hypotheses. In Project Epsom, this is precisely what was done.

In personality research, as with many areas of scientific enquiry such as medical research, there is also the phenomenon of the 'file-drawer effect' (e.g. Allison et al., 1996; Bauchau, 1997; Scargle, 2000). This effect describes the publication bias where only positive results are reported and published. If, for example, one were to develop a structured interview which demonstrates validity in measuring how successfully candidates are expected to perform in their job, these results are likely to be published as an academic paper. Where the interview is shown to demonstrate no validity, it is less likely to be written up and may be filed away. Similarly, where no correlations are found between a questionnaire and job performance, the results may simply not be published. Goldacre (2008) relates in his book *Bad Science* a quotation from Francis Bacon, who noted that 'it is the peculiar and perpetual error of the human understanding to be more moved and excited by affirmatives than negatives'.

In meta-analysis, where many existing studies are amalgamated into a large database for further study, if only affirmative results are included, this could lead to overestimations of the validity of a given procedure. With Bartram's (2005) meta-analytical data, this file-drawer problem may be one of a number of methodological issues, because the majority of the studies considered by Bartram (2005) are likely to have been conducted solely by SHL companies. It is not clear whether all studies considered were included in his final results. In Project Epsom, the complete results from one database are reported. Meta-analysis itself is an extremely powerful statistical procedure and in the opinion of the authors, the researchers who developed this methodology, Hunter and Schmidt, should have been considered for a Nobel Prize. Meta-analysis has had an enormous impact not only in psychology but also in many other areas of scientific research, including medicine. It is nevertheless important that all adequate studies are included in meta-analysis, not merely those which have been selected to support one's initial hypotheses.

The Great Eight model is one independent framework against which to measure the validity of all questionnaires on a level playing field. However, it is not necessarily the ultimate method. Against the more discerning Twelve Behavioral Performance Sections in the Saville Consulting Wave Performance Culture Framework, the Wave Styles questionnaires actually outperformed all other questionnaires by about 50%. This model was not used here in order to ensure absolute fairness across all questionnaires, but this model of work effectiveness is the subject of ongoing research.

Project Epsom clearly indicates that the Saville Consulting Wave Professional Styles predictions of competency demonstrate the greatest validities in measuring global job performance. It is rewarding to see such newly developed measures outperforming traditional measures by showing considerable increases in validity. The Saville Consulting Wave Styles questionnaires make use of contemporary technological and scientific advances in measurement to establish their position as the most effective personality questionnaires for measuring job performance.

The Saville PQ™ occupies the middle ground between the Saville Consulting Wave® questionnaires and other prominent personality assessments in the market. The Saville PQ is available online with no licence fee to pay, and offers users familiar with the OPQ the chance to use a comparable questionnaire which is more valid against the SHL criteria, takes less than 15 minutes, gives both normative and ipsative scores in that time, and provides separate measures of motives and talents. In terms of reliability of measure when compared to the OPQ32i, the combined normative and ipsative scales of the Saville PQ when mapped to their like-for-like OPQ32i counterparts have an average correlation exceeding +0.7. Nevertheless, as with the OPQ, the Saville PQ does rely on 1980s development methods and even better decision-making tools are offered in the Wave Focus or Wave Professional Styles questionnaires.

However, far from selecting the most valid measures of work performance, it seems that users of some questionnaires become attached to the tests that 'look right' or appear to be appropriate, which is known as faith validity (Saville, 1975).

Would you agree?		
99.3%	You are fair minded	
98.6%	You are kind	**% of people who agreed with statement**
96.5%	You are thoughtful	
97.2%	You are reasonable	
99.3%	You are co-operative	
99.3%	You value honest communication	
97.9%	You value sincere appreciation and recognition for a job well done	
97.9%	You like to be on good terms with other people, and will generally react to them in a friendly and open way	

FIGURE 9.10   Percentage of people who agreed that each statement accurately described them

This aspect of validity is where a test-user becomes familiar and happy with a tool and is very resistant to change, even though there may be more empirically valid modern alternatives available. To demonstrate this tendency, we returned to a classic experiment by Stagner (1958) which documents the 'Barnum Effect'. A series of statements were taken or adapted from the actual feedback reports of certain of the personality questionnaires used in Project Epsom and 144 participants were asked whether they thought the statements were an accurate description of them. Figure 9.10 above indicates the percentage of people who thought each statement was accurate of them.

Almost everyone said that these statements provided an accurate description of them. If the end result of some personality questionnaires is such generalised and socially desirable reports, it is perhaps no wonder that there is a perplexing level of appeal to these questionnaires which seems at odds with how poorly they differentiate people, and the limited validity they demonstrate in measuring performance at work. It seems that some questionnaire publishers confuse the number of people who think that a report is accurate with the validity of their questionnaire, but possession of faith validity does not mean that a questionnaire measures job performance well. As Descartes once remarked:

> Common sense is the best distributed commodity in the world, for every man is convinced that he is well supplied with it.

Saville (2008a) notes that where there is an unusual result in a study or questionnaire manual, it is often explained away by psychologists as 'neologistic gobbledigook', when in fact it is a simple error of scoring or in the data analysis. He refers to the effect known in the philosophy of science as the 'Crabtree Bludgeon', where 'no set of mutually inconsistent observations can exist for which some human intellect cannot conceive a coherent explanation, however complicated'.

Useful?	'Yes'	'Uncertain'	'No'
Interviews	41%	34%	26%
References	49%	37%	14%
Intelligence	56%	27%	17%
Personality	53%	34%	13%
Astrology	22%	28%	50%

FIGURE 9.11   The acceptability of different selection techniques (N = 1,000)

Personality questionnaires are actually viewed as useful and acceptable methods for selection by the public at large. In a sample of 1,000 participants, we found that only 13% of people felt that personality questionnaires were not effective for selection, whilst 26% of people were critical of the interview. The acceptability of various techniques in a selection context is shown above in Figure 9.11.

While the results indicate that personality questionnaires on the whole are acceptable to people and their use is surprisingly welcomed, this does not in itself indicate that personality questionnaires measure work performance well. It is also reassuring to see that evidence in the literature suggests that faking in question-naires does not materially affect their validities (e.g. Hough et al., 1990; Ones et al., 1996; Ellingson and Sackett, 2001) and may actually have minimal effects (Schmitt and Oswald, 2006). Ellingson and Sackett describe their results as providing 'addi-tional evidence in support of a growing literature that the incidence of applicant faking is lower than might be assumed'.

While some users develop a rigid loyalty to one particular test, as practition-ers making significant decisions about the careers and well-being of others, it is important to consider the specific functions for which any test is used. Some, like the Saville Consulting Wave Styles questionnaires, have been designed to max-imise the prediction of performance at work, while others were not originally designed to be used in industrial settings at all. Some have clinical origins and bring obscure, irrelevant and badly written items to the measurement of performance in the workplace.

By developing and sharing an understanding of performance and potential at work, it is possible to help more people self-actualise at work and to ensure that personality assessment will continue to become more efficient and valid in the future. Unfortunately, however, people continue to make extrapolations and state-ments from personality questionnaires which are backed up by no data whatsoever. Especially in a world where feedback and transparency of information is increas-ingly sought, we would do well to follow the guidance Shakespeare offers in his play *Othello, The Moor of Venice*:

Speak of me as I am; nothing extenuate, Nor set down aught in malice.

More recent predictive research on a subsample of 108 participants has also been carried out and the validity rank order of the seven key questionnaires considered in this paper was essentially maintained over a period of six months.

Of course, personality questionnaires are only one of the tools available for use. While Project Epsom shows that personality questionnaires which are modern and well-written can be valid measures of work performance, they should be used in conjunction with other techniques such as structured interviews, ability tests, in-tray tasks and job sample exercises. Indeed, personality questionnaires can be a most useful basis for structuring an interview through feedback as part of a multi-method approach. One criticism levelled at personality assessment is that it is just a self-perception with no practical application. The demonstration that personality questionnaires do have validity in measuring performance at work does not support this criticism. Aldous Huxley sagely and elegantly sums up the value of measuring personality in his 1954 work *The Doors of Perception*:

> To see ourselves as others see us is a most salutary gift. Hardly less important is the capacity to see others as they see themselves.

The authors would like to thank all the participants who took part in this study and look forward to future independent replication of this work in new and separate samples.

References

Allison, D. B., Faith, M. S. and Gorman, B. S. (1996). Publication bias in obesity treatment trials? *International Journal of Obesity*, 20, 931–7.

Angleitner, A., J., O. P. and Lö, F. J. (1986). It's what you ask and how you ask it: An item-metric analysis of personality questionnaires. In A. Angleitner and J. S. Wiggins (eds), *Personality Assessment via Questionnaires*. Berlin: Springer-Verlag, pp. 61–107.

Baron, H. (1996). Strengths and limitations of ipsative measurement. *Journal of Occupational and Organizational Psychology*, 69, 49–56.

Barrick, M.R. and Mount, M.K. (1991). The Big Five personality dimensions and job performance: A metaanalysis. *Personnel Psychology*, 44, 1–25.

Bartram, D. (2005). The Great Eight Competencies: A criterion-centric approach to validation. *Journal of Applied Psychology*, 90, 1185–203.

Bauchau, V. (1997). Is there a 'file drawer problem' in biological research? *OIKOS*, 19, 407–9.

Burisch, M. (1997). Test length and validity revisited. *European Journal of Personality*, 11, 303–15.

Cattell, R. B. (1965). *The Scientific Analysis of Personality*. London: Penguin.

Costa, P. T., Jr. and McCrae, R. R. (1992). Normal personality assessment in clinical practice: The NEO Personality Inventory. *Psychological Assessment*, 4, 5–13.

Cronbach, L. J. (1970). *The Essentials of Psychological Testing*, 3rd edn. New York: Harper & Row.

Digman, J. M. (1997). Higher-order factors of the Big Five. *Journal of Personality and Social Psychology*, 73, 1246–56.

Ellingson, J. E. and Sackett, P. R. (2001). Consistency of personality scale scores across selection and development contexts. Poster Session, Society for Industrial and Occupational Psychology, San Diego, California.

Ferguson, E., Payne, T. and Anderson, N. (1994). Occupational personality assessment: Theory, structure and psychometrics of the OPQ FMX5-student. *Personality and Individual Differences*, 17(2), 217–25.

Foster, J., Johnson, C. and Gaddis, B (2008). The predictive validity of personality: New methods produce new results. Presented at the 23rd annual conference of the Society for Industrial-Organizational Psychology, April.

Goldacre, B. (2008). *Bad Science*. London: Fourth Estate.

Hogan, J., Davies, S. and Hogan, R. (2008). Generalizing personality-based validity evidence. In S. Morton McPhail (ed.), *Alternative Validation Strategies: Developing New and Leveraging Existing Validity Evidence*. San Francisco: Jossey Bass, pp. 181–233.

Hough, L., Eaton, N. K., Dunnette, M. K., Kemp, J. D. and McCloy R. A. (1990). Criterion related validities of personality constructs and the effect of response distortion on those validities. *Journal of Applied Psychology*, 75(5), 581–95.

Hurtz, G. M. and Donovan, J. J. (2000). Personality and job performance: The Big Five revisited. *Journal of Applied Psychology*, 85, 869–79.

Huxley, A. (1954). *The Doors of Perception*. New York: Harper & Row.

Kurz, R. and Bartram, D. (2002). Competency and individual performance: Modelling the world of work. In I. T. Robertson, M. Callinen and D. Bartram (eds), *Organizational Effectiveness: The Role of Psychology*. Chichester: Wiley, pp. 227–58.

Kurz, R. MacIver R. and Saville, P. (2008). Coaching with Saville Consulting Wave™. In J. Passmore (ed.), *Psychometrics in Coaching*. London: Kogan Page, pp. 132–50.

Kurz, R., Saville, P., MacIver, R., Mitchener, A., Parry, G., Oxley, H., Small, C., Herridge, K. and Hopton, T. (2009). The structure of work effectiveness as measured through the Saville Consulting Wave ® Performance 360 'B-A-G' Model of Behaviour, Ability and Global Performance. *Assessment and Development Matters*, 1(1), 15–18.

Lie, D. (2008). A single subjective question may help screen for excessive daytime sleepiness. *Journal of Clinical Sleep Medicine*, 4, 143–8.

MacIver, R., Saville, P., Kurz, R., Mitchener, A., Mariscal, K., Parry, G., Becker, S., Saville, W., O'Connor, K., Patterson R. and Oxley, H. (2006a). Making waves: Saville Consulting Wave Styles questionnaires. *Selection and Development Review*, 22(2), 17–23.

MacIver, R., Saville, P., Kurz, R., Henley, S., Mitchener, A., Mariscal, K., Parry, G., Becker, S., Hurst, E., Saville, W., O'Connor, K, Patterson R., McLellan, S. and Blakesley, M. (2006b). The validation centric development of the professional styles questionnaires. Presented at the BPS Occupational Psychology Conference, Glasgow.

MacIver, R., Saville, P., Kurz, R., Anderson, N. and Evers, A. (2008). New aspects of validity: User available and user received validity. Presented at the ITC Conference.

Morgeson, F. P., Campion, M. A., Dipboye, R. L., Hollenbeck, J. R., Murphy, K. and Schmitt, N. (2007). Reconsidering the use of personality tests in personnel selection contexts. *Personnel Psychology*, 60(3), 683–729.

Nyfield, G., Gibbons, P. J., Baron H and Robertson, I. (1995). The cross-cultural validity of management assessment methods. Paper presented at the 10th Annual SIOP Conference Orlando, May.

Ones, D. S., Viswesvaran, C. and Reiss, A. D. (1996). The role of social desirability in personality testing for personnel selection: The red herring. *Journal of Applied Psychology*, 81, 660–79.

Plake, B. S. and Impara, J. C. (eds) (2001). *The Mental Measurements Yearbook*, Lincoln, NE: University of Nebraska Press.

Robertson, I. T. and Smith, M. (2001). Personnel selection. *Journal of Occupational and Organizational Psychology*, 74(4), 441–72.

Saville, P. (1975). *Occupational Testing*. London: HDS Management Consultants.

——. (2008a). Personality questionnaires – Valid inferences, false prophecies. Presented at the Division of Occupational Psychology of the British Psychological Society Annual Conference, Stratford-upon-Avon, January.

——. (2008b). Does your test work? Presented at the Psychological Society of South Africa Annual Conference, Johannesburg, August.

——. (2008c). A comparison of leadership in business and elite athletes. Presented at the A&DC Conference, Institute of Directors, London, November.

Saville, P., Holdsworth, R., Nyfield, G., Cramp, L. and Mabey, W. (1984). *Occupational Personality Questionnaire Manual*. Thames Ditton: Saville-Holdsworth, Ltd.

Saville, P, MacIver, R., Kurz, R. and Hopton, T. (2008a). *Saville PQ Manual and User Guide*. Jersey: Saville Consulting Group.

Saville, P., MacIver, R. and Kurz, R. (2008b). *Saville Consulting Wave Professional Styles Manual and User Guide*. Jersey: Saville Consulting Group.

Saville, P., MacIver, R. and Kurz, R. (2008c). *Saville Consulting Wave Focus Styles Manual and User Guide*. Jersey: Saville Consulting Group.

Saville, P. and Willson, E. (1991). The reliability and validity of normative and ipsative approaches in the measurement of personality. *Journal of Occupational Psychology*, 64, 219–38.

Scargle, J. D. (2000). Publication bias: The 'file-drawer' problem in scientific inference. *Journal of Scientific Exploration*, 14(1), 91–106.

Schmidt, F. L. and Hunter, J. E. (1998). The validity and utility of selection methods in personnel psychology: Practical and theoretical implications of 85 years of research. *Psychological Bulletin*, 124(2), 262–74.

Schmitt, N., Gooding, R. Z., Noe, R. A. and Kirsch, M. (1984). Meta-analyses of validity studies. *Journal of Applied Psychology*, 70, 280–9.

Schmitt, N. and Oswald, F. L. (2006). The impact of correction for faking on the validity of noncognitive measures in selection settings. *Journal of Applied Psychology*, 91(3), 613–21.

SHL (1999). OPQ32 *Manual and User's Guide*. Thames Ditton: SHL Group plc.

Stagner, R. (1958). The gullibility of personnel managers. *Personnel Psychology*, 11, 347–52.

Wiggins, J. S. (1973). *Personality and Prediction: Principles of Personality Assessment*. Reading, MA: Addison-Wesley.

10

APPLICATIONS OF ASSESSMENTS

This chapter is based on a presentation I gave in 2011 at an event held by the Psychometrics Forum group:

> Saville, P. (2011). Personality, Leadership and Organizational Effectiveness. Presented at the Psychometrics Forum Meeting, June.

The presentation focused on how psychometric tools, such as Saville Consulting's Wave assessment, could be used in diverse applications, including leadership assessment and the assessment of entrepreneurial potential. In this presentation, I discussed our (then brand new) model of leadership effectiveness and covered the background leadership literature which underpinned our research. I then moved on to discuss the specific model itself in greater depth.

The second part of the presentation moved on to consider the other application in question, namely entrepreneurial potential. I introduced the Entrecode® model which we developed with Professor David Hall, a renowned expert on entrepreneurship. To illustrate my points about the entrepreneurial model, I delivered a case study about the highly successful entrepreneur Ajaz Ahmed. His fascinating story forms the latter half of the present chapter. My discussion of Ajaz's story at this event was based on extracts from a chapter that featured in our 2009 book, *Talent* (Saville and Hopton, 2009).

Personality, leadership and organizational effectiveness

Leadership

Saville Consulting's new leadership model expands on the individual differences, situational and people/task concepts which are commonplace in many existing leadership theories. The focus in this model shifts to assess the impact of leadership not only on the management of people and tasks, but also on leadership characteristics which contribute to the growth of an organization. The development of the Saville Consulting Leadership Model has been guided by empirical research from conception to conclusion based around international research on thousands of individuals working across hundreds of different organizations.

The Saville Consulting Leadership Model is designed to harness leadership potential, leadership styles and the situational aspects of leadership in order to provide a comprehensive picture of an individual's likely effectiveness as a workplace leader. The model features 24 leadership styles which are effective in different circumstances and in parallel matches each of these styles to a situation in which a given leader is most likely to be suited. The model also presents six LEADER bases which underpin the general characteristics important for effective leadership across situations.

As the Saville Consulting Leadership Report measures leadership using the Wave Professional Styles online assessment, it also allows for the separation of motives and talents and highlights where an individual may be over- or under-estimating their leadership styles.

This combined approach of identifying both the qualities required of all leaders and the styles and situations which a specific leader may be suited to brings many advantages. Amongst other things, the Saville Consulting Leadership Model addresses the major issues of identifying who has the underlying potential to become a leader, whose leadership style is appropriate for a given situation and where to place chosen leaders in order to enhance organizational effectiveness. The use of the Leadership Model helps to answer questions about both general leadership potential and leadership effectiveness in specific situations.

Theoretical background

The Saville Consulting Leadership Model is a performance-driven model of workplace leadership. During its development, workplace performance data collected through international research were used as independent outcome criteria in order to empirically validate the model. It was designed using a hypothetico-deductive method, whereby established and contemporary research literature, along with empirical data, was used to define and refine the model.

In order to better understand the new Saville Consulting Leadership Model and its advance, it is useful to consider briefly both the evolution of leadership theory and the history of the assessment of individual differences.

The evolution of leadership theory

Well before leadership was seen as a subject worthy of modern scientific enquiry, many cultures and peoples have striven to define what makes people effective leaders:

> *'You are what you repeatedly do. Excellence, then, is not an act, but a habit.'*
>
> Aristotle, 384–322 BC (presented in Bekker, 1831–70)

> *'Some are born great, some achieve greatness and some have greatness thrust upon them.'*
>
> Shakespeare, 1601

Psychology as a modern discipline has from the nineteenth century to the present day examined leadership from a range of different angles.

The Great Man theory

The Great Man theory of leadership suggests that effective leaders are born rather than made and rise to the occasion when they are required to do so. Research from this perspective has tended to focus on individuals who are already in positions of leadership. In the nineteenth century the lower classes had very little opportunity to lead in those countries where leadership was being studied. The aristocracy was able to convince itself that leadership was simply a matter of good breeding and many so-called Great Men have taken on an almost mythical status of reverence. Looking back, we can undertake nothing more rigorous than to speculate how other individuals would have fared in the same circumstances.

When the Great Man theory was developed, there was little consensus on a common taxonomy of personality traits and so researchers' capacity to differentiate between personality traits, intelligence and sociological factors such as social class was limited. More modern research has suggested that there are clear links to leadership from both personality and intelligence. This topic is raised during a discussion of the contribution of individual differences to leadership.

The Ohio studies and people-task differentiation

In the 1950s a series of studies carried out at the Ohio State University identified two independent and critical characteristics of leaders – 'Consideration' towards subordinates and 'Initiating Structure' to promote the achievement of goals. This frequently became rendered as the People-Task division in leadership, which is seen today in a number of different leadership models.

Building on the work of Katz et al. (1950), Blake and Mouton (1964) produced the Managerial Grid Model, which considered the two variables 'Concern for people' and 'Concern for production'. According to their original model, different scores on the two variables in this grid identified five distinct leadership types. In 1978, Blake and Mouton added 'Flexibility' to the Managerial Grid Model as a third important determinant of a leader's approach.

Judge and Bono (2004) conducted a meta-analysis which revealed a moderately strong correlation with leadership and initiating structure/individual consideration. Initiating structure was seen to be slightly more strongly related to the work performance of the leader and of the group, and consideration was slightly more strongly related to follower satisfaction, follower motivation and leader effectiveness.

The People-Task distinction derived from such theories is a useful one. However, as with many approaches to leadership, making these kind of distinctions doesn't take account of the changing situation in which leadership occurs. To a certain extent, there is an assumption that leadership occurs in a static environment, when of course the situation which the leader is in and the need to vary one's approach depending on the prevailing situation are important. Similarly, the distinction between 'people-' and 'task-'oriented leadership presents a coarse division between leadership styles which lacks the finer-grained distinctions made possible from the breakdown of the different styles into sub-styles. Based on recent research, Saville Consulting added the concept of 'Growth' – a more active variant on the 'Flexibility' construct (Kurz et al., 2010) – and have integrated this with situational aspects of leadership in our model.

Situational leadership and contingency theories

By the late 1960s, researchers were focusing on what came to be known as Contingency Theory. The basis of such an approach is that the optimal course of leadership is dependent upon both internal and external situational factors. Several different contingency taxonomies have been developed (e.g. Fiedler's, 1967) and converge upon the view that much of the previous leadership research had neglected the influence of environmental (contingency) factors on leadership effectiveness. Contingency Theory is still widely used today and modern formulations include variables such as organizational culture as contingency factors (Schimmoeller, 2010).

The importance of the context of leadership is clearly demonstrated in work such as that of Hersey and Blanchard (1969). Perhaps the most important contribution from the Hersey-Blanchard Situational Leadership Theory was that there was no single best style of leadership and the most effective leaders are those who adapt their style to the task at hand. Furthermore, these researchers characterized leadership styles in terms of Task Behaviour and Relationship Behaviour, building on the people-task dichotomy common to many existing leadership models.

Situational Leadership Theory emphasized that the most appropriate leadership style to use depends on the nature of the individuals being led (Ashour and Johns, 1983), amongst other contextual factors. Initially, the focus was on follower 'maturity', ranging from immature individuals who take no responsibility for their work and who may lack the skills required through to mature individuals who are experienced, willing and who do take responsibility for their work (Hersey, 1985).

In proposing that the context for leadership can influence the type of leadership which is most effective, situational and contingency theories of leadership went some way to undermining the earlier Great Man hypothesis that certain people were likely to be effective leaders across all situations merely by virtue of their 'greatness'. Vroom and Jago, two of the researchers responsible for major approaches to Contingency Theory, reiterated plainly in 2007 that 'leadership depends on the situation'. It is also true, however, that focusing on the situational and contingency factors can result in neglect of the empirical findings that people often do exhibit behavioural consistency across situations (e.g. Furr and Funder, 2004; Mischel et al., 2002). Zaccaro (2007) adds that combinations of traits and attributes, integrated in conceptually meaningful ways, can reflect a stable tendency to lead across 'disparate organizational domains'. While leadership research on the whole has tended to move away from 'heroic leadership' to situational approaches, it seems that some traits, to a certain extent at least, do offer predictive value in terms of underlying leadership potential.

At their extreme, situational and contingency leadership theories have been taken to suggest that anyone can become an effective leader provided they are put in the correct situation and given the necessary training and resources to perform appropriately. Yet many individuals do fail as leaders when it appears that all conditions are favourable to them and equally there are people who can still be effective leaders when the situation is not in their favour. In addition, situational and contingency theories of leadership tend not to consider how leaders can adapt their approach to fit the situation they are in, or how they might go about changing the situation itself.

Emergent and servant leadership

Emergent leadership research focuses on how leaders surface from their peer group. Sometimes a leader may emerge through informal appointment by their followers, rather than a formal appointment by other leaders. There are different ways a leader can emerge. It may be through a conscious attempt to dominate their peer group, while at other times it may be by merit of their performance and the respect of their peers. This area of research has origins in Leader-Member Exchange theories and the Path-Goal theory of House (1971). Here, the leader's approach is tailored to the specific needs of followers and the preferred unit of analysis is the leader and each individual follower, rather than the leader and the followers as a collective.

Nevertheless, the central emergent leader approach relates closely to the concept of Servant Leadership (Greenleaf, 1977) which identifies two different kinds of leaders – Strong Natural Leaders (who are assertive and driven by a need for dominance) and Strong Natural Servants (who are driven by the need to serve a cause).

Bolden (2004) argues that the servant leader is a servant first and leader second. Servant Leaders want to serve a cause and often this means they need to represent other people in their quest.

Leading is thus a secondary aspect of the implementation of service, rather than arising out of a desire to lead and dominate others per se. In this paradigm, the leader can sometimes take the role of a partner or confidant to his or her followers. This also relates to the concept of 'authentic leadership', which involves shared values between the leaders and their followers in terms of balanced processing, relational transparency, self-awareness and an internalized moral perspective (Avolio, 2007).

While Servant Leadership is effective as a style in certain situations, its wide generalizability and the predictability of its effectiveness is contentious. As with many other leadership styles, its usefulness is to some degree dependent on the context in which leadership occurs.

Transformational and transactional leadership

Perhaps the prevailing approach to leadership is based on the concepts of transformational and transactional leadership. Burns (1978) introduced 'Transforming Leadership' and his work was furthered by Bass (e.g. Bass, 1985, 1990) and others. Transformers engender success by inspiring their followers, enhancing motivation, promoting individual responsibility and ownership of work, and by giving individualized consideration to the strengths and weaknesses of the people who work for them. Transactors focus on achieving success by exchanging and negotiating benefits with their followers, as well as clarifying their role and responsibilities through a reward and punishment system.

In one of the most widely used transformational leadership models, Bass and Avolio (1989) include the transactional concept of 'laissez-faire' leadership. This is the hands-off approach to leadership, whereby individuals are given freedom and autonomy in their work to set their own goals and drive their own success. Such a style may be useful in certain circumstances, for example, where individuals are competent, motivated and trustworthy, but some researchers such as Gill (2006) have questioned whether a laissez-faire approach is a leadership style at all.

A number of researchers (e.g. Sergiovanni, 1992) have suggested that the transformer-transactor distinction may reflect the difference between leadership and management, with the transformational style representing leadership and the transactional style being more closely aligned to management. Good management is sometimes viewed as 'doing things right', while good leadership is 'doing the right things'. It has also been suggested that leadership is more important at the highest levels of an organization's function, whereas management is more important at intermediate levels, although there is evidence which suggests that transformational leadership is effective at all organizational levels (Lowe and Kroeck, 1996), but simply occurs less commonly at lower levels (e.g. Tichy and Uhich, 1984).

Such findings suggest that management and leadership are perhaps more closely aligned than some researchers have previously indicated. While the differences between transformational and transactional leadership are relevant, the distinction between management and leadership is perhaps less important in the modern, distributed and global work environment.

Many researchers have linked personality to transformational/transactional leadership and Judge and Bono's (2004) meta-analysis showed 'some support for the dispositional basis of transformational leadership'. However, it is worth noting that these authors also suggested that non-dispositional factors are also likely to be determinants of transformational/transactional leadership.

Alimo-Metcalfe and Alban-Metcalfe produced a model of transformational leadership which focuses on 'nearby' rather than 'distant' approaches to leadership and which introduces concepts such as Servant Leadership, distributed leadership and an individual's workplace development to the transformational leadership literature (e.g. Alimo-Metcalfe and Alban-Metcalfe, 2005). An important contribution from these researchers was to recognize the prevalence of white American male leaders in research samples and to move to more representative samples including leaders who are female and/or from minority ethnic groups. Some researchers are now investigating transformational leadership in female-dominated groups (e.g. Moss and Ngu, 2006).

Charismatic/visionary leadership and leadership by engagement

The concept of the transformational leader has led to research focusing in greater depth on a leader's charisma and how they instil engagement and motivation in their followers. The transformational and charismatic leadership concepts overlap in a number of ways, but perhaps the main difference is that while transformational leaders are likely to want to induce change in order to improve performance, a charismatic leader may not wish to change anything. Charismatic leaders engage their followers using such styles as charm, persuasion and self-confidence (Bryman, 1992). Musser (1987) suggested that charismatic leaders instil commitment to ideological goals and devotion to the cause and Sashkin (1988) speaks of visionary leaders who can change the culture of an organization to bring it in line with their vision.

Some research has suggested that charismatic leadership does bring demonstrable advantages as a style of leadership. Rowold and Laukamp (2009), for example, showed that charismatic leadership has a direct and positive association with a business' profit. However, perhaps more so than with other leadership styles, there is a fine line of effectiveness with charisma which can readily lead to unintended negative side-effects and may become 'toxic'. Strongly charismatic leaders may be viewed by others as self-promoting, supercilious or even insincere and so charisma may not, in some circumstances, be a leadership style which is desirable.

There are also issues around the fact that 'charisma' itself is difficult to define. From a trait approach, it is difficult to describe charisma as anything other than an outcome of a complex interaction between the leader and the followers. It needs to be conceptualized primarily as dependent upon the particular and varying values/ desires of the followers. To say that someone is charismatic is to describe the effect they have on you or others rather than to describe any tangible personality traits that they possess. Put simply, being charismatic means different things to different people in different contexts and this, combined with other concerns, highlights that there are limitations of adopting a charismatic leadership style, which cannot easily be overlooked.

Individual differences and leadership effectiveness

Leadership research has certainly come a long way since its beginnings and the recent move to focus on the impact of leadership in work-relevant contexts is an important step. However, the field is still liable to focus only on gross concepts and leadership theories often tend towards the descriptive rather than the explanatory. There may well be people who are great/transformational/charismatic/well-aligned with corporate values, and these people may well be effective leaders, but what are the individual differences which make one person great/transformational/charismatic/well-aligned with corporate values and another person not so? The evolution of leadership theory reaches something of an impasse if one does not appeal to the psychological study of individual differences in greater detail.

At the turn of the nineteenth century, researchers had begun to notice that leadership had some cross-situational consistency. Terman (1904), for example, reported that children who emerged as leaders consistently across different situations could be differentiated from their peers according to several individual characteristics, including speech and fluency. Thanks in part to the more recent achievement of a consensus on a taxonomy of personality characteristics and the increased accuracy of measurement of individual difference variables, a number of individual differences have been shown to impact on leadership. I'd now like to introduce some of the contributions of individual difference research to our understanding of leadership.

Intelligence and leadership

Various researchers have proposed a link between intelligence and leadership effectiveness. In 1917, Yerkes developed two intelligence tests, the Army Alpha and the Army Beta, which were administered to over two million soldiers in order to identify those men who were suited to specific roles, including leadership positions (Yoakum and Yerkes, 1920). In a classic paper of 1948, Stogdill noted intelligence showed a modest but consistent link with leadership.

Many well-known models or measures of intelligence (e.g. those of Spearman, 1904; Binet and Simon, 1905; Weschsler, 1958) have been applied to research investigating leadership. Judge, Colbert and Ilies (2004) carried out a meta-analysis of 151 different samples of leadership data from 96 different sources. These researchers reported an overall correlation of .27 between intelligence and leadership (corrected for range restriction). It should be noted that this correlation suggests that there is a moderate relationship between intelligence and leadership effectiveness and is actually one of the lower estimates available in the literature.

It seems that while intelligence does have an important role to play in leadership, it certainly is not an individual difference factor acting in isolation on leadership effectiveness. Sternberg (2003) proposed that wisdom, intelligence and creativity are the three key components of leadership and it is the successful synthesis of these ideas which results in effective leadership.

Personality and leadership

As far back as 1884, Francis Galton stated in an edition of the *Fortnightly Review* that personality is a 'definite and durable "something" and therefore . . . it is reasonable to attempt to measure it'. Cattell (1965) emphasized the criticality of validity when he stated that personality is 'that which enables us to predict what a person will do in real-life situations'. In the present context, the real-life situation is being an effective leader.

Personality questionnaires have their origins in the early 1900s when Woodworth (1919) published the Personal Data Sheet he had recently developed for screening out potentially neurotic soldiers from front-line action in the First World War. In the first half of the twentieth century, researchers such as Cattell and Eysenck sought to delineate the structure of personality and intelligence. One of the most famous early personality questionnaires is R. B. Cattell's 16 Personality Factor Questionnaire (16PF, 1946), which contains a reasoning ability scale in addition to 15 factors of personality.

In 1968, Mischel published a landmark monograph which asserted that personality psychology should not try to look for stable traits in isolation, but instead should embrace the influence of situational/contextual factors on individual differences. At a time when pieces of research into leadership and individual differences was still largely separate, both fields were realizing the importance of the situation in determining outcome behaviours. Researchers began to recognize that organizational cultures, values and social norms did influence personality, just as others were noting that these same contextual factors did influence leadership (Fiedler et al., 1976).

One of the great achievements of personality psychology during the twentieth century was the development of the Big Five taxonomy, which distinguishes personality using five major factors of Openness to Experience, Conscientiousness, Extraversion, Agreeableness and Neuroticism/Emotional Stability (e.g. Costa and McCrae, 1985). The Occupational Personality Questionnaires (OPQ®, developed in 1984 by Peter Saville and his team including Roger Holdsworth, Gill Nyfield, Lisa Cramp and Bill Mabey) featured the Pentagon model, potentially the first commercially available measure of the Big Five. During the UK standardization of the 16PF, Saville (1978) also factor-analysed this questionnaire to show a Big Five plus Intelligence structure. While the Big Five personality factors lack the detail of narrower personality scales which can give better validity, they provide a useful framework for researching personality characteristics using different tools and different samples of leaders.

A meta-analysis carried out by Judge et al. (2002) improved upon the limitations of many previous individual pieces of research and revealed relatively strong correlations between the Big Five factors and leadership success. With a multiple correlation across all five factors of .48, the strongest single factor was Extroversion (.31), followed by Conscientiousness (.28), Openness to Experience (.24), Emotional Stability (.24), and finally Agreeableness (.08). It seems therefore that Extroversion is the best Big Five predictor of someone's likelihood of being a successful leader, from this research at least.

Moreover, recent research has suggested that breaking the Big Five down into more specific facets of personality produces increased validity over the higher level of five factors. Dudley et al. (2006) showed, for example, that when Conscientiousness was broken down into Detail Consciousness and Drive, criterion-related validity increased.

Use of more specific facets and a validation-centric approach to questionnaire development was pioneered in the development of the Saville Consulting Wave Professional Styles and Focus Styles questionnaires. During the development of the Wave questionnaires, the focus was on maximizing the prediction of the 'criterion space', i.e. work-relevant competencies of effective performance. This is seen in work such as that of Kurz et al. (2009), which defines competencies as specific behaviour sets.

Other research by individuals such as Goleman (1998) and Boyatzis (1982) has also reinforced that work-specific competencies can be some of the most powerful variables for predicting effective performance at work.

To summarize, it appears that there are certain personality traits which tend to underlie successful leadership. As a range of researchers and commentators (e.g. Levin and Turner, 2009) have noted, successful leaders are more likely to emerge when they are extroverted and conscientious.

The structure of the Leadership Model

There are three main components of the Leadership Model:

1. Leadership Styles (Styles Profile).
2. Leadership Situations (Predicted Situational Leadership Effectiveness).
3. General Leadership Potential (LEADER Base profile).

These three components are shown below.

The Saville Consulting Leadership Model has the following features:

- It goes beyond the established measures of task and people-oriented leadership to consider growth/pioneering-oriented leadership.
- It pulls together disparate strands of research into leadership, individual differences and workplace effectiveness, performance and potential.
- It is performance-driven and has been empirically validated from conception and throughout its development.
- It is highly predictive of leadership effectiveness.
- It provides information about the leadership styles an individual is likely to adopt.
- It differentiates between leadership motives and leadership talents.
- It specifically indicates where individuals may have over-estimated or under-estimated their orientation towards particular leadership styles.

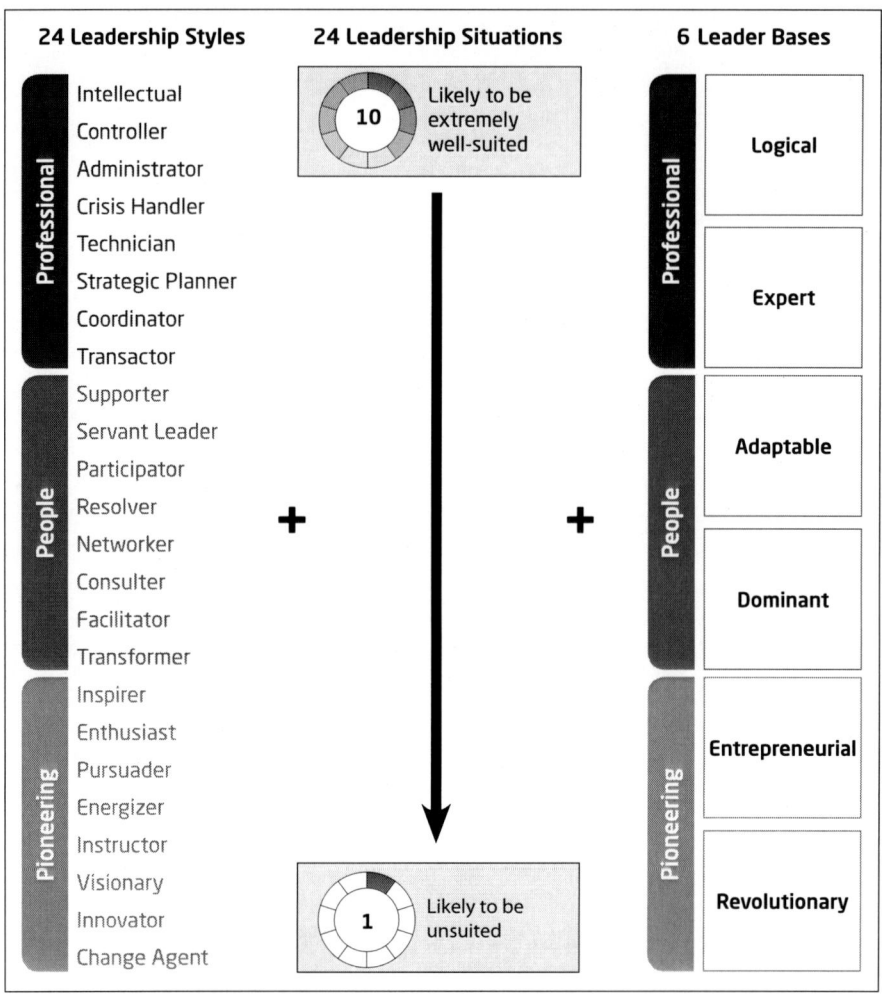

FIGURE 10.1 The three components of the Saville Consulting Leadership Model

- It highlights those situations in which individuals are likely to be effective leaders and where they are likely to be less effective.
- It allows for the effective identification and placement of leaders.
- It provides an indication of an individual's level of potential in a number of general characteristics which have been shown to be integral to effective workplace leadership across situations.

It is evident from many years of research that a range of individual difference variables, a person's underlying potential and the nature of the situation/context interact to influence the effectiveness of leadership. While other leadership models tend to focus on one or just a few of the factors which impinge upon leadership effectiveness, new and work-relevant leadership models should integrate the empirically verified aspects of the many different approaches, and this was one of the key aims in the development of the Saville Consulting Leadership Model.

Additionally, many established leadership models capture task- and people-oriented approaches to leadership, but a large number do not consider the organizational-level impact of leadership. The Saville Consulting Leadership Model has integrated the measurement of 'Pioneering Leadership' – which looks at individual motivation to grow and develop organizations that embody and realize the vision of the leader.

Saville Consulting have previously developed the Wave Performance Culture Framework which combines measures of Behavior, Ability and Global areas of workplace performance and potential. The Performance Culture Framework has been extensively researched and forms the basis of all new Saville Consulting product development because its elements have been empirically validated as important correlates of performance at work.

The 'Behavior' element describes work-relevant behavioural styles and competencies, thus capturing various individual differences via a range of personality factors and competencies. The 'Ability' element describes various intellectual and cognitive work-relevant competencies. Finally, the 'Global' element describes broad overall effectiveness characteristics in key areas of workplace effectiveness – 'Applying Specialist Expertise', 'Accomplishing Objectives' and 'Demonstrating Potential'. It is this combination of empirically validated areas which the Leadership Model capitalizes on in order to offer a richer understanding of individual differences, situations, potential and effectiveness in a workplace leadership context.

I'd now like to provide a more specific overview of the three components of the leadership model.

Leadership styles (styles profile)

The Saville Consulting Leadership Model encompasses 24 leadership styles which are built from the 108 facets of the Wave Professional Styles model. Individuals who complete Wave Professional Styles receive a score on each of the 24 leadership styles, indicating which styles they are more or less likely to adopt based on the responses that they have given to the questionnaire.

The styles reflect a large range of different factors previously discussed in other leadership models/theories, and the Saville Consulting Leadership Model synthesizes these factors to provide a coherent framework of leadership styles grouped under the four clusters of the Wave Professional Styles model. These four clusters – Thought, Influence, Adaptability and Delivery – are aligned to the Big Five factors of personality traits and thus the principal taxonomy of personality psychology is interwoven through the Saville Consulting Leadership Model and is important for its interpretation.

The leadership styles were validated throughout their development to ensure that the constructs being accepted into the Saville Consulting Leadership Model possessed both theoretical and empirical justification.

Leadership situations (predicted situational leadership effectiveness)

Each of the leadership styles is matched to a workplace situation, so it is possible to see which situations individuals are likely to be effective in given their preferred leadership styles. The Saville Consulting Leadership Report provides a list of 24 situations and a score indication of an individual's suitability as a leader in each of these situations.

The 24 leadership situations are an integral aspect of the Leadership Model and reflect a range of the contextual factors covered by various theories and models, for example, the Hersey-Blanchard Situational Leadership Theory and Fiedler's Contingency Theory. People, Professional (task) and Pioneering-related situations are covered and the degree of fit of an individual to each situation is shown in the Leadership Report. Contextual variables such as Fiedler's 'situational favorableness' (covering leader-member relations, task structure and leader positions) and Hersey and Blanchard's situational 'maturity' (covering the extent to which the followers are skilled, motivated and responsible for their work) are also reflected within the 24 situations.

Different workplace situations are important moderators of a leader's effectiveness. By displaying individuals' suitability to lead in 24 different situations, it is possible to link these contextual variables with the other factors being considered in the overall Saville Consulting Leadership Model. For example, an individual may demonstrate general leadership potential for being entrepreneurial at work, but if they are in an environment in which entrepreneurship is not valued, this may not be an effective leadership style to adopt.

Through its display of 24 different leadership styles and matched situations, users of the Saville Consulting Leadership Model can identify the situation the leader is currently in and compare their effectiveness in this context to their likely effectiveness in other contexts. This can be used to inform both changes to leadership styles and/or the situation in which leadership occurs.

General leadership potential (LEADER Base profile)

The third component of the Leadership Model is the LEADER Base profile. In the sphere of leadership research a classic debate has been framed around the extent to which effective leadership can be learned or imposed. At one end of the extreme, the view is held that there are certain people who have the necessary X factor to become leaders across all situations (the very strongest view being based around the assumption that leadership skills are innate – leaders are born and not made); at the other end of the extreme is the view that leadership is almost entirely situational and anyone can be taught to become an effective leader given the right context, circumstances and teaching.

As is often the case, it appears that both approaches have something to offer, but yet struggle to offer a parsimonious account of all of the evidence. Saville Consulting's reconciliation of these approaches acknowledges that, while situational factors clearly can influence whether a person's preferred leadership styles are effective or not in a given context, there does equally seem to be certain underlying behavioural characteristics which reappear time and again in the literature and empirical data surrounding effective leadership. These are broad aspects of a person's workplace behavioural style which underlie leadership potential with empirically demonstrable regularity.

The newly developed LEADER Base is founded on a model of an individual's level of potential to be Logical, Expert, Adaptable, Dominant, Entrepreneurial and Revolutionary in leadership. These six bases are general behavioural characteristics underpinning leadership effectiveness across different situations. The six bases are grouped in pairs under three themes – Professional, People and Pioneering.

The Professional, People and Pioneering concepts originate in the People-Task-Flexibility variables included in a number of different leadership models. The 'Professional' concept is composed of the Logical and Expert scales and is concerned with a leader's capacity to demonstrate capability in terms of workplace tasks. 'People' is composed of Adaptable and Dominant, and is about working together with others. 'Pioneering' forms a more active version of 'Flexibility', which may be seen as too reactive/passive and can under-emphasize growth aspects of a business (e.g. ideas, vision, enterprise). It is composed of the Entrepreneurial and Revolutionary scales, and is about promoting change across organizations, harnessing intuitive instincts and motivational energy.

'Pioneering' captures the important concept of the need for achievement and power in leadership as proposed by McClelland (1968). Crucially, these are areas which are under-emphasized in the Big Five model of personality, despite showing good validity. Furthermore, Collins (2001) defined Level 5 leadership as 'the highest level of executive capability' and explained that a Level 5 leader drives sustained organizational growth through inner intensity, drive and dedication. This is captured using the Entrepreneurial and Revolutionary scales in the LEADER Base. 'Pioneering' LEADER bases also emphasize the importance of the group/organizational level of analysis, an approach shared to some extent with the modern authentic view of leadership (Avolio, 2007).

Kurz et al. (2010) developed a three-factor model of effectiveness featuring 'Working Together', 'Demonstrating Capability' and 'Promoting Change' as factors which broadly correspond to the Professional, People and Pioneering orientations in the Leadership Model.

In essence, the LEADER Base provides an empirically researched overview of the general characteristics which underpin leadership effectiveness across different situations. However, the LEADER Base is not merely a modern version of the Great Man approach, but instead should be seen as an index of the breadth of leadership potential.

It is clear that in some situations certain LEADER bases will not reflect the most appropriate forms of leadership. The potential to be revolutionary may not be desirable in some highly regulated administrative leadership roles, for example. Likewise, selecting individuals who have a high potential to become expert leaders may be less preferable in some contexts to selecting individuals who already have years of relevant leadership experience. However, it is true to say that, on the basis of the validity evidence for the Leadership Model, an individual who has high potential in all six LEADER bases is more likely to adopt a broader range of different leadership styles than an individual who has high potential in just one of the LEADER bases. The latter is likely to become a highly specialized leader and may adopt a much narrower range of leadership styles. In some contexts the specialist leadership styles may be more effective than a broad range of possible styles. As ever, situational and contingency factors moderate the influence of general potential for leadership.

Summary of the Leadership Model

The leadership literature which we have explored here has provided a wealth of useful information that has been consolidated into the new model of leadership. Our review of the existing literature has culminated in the combined approach of having both a broad leadership overview in the Saville Consulting model, as well as more specific information about the styles and situations to which a specific leader may be suited. Our Leadership Model therefore draws extensively on established theory to help answer questions about both general leadership potential and leadership effectiveness in specific situations.

This combined approach has clear practical implications. Among other things, such a leadership model addresses the major issues of identifying which individuals possess the behavioural tendencies that increase their chances of becoming a successful leader, whose leadership style is appropriate for a given situation and where to place chosen leaders in order to enhance organizational effectiveness. We would argue that these are critical considerations for any practitioner working in the leadership space. Our model provides a means to support such activities as selecting leaders, succession planning, coaching and development, and assessing leader-environment fit.

Our new model consolidates many fascinating and useful strands of extant research to create a demonstrably valid, practical and intelligible method for assessing leadership effectiveness.

Entrepreneurship

Having now provided a broad overview of the leadership application of our work, I'd like to turn to entrepreneurship, in the form of a case study.

Ajaz Ahmed is a man on a quest for his next eureka moment. Ten years ago, he had just such a moment in a computer store in the north of England. He discovered that having just bought a new PC, none of the staff could explain to him how to get on to the internet. To solve this problem, which he presciently supposed to be shared by thousands of people around the UK, he set up the company Freeserve with his employer, The Dixons Group. This allowed people to simply and quickly install the internet on their computer. Freeserve rapidly became the UK's largest internet service provider. Within one year it floated on the London Stock Exchange at £1.5 billion. Within six months of flotation, Freeserve had entered the FTSE 100. At its peak it had a value of £9 billion.

Born in Lahore, Pakistan, Ajaz moved to Huddersfield in the north of England at the age of three. He grew up in the humblest of surroundings. His father worked at a textile mill and his family lived in a terraced house with an outside toilet. Neither luxury nor success was forthcoming at an early age. Ajaz left school without anything to show for himself, having failed every exam. Because of this, he was unable to attend university, but points out that a number of very successful individuals such as Sir Richard Branson, Bill Gates and Larry Ellison never received a degree. Ajaz is also keen to stress a clear distinction between academic prowess and business savvy. Despite any academic shortcomings, the young Ajaz needed to earn a living and in 1979 he was offered a job at Dixons. A well-known British high street electronics retailer, Dixons offered Ajaz £30 per week as a sales assistant. He was a successful salesman and in his twenties he became a manager, rising to take charge of the biggest store in the north of England within one year.

It was here that he inadvertently received his inspiration. The idea he had would go on to make him one of the most successful internet entrepreneurs of his time. He recalls having heard about 'this thing called the internet' which he felt he had to try. But he soon discovered, much to his personal frustration, that there was no simple way for the average person with a limited technological understanding to get online. The idea that was to become Freeserve began to crystallize. Ajaz realized that at Dixons he could do something that none of his competitors could do. He could physically talk to the customer about the internet precisely when they were buying a computer in order to gain internet access. His team could get to those customers first. Ajaz worked hard to convince his seniors of the growing importance of the internet as a revolutionary technological medium. He conceived a simple system for getting people online. At a time when all internet access in the UK was via dial-up access through telephone lines, Freeserve was one of the first internet service providers to dispense with a monthly subscription fee. Customers typically had to pay a monthly fee and then the price of a local rate phone call for every minute they were connected to the internet. But Freeserve customers could just pay the local rate and the company collected a share of that call cost.

When Freeserve was bought in 2001 by the France Telecom-owned group Wanadoo, this gave Ajaz the opportunity to turn his attention to other areas. Since this time, he has remained a successful entrepreneur. He has worked particularly with a number of companies in the science and technology fields. Having started in electronics, Ajaz feels his understanding of these areas is a useful strength. He prefers to focus his efforts into such businesses. He thus sits on the boards of several technology companies. He is also involved in a project called Jumble Aid, which encourages people and businesses to post unwanted items on a website. It works a little like eBay. When a customer buys an item on the site, all of the money goes to a charity nominated by the seller. This is a simple and effective way to both raise money for charity and to reduce landfill. Notwithstanding his earlier academic shortcomings, Ajaz also sits on the Governing Council of the University of Huddersfield. In another role which affords him something of an opportunity to return to his retail roots, he is also a partner in Abdul's, a chain of Asian restaurants.

Ajaz completed our Wave Professional Styles questionnaire and his profile provides a fascinating insight into an immensely successful individual. He is extremely inventive and creative and also has exceptional abilities which help him influence and interact with people. From his responses, we can probe deeper into what motivations and talents underlie entrepreneurial success. We can also look at Professor David Hall's Entrecode™ Model of Entrepreneurial Potential, another report produced following Ajaz's completion of the Wave questionnaire. The Entrecode™ Entrepreneurial Potential Profile is validated against a model developed to identify successful entrepreneurs. In order to do this, it predicts potential in six core areas which are of importance to entrepreneurs.

It is noteworthy that Ajaz has a higher indicated potential than 99 per cent of people who complete the Wave Professional Styles questionnaire in two of these key areas: Seeing Possibilities and Opening Up to the World. Seeing Possibilities refers to the ability to take in information and create insights. The graphic here shows three of the ways that Ajaz achieves this.

Ajaz is clearly focused on seeing the full extent of issues. From his Wave Professional Styles profile we can see that Ajaz nurtures a very clear vision for the future and takes a very long-term view. He also is able to explore a wide range of different options. All of these are skills that would no doubt be of crucial usefulness to a self-made entrepreneur. Ajaz's role requires him to work out which ideas are worth pursuing and which are not. To give an example of his commercial savvy and ingenuity, when he and his friend Abdul set up a chain of Asian restaurants, Ajaz made the radical decision to invite British comedian Bernard Manning to officially open the venture. The presence of Manning, who was well-known for a stage act that many felt to be racist and intolerant of other cultures, ensured that national press coverage was devoted to the simple opening of a restaurant. The

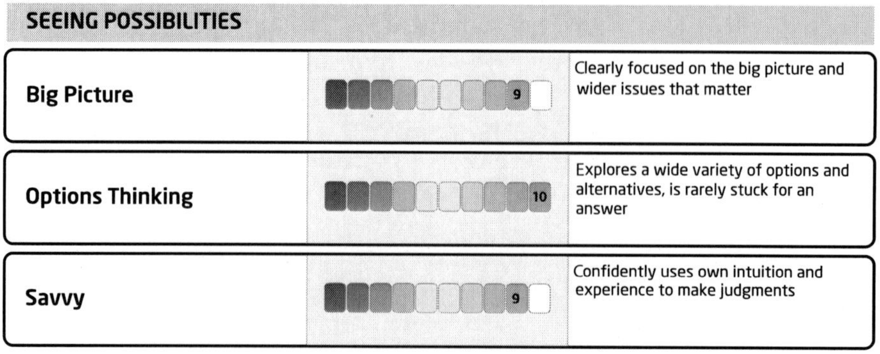

SEEING POSSIBILITIES		
Big Picture	9	Clearly focused on the big picture and wider issues that matter
Options Thinking	10	Explores a wide variety of options and alternatives, is rarely stuck for an answer
Savvy	9	Confidently uses own intuition and experience to make judgments

FIGURE 10.2   Ajaz Ahmed's 'Seeing Possibilities' scores

headline in best-selling British newspaper *The Sun* the following morning quipped 'Who's a cheeky chapatti?'

By inviting Bernard Manning to open an Asian restaurant, Ajaz was clearly thinking 'outside of the box'. He evidently considered a variety of options to work to his advantage. His responses place him in the top 1 per cent of people for Options Thinking, according to the Entrecode™ model. Similarly, Ajaz and Abdul marketed an aphrodisiac-themed curry for Valentine's Day, having discovered that many of the ingredients in curry did have aphrodisiac qualities. This enterprise led to people queuing around the block and proved so successful that they subsequently extended the offer to include the two days either side of Valentine's Day. Ever since, this has been their busiest time of the year and nobody has ever disagreed with their claim that curry is an aphrodisiac. Ajaz confirmed, with a glint in his eye, that none of the couples who'd eaten at Abdul's has ever got in touch and disputed the claimed aphrodisiac properties. 'Well, they couldn't, could they?' he joked.

From Ajaz's profile, another aspect of his behavioural style that is highlighted is his ability to use his own intuition and experience when making decisions. Ajaz particularly embodies this principle of successful entrepreneurship. He likes to focus on companies specializing in science and technology, as he has considerable experience in this area. Ajaz is keen to emphasize the importance of his extensive retail experience in guiding his decisions, as his grounding in this field allows him to speak to customers in jargon-free, succinct terms. He is mindful of the importance of mirroring a customer's language when dealing with them, regardless of the context. In his role, Ajaz often needs to take people's ideas and articulate them in a way that customers understand. He also demonstrates an aptitude for recognizing opportunities and the signals people give off when they're about to make a purchase. To give a simple example, Ajaz explains that as a salesman at Dixons, he recognized that customers who put their bags down on the floor were more likely to make a purchase than people who kept their bags in hand.

While he is savvy and prepared to use his own experience to guide judgments, it seems that Ajaz is also receptive to feedback from others. He recovers quickly from setbacks, as can be seen in the Receptive and Positive sections of his Wave Professional Styles Psychometric Profile.

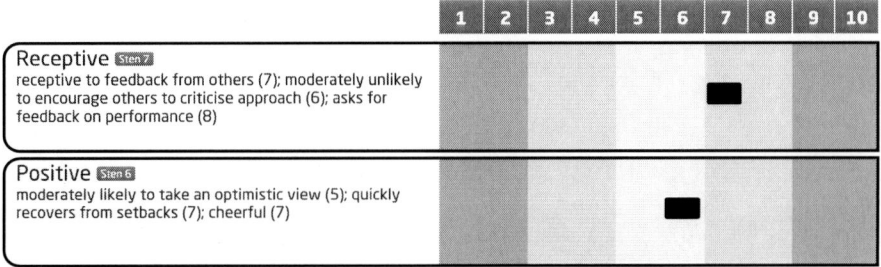

FIGURE 10.3 Ajaz Ahmed's 'Receptive' and 'Positive' scores

This combination of using one's own experience to make judgments, while at the same time being prepared to listen to others and learn from mistakes, could be of great use to a self-made entrepreneur. Many truly successful individuals learn just as much from their experiences of failure as they do from their triumphs. Certainly Ajaz was keen to ask for feedback from others as a manager at Dixons. He frequently monitored and asked for reactions from his salespeople about their communications with customers. He even recalls asking his staff to find out from prospective customers where they might have gone wrong in their dealings. He sometimes asked sales people to go out and bring customers back into the store so that a deal could be closed that day, instead of letting customers go away and 'think about it'.

Ajaz furthermore admits that he has lost hundreds of thousands of pounds and has had some failures, but his outlook is such that he is keen to learn something from every one of these experiences. We can see that Ajaz is adept at recovering from poor performances and has a flexible, adaptive style. He takes this ability to adapt and learn from any situation and applies it in his personal life. His world was profoundly changed when he discovered that he had oral cancer, despite never having been a drinker or a smoker. Happily, this was successfully treated by laser surgery, but the experience provided a prompt for Ajaz to make some lifestyle changes. He started going to the gym and lost a total of 30 pounds in weight. He's also a dedicated soccer and cricket enthusiast. Following the first time I met Ajaz, he made for the gym and regards his healthy lifestyle as a contributing factor to his business success.

The second of the six core competencies in the Entrecode™ Entrepreneurial Potential Profile where Ajaz demonstrates higher potential than 99 per cent of people is Opening Up to the World. This refers to his ability to present appropriate information to the appropriate people. It also concerns building networks and forming those relationships that enable a business to develop. Ajaz has a very high potential for networking purposefully and is skilled at negotiating with people. He builds strong commercial partnerships. However, what must be of particular use

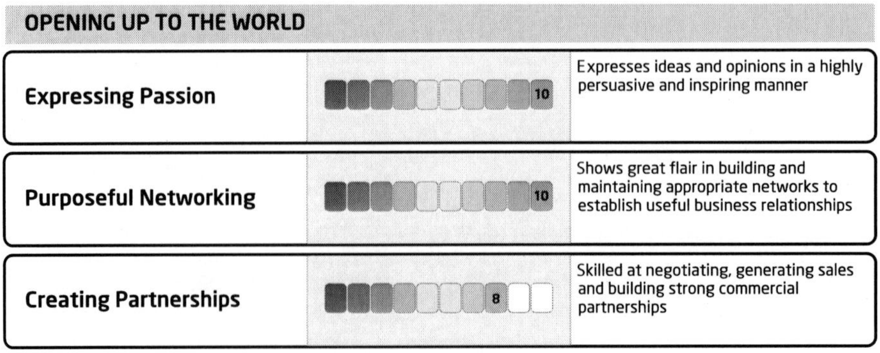

OPENING UP TO THE WORLD		
Expressing Passion	■■■■□□□□□ 10	Expresses ideas and opinions in a highly persuasive and inspiring manner
Purposeful Networking	■■■■□□□□□ 10	Shows great flair in building and maintaining appropriate networks to establish useful business relationships
Creating Partnerships	■■■■□□□ 8 □□	Skilled at negotiating, generating sales and building strong commercial partnerships

FIGURE 10.4 Ajaz Ahmed's 'Opening up to the World' scores

to him is that he is skilled at conveying passion for what he does. He is therefore able to express his ideas persuasively and inspires people. The particular methods by which Ajaz is able to effectively open up to the world are shown in the next extract from his profile.

We have seen that Ajaz is adept at seeing possibilities, influencing people appropriately and also can use his own intuitions and experiences when judging a wide range of options. However, he reports that he is less organized, meticulous and reliable than most people. As Ajaz *is* so successful, it is clear that these areas aren't so important to his success. In his job, Ajaz makes judgments about whether something will be successful or not and forms profitable relationships with others. He is not required to pay close attention to detail or to work to regular deadlines. Ajaz believes in the principles of Monkey Management. If a problem is thought of as a monkey, it is important to prevent other people passing their monkeys on to you for feeding. Ajaz is the ideas man and can't let people pass the monkeys on their shoulders to him. His skill is in persuading and empowering people to get their own monkeys off their backs.

When considered with his ability to create a clear vision for the future, it would be interesting to see whether developing his planning abilities would help Ajaz recognize business opportunities even more. Given that Ajaz reports that he is very interested in identifying business opportunities, as can be seen in the Enterprising section of his profile, this may well prove to be an area he would be keen to develop. For example, he might find that planning could enhance his ability to identify the goals he wants to achieve from a particular project.

As has already been touched upon from looking at Ajaz's Entrepreneurial Potential Profile, his interpersonal skills are a key factor in his successful behavioural style. He is very persuasive and assertive in putting his points across, explaining things well. This suggests that he has an effective impact on people. Combined with his very strong networking skills, it appears that Ajaz projects himself to the appropriate people as an articulate and convincing individual. He remains very liberal and likes to be tolerant of other people and cultures. There is no doubt that this outlook also helps him to interact well with others. Ajaz also knows when to tell people about his achievements and is comfortable being the centre of attention if necessary, as indicated in the Self-Promoting section of his profile. Such useful skills, employed judiciously, no doubt aid Ajaz in his interactions with others.

It is interesting to explore further the exact nature of Ajaz's influence over others. He reports that he is adept at finding ways to influence people, is inspirational

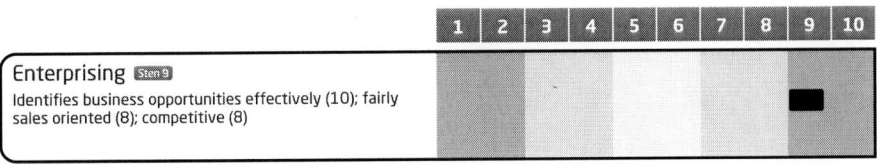

FIGURE 10.5 Ajaz Ahmed's 'Enterprising' score

and is clearly oriented towards leadership. But he also says that he is less team-oriented than many people and has little desire to coordinate people. Ajaz affirms that he wouldn't want to be a CEO again, because his interests lie in vision and creativity rather than in coordinating people and 'their monkeys'. This, he admits, he can find frustrating. In his day-to-day work he is primarily responsible for himself only and doesn't actually have much involvement with teams of people. His profile responses seem to reflect that team working skills aren't important to him rather than that he lacks these skills per se.

Looking at his Wave profile, an interesting motive-talent split becomes apparent in the Purposeful section of his leadership style. In Ajaz's Purposeful section (below), he is more motivated by, rather than talented in, this area. His talent for making quick decisions and to take responsibility for decisions is typical of many people, but he is somewhat more motivated by this than many people are. It may well be that this is an area that Ajaz is considering as an area for further development.

What is perhaps so fascinating about Ajaz's profile is that he demonstrates many areas of strength which interact in unique ways. As we have seen, he combines a powerful set of skills that allow him to influence people effectively. Yet, while he is quick to state that his work involves articulating other people's ideas in a persuasive way, it is eminently clear that Ajaz excels at generating his own ideas too. Perhaps his greatest strength as illustrated in his Wave profile is his inventive and strategic thought style. Ajaz generates many original ideas and is prepared to adopt radical solutions to problems. This makes him far more inventive than most people report they are. He develops concepts, theories and strategies with ease. Ajaz's personal view is that it is the ideas that matter, not the business plan. As we have already encountered from his Entrepreneurial Potential Profile, Ajaz creates a compelling future vision. The prevailing areas of his thought style are summarized in the next graphic.

In the Abstract section, Ajaz has indicated that while he is very good at developing concepts and applying theories, he is much less interested in studying the principles underlying issues. Most people find that developing concepts, theories and underlying principles are allied much more closely than Ajaz sees them. Consequently, his profile highlights a unique aspect of his preferred behavioural style. Taken in conjunction with the motive-talent split in the Abstract section, Ajaz's profile suggests that he has a distinct motivation to develop his conceptual and theoretical thought skills. Because his reported understanding of underlying

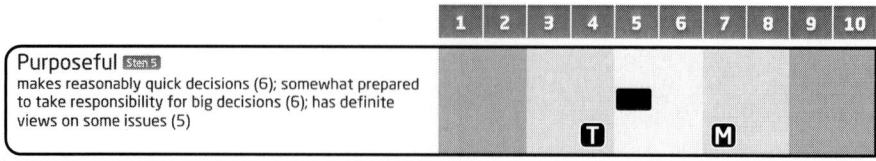

FIGURE 10.6 Ajaz Ahmed's 'Purposeful' score

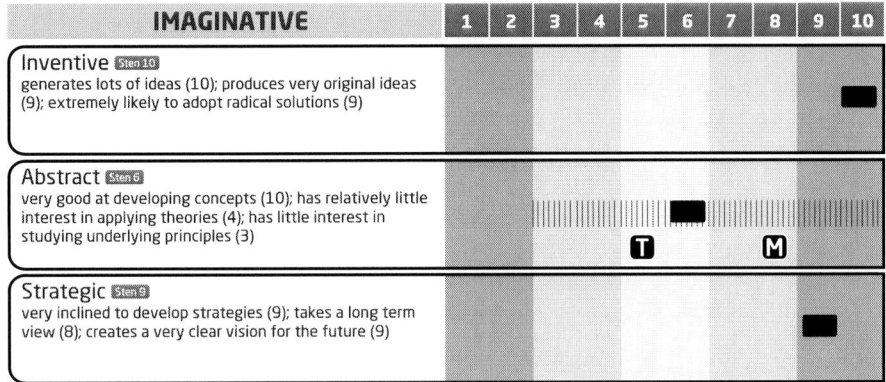

FIGURE 10.7 Ajaz Ahmed's 'Imaginative' scores

principles is somewhat lower than for the other areas, this might be an area that Ajaz could choose to focus on in order to further develop his capability for abstract thought.

Being practically minded, factual and rational is quite different from being good at abstract thought. These practical areas are prioritized a good deal lower in Ajaz's responses. Ajaz is much less inclined to follow the rules than many people. We can see that Ajaz has creative ideas and is talented at empowering people. His empowering skills may be the key to explaining how he is so good at realizing creative ideas despite being less interested in the practicalities of those ideas. Quite simply, he is very good at empowering others to help realize his ideas. Speaking to Ajaz himself corroborates this hypothesis. He believes that many people are capable of having 'eureka' moments, but that a key skill is acting appropriately on these ideas. For him, entrepreneurs are those who are able to do this and direct others to align with their vision. He read and studied how other people achieved success and believes that aspiring individuals should do the same.

It is also interesting to speculate how Ajaz's very abstract thought style might contribute to his success. Perhaps the fact that he is less rule-bound, factual and risk-averse than many people helps him to produce exceptionally creative ideas, unconstrained in the ways that many people commonly are. Ajaz's Conforming section of his profile can be seen here.

In Ajaz's view: 'History is littered with examples of ordinary people achieving extraordinary things because they could see things that were completely obvious

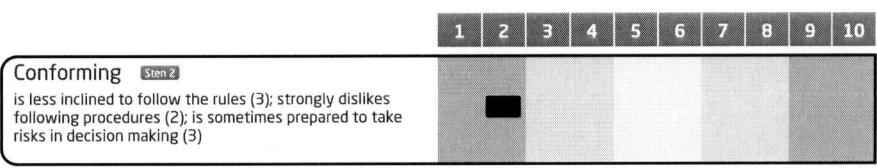

FIGURE 10.8 Ajaz Ahmed's 'Conforming' score

before anyone else could. That's what life is about, doing the obvious before everyone else and not trying to complicate everything.' It seems that this combination of a lack of constraint by rules and a very strong creative vision helps Ajaz to see things that are 'obvious' before other people do. Ajaz muses: 'How many times have I heard people say to me "I had that idea!"? But the problem is that they didn't do anything about their idea. That's the tragedy.'

We can also use the various reports from the Wave Professional Styles questionnaire as tools for guiding feedback in a variety of ways. For example, we have seen that Ajaz's Entrecode™ Entrepreneurial Potential Profile indicates that he has great flair for maintaining the networks needed for the business and that he is inspiring and persuasive.

However, while Ajaz's reported talent for resolving situations is lower than that for many people, his reported motivation to resolve situations is somewhat higher. He may therefore already be inclined to focus on these supportive skills. Ajaz is an immensely successful individual, so it is likely that he can effectively self-regulate changes in his behavioural styles in order to maximize success in a range of different situations.

From Ajaz's profile, we can also consider areas where his success might be used to extend advice to others. There is a large facet split on Composed, where Ajaz reports that he is very calm before important events. He is only slightly anxious during important events, but dislikes having to work under pressure.

In some situations, such anxiety can help and in others it can be a hindrance. Ajaz is certainly very comfortable giving presentations. He reports disliking working under pressure and in a busy working environment, but appears able to flourish in other situations such as networking and giving presentations. Crucially, Ajaz believes that 'success is an attitude', so if you can go into a difficult situation believing that you will be successful, this is half of the battle won.

The Wave Professional Styles reports for Ajaz Ahmed are a fascinating case study into the unique behavioural styles of an immensely successful and self-motivated entrepreneur. Clear strengths for Ajaz are indicated in his creative thought and interpersonal skills, which allow him to effectively influence people in order to develop his business. He also demonstrates a remarkable ability to invoke his own experience and intuitions to make discerning commercial judgments. He is at pains to stress the importance to him of this particular skill.

However, what is perhaps heartening for others is that Ajaz believes that ordinary people can do extraordinary things with the right motivations. He explains

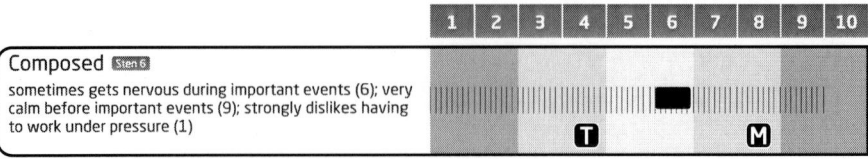

FIGURE 10.9 Ajaz Ahmed's 'Composed' score

how one famous British television commercial affected him profoundly. An advertisement for Hovis bread showed a millworker walking down a cobbled street as he retires from a hard life's work. He clutches the clock that has been given to him as a leaving gift and looks back at the mill where he has faithfully served his whole life. He returns home and cuts a slice of Hovis bread, when the commercial reveals that Hovis is as good today as it has always been. The message conveyed was one of good old-fashioned values and tradition, but Ajaz saw the advertisement in a rather different light.

Millworkers like his father left with nothing but a token gift to show for their life's work. Ajaz wasn't going to retire with nothing to show for his toil. For him, success is about wanting to have something to show for your life's work. He believes that most people at work spend six months of the year thinking about the vacation they're going to take and then six months talking about what they did on that vacation. They don't try to make a difference. This was a driving force for his success; the desire to make a difference.

Amusingly, Ajaz's colleagues at Dixons presented him with a clock as a leaving gift, but his drive, determination, creativity and influencing skills have carried him much further than that humble millworker. For many people, the advice, beliefs and behaviours demonstrated by Ajaz Ahmed form the cornerstone of a successful entrepreneur. There is no doubt that he embraces them with verve and aplomb.

Thank you very much for your time and it was a pleasure to be able to share this with you.

References

Alimo-Metcalfe, B. and Alban-Metcalfe, J. (2005). Leadership: Time for a new direction? *Leadership*, 1(1), 51–71.

Ashour, A. S. and Johns, G. (1983). Leader influence through operant principles: A theoretical and methodological framework. *Human Relation*, 36(7), 603–26.

Avolio, B. J. (2007). Promoting more integrative strategies for leadership theory-building. *American Psychologist*, 62(1), 25–33.

Bass, B. M. (1985). *Leadership and Performance Beyond Expectation*. New York: Free Press.

——. (1990). *Bass and Stodgill's Handbook of Leadership*, 3rd edn. New York: Free Press.

Bass, B. M., and Avolio, B. J. (1989). *Manual for the Multifactor Leadership Questionnaire*. Palo Alto, CA: Consulting Psychologists Press.

Bekker, I. (1831–70). *Aristotelis opera edidit Academia Regia Borussica*. Berlin: Prussian Academy.

Binet, A. and Simon, T. (1905). Méthodes nouvelles pour le diagnostic du nouveau intellectuel des anormaux. *L'Année Psychologique*, 11, 191–244.

Blake, R. and Mouton, J.S. (1964). *The Managerial Grid: The Key to Leadership Excellence*. Houston, TX: Gulf Publishing Co.

Bolden, R. (2004). *What is Leadership?* Leadership South West, Research Report, 1–36.

Boyatzis, R. E. (1982). *The Competent Manager*. Hoboken, NY: Wiley.

Bryman, A. (1992). *Charisma and Leadership in Organizations*. London: Sage Publications.

Burns, J. M. (1978). *Leadership*. New York: Harper & Row.

Cattell, R. B. (1946). *The Description and Measurement of Personality*. New York: World Book.

Cattell, R. B. (1965). *The Scientific Analysis of Personality*. London: Penguin.

Collins, J. (2001). Level 5 leadership: The triumph of humility and fierce resolve. *Harvard Business Review*, 79(1), 66–76.

Costa, P. T. and McCrae, R. R. (1985). *The NEO Personality Inventory Manual*. Odessa, FL: Psychological Assessment Resources.

Dudley, N. M., Orvis, K. A., Lebiecki, J. E. and Cortina, J. M. (2006). A meta-analytic investigation of conscientiousness in the prediction of job performance: Examining the intercorrelations and the incremental validity of narrow traits. *Journal of Applied Psychology*, 91(1), 40–57.

Fiedler, F. E. (1967). *A Theory of Leadership Effectiveness*. New York: McGraw-Hill.

Fiedler, F. E., Chemers, M. M. and Mahar, L. (1976). *Improving Leadership Effectiveness: The Leader Match Concept*. New York: John Wiley & Sons.

Furr, R. M. and Funder, D. C. (2004). Situational similarity and behavioural consistency: Subjective, objective, variable-centred, and person-centred approaches. *Journal of Research in Personality*, 38, 421–47.

Gill, R. (2006). *Theory and Practice of Leadership*. London: Sage Publications.

Goleman, D. (1998). *Working with Emotional Intelligence*. New York: Bantam Books.

Greenleaf, R. K. (1977). *Servant Leadership*. Mahwah, NJ: Paulist Press.

Hersey, P. (1985). *The Situational Leader*. New York, NY: Warner Books.

Hersey, P. and Blanchard, K. H. (1969). Life cycle theory of leadership. *Training and Development Journal*, 23(5), 26–34.

House, R. J. (1971). A path-goal theory of leader effectiveness. *Administrative Science Quarterly*, 16, 321–38.

Judge, T. A., Bono, J. E., Ilies, R. and Gerhardt, M. W. (2002). Personality and leadership: A qualitative and quantitative review. *Journal of Applied Psychology*, 87(4), 765–80.

Judge, T. A. and Bono, J. E. (2004). Personality and transformational and transactional leadership: A meta-analysis. *Journal of Applied Psychology*, 89(5), 901–10.

Judge, T. A., Colbert, A. E. and Ilies, R. (2004). Intelligence and leadership: A quantitative review and test of theoretical propositions. *Journal of Applied Psychology*, 89(3), 542–52.

Katz, D., Maccoby, N. and Morse, N. (1950). *Productivity, Supervision, and Morale in an Office Situation*. Ann Arbor, MI: Institute for Social Research.

Kurz, R., Saville, P. and MacIver, R. (2009). The structure of work effectiveness as measured through the Saville Consulting Wave® Performance 360 'B-A-G' Model of Behaviour, Ability and Global Performance. *Assessment and Development Matters*, 1(1), 15–18.

Kurz, R., Saville, P., MacIver, R. and Hopton, T. (2010). Stakeholder perspectives on behaviour, ability and global performance: Evidence for a three-factor model. Presented at the BPS DOP Conference, Stratford-upon-Avon, January.

Levin, I. and Turner, R. (2009). Can leaders really be 'developed?' *The California Psychologist*, 42(1), 17–19.

Lowe, K. B. and Kroeck, K. G. (1996). Effectiveness correlates of transformation and transactional leadership: A meta-analytic review of the MLQ literature. *Leadership Quarterly*, 7(3), 385–425.

McClelland, D. C. (1968). *Human Motivation*. New York: Irvington Publishers.

Mischel, W. (1968). *Personality and Assessment*. New York: Wiley.

Mischel, W., Shoda, Y. and Mendoza-Denton, R. (2002). Situation-behavior profiles as a locus of consistency in personality. *Current Directions in Psychological Science*, 11(2), 50–54.

Moss, S. A. and Ngu, S. (2006). The relationship between personality and leadership preferences. *Current Research in Social Psychology*, 11(6), 70–91.

Musser, S. J. (1987). *The Determination of Positive and Negative Charismatic Leadership*. Grantham, PA: Messiah College.

Rowold, J. and Laukamp, L. (2009). Charismatic leadership and objective performance indicators. *Applied Psychology: An International Review*, 58(4), 602–21.

Sashkin, M. (1988). The visionary leader. In J. A. Conger and R. N. Kanungo (eds), *Charismatic Leadership: The Elusive Factor in Organizational Effectiveness* San Francisco: Jossey-Bass, pp. 122–60.

Saville, P. (1978). *The National Adult Standardisation of 16 Personality Factor Questionnaire (16PF)*. London: NFER.

Saville, P. and Hopton, T. (2009). *Talent: Psychologists Personality Test Elite People*. Saville Consulting Group, Jersey.

Saville, P., Holdsworth, R., Nyfield, G., Cramp, L. and Mabey, W. (1984*). The Occupational Personality Questionnaire (OPQ)*. London: SHL.

Schimmoeller, L. J. (2010). Leadership styles in competing organizational cultures. *Leadership Review*, 10(2), 125–41.

Sergiovanni, T. J. (1992). *Moral Leadership: Getting to the Heart of School Improvement*. San Francisco: Jossey-Bass.

Shakespeare, W. (1623). *First Folio*. London: Isaac Laggard and Ed Blount.

Spearman, C. (1904). General intelligence objectively determined and measured. *American Journal of Psychology*, 15(2), 201–93.

Sternberg, R. J. (2003). WICS: A model for leadership in organizations. *Academy of Management Learning and Education,* 2, 386–401.

Stogdill, R. (1948). Personal factors associated with leadership: A survey of the literature. *Journal of Psychology*, 25, 35–69.

Terman, L.M. (1904). A preliminary study in the psychology and pedagogy of leadership. *Journal of Genetic Psychology*, 11, 413–51.

Tichy, N. and Uhich, D. (1984). The leadership challenge: A call for the transformational leader. *Sloan Management Review*, 26(1), 59–68.

Vroom, V. H. and Jago, A. G. (2007). The role of the situation in leadership. *American Psychologist*, 62(1), 17–24.

Wechsler, D. (1958). *The Measurement and Appraisal of Adult Intelligence*, 4th edn. Baltimore: Williams and Witkins.

Woodworth, R. S. (1919). *Personal Data Sheet*. Chicago, Stoelting Co.

Yoakum, C. S. and Yerkes, R. M. (1920). *Army Mental Tests*. New York: H. Holt and Company.

Zaccaro, S. J. (2007). Trait-based perspectives of leadership. *American Psychologist*, 62(1), 6–16.

11

THE ISSUE OF CHEATING

This chapter is based on a presentation which I gave at the 14th South African Psychology Congress in Johannesburg, South Africa in 2008:

> Saville, P. (2008). Improving security of assessments delivered by the internet. Presented at the 14th South African Psychology Congress, Johannesburg, South Africa, August.

During this presentation, I reflected on a number of key concepts and issues in test security, as well as some of our own research about potential solutions to this problem.

Improving security of assessments delivered by the internet

The security of online testing is often one of the main criticisms that is levelled at psychometricians. Unfortunately, we do know that it is an increasing problem, both in educational and workplace settings. It is true that there will always be a percentage of individuals who will try to beat the system and engage in strategies which work to their advantage. I'd like to discuss a number of the potential issues, as well as some possible solutions, based on our research.

The first thing to say is that we have to be realistic and accept that there is no 100 per cent solution to stopping all forms of cheating, but is there ever a 100 per cent solution in anything we do in life? We need to be pragmatic and reduce cheating as much as we can, but also acknowledge that there will almost always be someone who gets around the system.

The British newspaper *The Telegraph* once featured a cartoon on the subject of online testing (designed by Peattie & Taylor of www.alexcartoon.com). Two managers are sitting at their desks in an office when one turns to the other and notes that a graduate applicant they're currently discussing appears to possess the necessary qualities that they're looking for.

'Just look at some of his scores in the assessment tests – he got 98 per cent in maths', he notes. His colleague replies that this score was achieved on the online test which candidates have to complete from home. He notes that when the candidate had to sit a similar numeracy test under supervision, he only scored 62 per cent, suggesting he must have got a more mathematically able friend to take the online version for him. To this, the first retorts: 'Exactly – proving that he has grasped the concept of delegation . . . so I'm sure he'd respect us when we offload all the coffee- and sandwich-fetching duties to him.'

Or take, for example, the 11+ examination which was a feature of British education some years ago. Every child at the age of 11 took an IQ test, which served as a selection test to enter more or less academic schools at that age. In the English county of Wiltshire, it was found that IQ apparently declined by 15 points when the 11+ system stopped, which was one of several suggestions that certain parents were using various methods to get around the system. For example, some parents were moving their families from highly competitive and socio-economically developed areas to less socio-economically developed areas before the 11+ exam, and then moving back again afterwards. This would increase the chances of their children scoring well compared to others from the same area, and this maximised their chances of getting into the best schools.

In 2009 we also carried out some research with our colleague Rab MacIver on cheating, using a sample of 1012 UK students. In this research, we found that 35.9 per cent of respondents reporting knowing at least one male student who had cheated on an unsupervised test, and 29.2 per cent knew at least one female student who had done the same. Over three-quarters of respondents (76.9 per cent) agreed that they would feel negatively towards an organisation which had appointed a cheat if they had applied honestly and been rejected. Similarly, more than one in eight (81.5 per cent) disagreed that it would be fair for university examinations to be delivered unsupervised via the internet.

Nevertheless, let's not throw out the baby with the bath water – online testing is here to stay and can be effective if done properly. In many cases, organisations are faced with large numbers of applicants to decide between, and ability testing is among the most valid methods available for reducing these numbers. Often it is simply not practical to assess each candidate in a supervised manner and/or to interview all of them. This is particularly the case with large, global assessment processes where candidates may be geographically dispersed and/or in especially large numbers. The assessors may simply need a practical way to reduce the numbers of candidates before they can start the more labour-intensive assessment activities such as interviews or assessment centres. Ability tests are among the most valid ways of reducing candidate numbers, so are often particularly useful as initial screening tools in an assessment process.

Thankfully, the situation isn't quite as bleak as the cartoon, the 11+ data and our own research might initially suggest. There are certainly things we can do to counteract cheating on workplace assessments. Our research suggests that simply letting respondents know that there are checks and balances in the assessment can reduce their tendency to fake or distort results. In terms of cheating on unsupervised assessments, there are various sophisticated statistical methods and ways to randomise content so that different candidates see different versions of an assessment. Such techniques are typically deployed for ability tests rather than personality or behavioural questionnaires. Randomisation methods can help prevent people getting access to the correct answers before completing an assessment.

However, the main point to make with regard to such methods is that they do nothing to prevent identity deception, i.e. where a candidate receives help from others when completing the unsupervised tests or even, as in the cartoon, 'delegates' the test completion to a smarter friend. Some have suggested that the use of monitoring equipment such as webcams are effective, but in my view it'd be very easy for the webcam to be positioned in a way so that anybody giving additional assistance wasn't visible. As I've said before, if you assess enough people, there'll always be someone who can beat the system!

Nevertheless, there is a method which does get around these potential identity deception issues – *supervised retesting*. We would argue that, wherever possible, organisations should retest candidates in a supervised manner prior to appointment. This can reassure the assessors that the candidate is who they said they are before they are offered a job.

Indeed, our 2009 research on UK students suggested that the existence of supervised retests remains the most effective deterrent for explicit cheating on an unsupervised assessment. Eight out of ten respondents (82 per cent) agreed that an organisation following unsupervised internet tests with longer supervised tests prior to appointment was an effective method for preventing cheats from being selected for a job. The effectiveness of retesting has been known outside of industry for a long time. The ancient Chinese – and Mensa – always retested with a parallel form of a test.

If you are using ability tests in this manner, we would argue that the premier solution which provides maximum security in testing is to follow the method below:

- Screen all applicants using an initial unsupervised test (and potentially other assessments too).
- Communicate to them *before they complete the first test* that they will be retested, under supervised conditions, using a more rigorous parallel form of the test if they make it to the later stages of the assessment process.
- Retest the remaining applicants in a supervised testing environment at a later stage.

If it is not possible to retest all applicants using a more rigorous version of a test, the next best option is to retest all applicants, under supervised conditions, using a test which is of a comparable quality to the initial screening test.

Again, if this is not possible, the next best option is to randomly retest a number of applicants at a later stage (and let them all know beforehand that this will occur). Interestingly, if they definitely knew they would later be retested in a supervised situation, just 9 per cent of students in our 2009 research also said that they would cheat. Of course, if that 9 per cent did cheat on an unsupervised test, they would still be faced with passing the supervised test prior to being appointed. We would argue that supervised retesting is frequently desirable for personality or behavioural assessments and essential with ability tests.

Given that supervised retesting is an effective addition to many assessment processes, there are still a number of possible ways in which the supervised retesting could be done. Broadly speaking, there are two approaches to supervised retesting – the so-called *verification* approach and the *screen-out/select-in* approach.

The verification approach involves inviting candidates who are successful in the earlier unsupervised testing phase to complete another assessment in a supervised environment and to compare the consistency of scores between the two tests. Although this may sound intuitively like a good approach, the potential problem is that no assessment method is perfectly reliable. As with virtually every measurement method in the universe (not just psychometrics!), we have to accept that there will be a degree of error in our measurement. This can be quantified as the reliability of the measurement method – a way of describing how consistently it is in making its measurements. We'll return to this concept shortly, but suffice it to say for now that psychometric tests are far from perfectly reliable.

The screen-out/select-in approach involves inviting candidates who are successful in the earlier unsupervised testing phase to complete another assessment in a supervised environment, but treating the scores from the two assessments completely separately. In this approach, the two testing stages are treated completely separately as two 'hurdles', and scores are not compared across the two approaches.

I'd like to briefly summarise some empirical research which I recently carried out with my colleague Rab MacIver that compared these two different approaches. Based on this, I'd like to offer my thoughts on why I believe the screen-out/select-in approach is the superior one.

We wanted to simulate the quality of possible decisions that could be made through a retesting scenario with the two possible approaches: verification and screen-out/select-in. To do this, we created some simulation data representing two different test completions. Throughout the discussion below, it is important to bear in mind that we are not representing candidates who cheated. We are simply showing what would happen to scores across two different test completions *assuming all candidates have been completely honest on both testing occasions*.

In the graph below, the two axes use a 1–10 scale to represent the score achieved on each test. The scale used is not important in itself; it could be any scoring scale at all, but here we've favoured the commonly used standardised 1–10 (sten) scale for simplicity. Each dot represents the scores achieved by one candidate on both tests. As we move vertically up the graph from bottom to top, we encounter candidates who do progressively better on the first test. Similarly, as we move

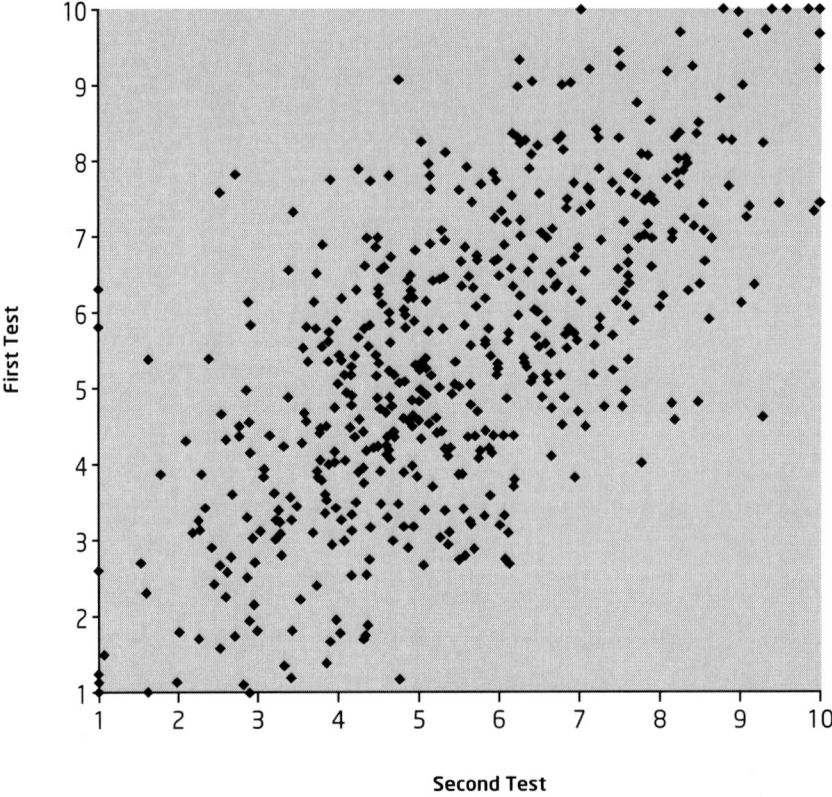

FIGURE 11.1 Simulated concordance between two aptitude tests correlating .70

horizontally across the graph from left to right, we encounter candidates who do progressively better on the second test.

Clearly, just from looking at the graph, we can see that there's a general trend to the data points – the scores on the two tests tend to be relatively consistent. Thus, candidates who do better on the first test tend to do better on the second test. Conversely, the lower scores on the first test tend to be matched by similarly low scores on the second test. There are relatively fewer candidates who do really well on one test, but not the other. It is worth pointing out that such candidates *do* exist, but they aren't especially numerous in this data set. More specifically, there's a fairly strong positive relationship between the two variables measured here (i.e. people's scores on the two tests). In fact, to be more precise, this simulation data set has a correlation coefficient of .70. This value of .70 has been specifically chosen for our present purposes because this is a very typical reliability figure for two different ability tests. In the psychometrics industry, we speak of .70 being the benchmark of reliability for two parallel forms of an ability test. If we're doing supervised testing, we want the scores from the first test to correlate with the scores from the second test at this kind of level. If the reliability was considerably lower, there would be little relationship between the scores on the two tests. In such a case, it would be very common for candidates to score well on one, but poorly on the other test.

If we're trying to do a supervised *retest*, i.e. to measure the same thing twice, low correlations between tests would be undesirable. We would want to see a correlation of .70 or above to reassure us that the scores on the two tests are likely to be pretty consistent with each other. In short, this simulation data set is very typical of what we'd expect to see if we put a large sample of candidates through two tests designed to measure the same thing. Bear in mind that in our simulation data set, we haven't represented any cheating at all. These score differences are simply what we should expect when people complete two different tests which correlate .70, to the best of their ability on both occasions. From a more technical perspective, this is because there is error inherent in any measurement method, including both of our tests, as we've already seen.

In terms of practical significance, in the above data set just simply because of the statistical random error inherent in any methods that are not perfectly reliable (here, our methods are .70 reliable), 26 per cent of candidates would have the identical sten score on the first and second test completions. Of the remaining 74 per cent that had changed scores:

- 21 per cent drop by one sten between the first and second tests;
- 10 per cent drop by two stens between the first and second tests;
- 4 per cent drop by three stens between the first and second tests;
- 2 per cent drop by four or more stens between the first and second tests.

Equally:

- 21 per cent increase by one sten between the first and second tests;
- 10 per cent increase by two stens between the first and second tests;
- 4 per cent increase by three stens between the first and second tests;
- 2 per cent increase by four or more stens between the first and second tests.

These values have simply been taken from the graph – by looking at the pairs of scores for each candidate and then categorising them into the various groupings above.

Given that this data set is, by design, extremely representative of what happens in real supervised retesting situations, there are some striking implications here. If we were following a 'verification' approach, we might set a specific criterion as our way of saying if the two scores achieved by a candidate are sufficiently similar (often termed 'verified') or sufficiently different that they cannot be verified as suitably consistent with each other.

Often, psychometric tests which work on such a verification method tend to use a sten difference between the two sets of test scores of three or more stens as the cut-off point. This degree of difference is typically chosen based on the expected degree of error in any score – from the practical point of view, it is where the two scores could be said to be significantly different from each other. If this was applied, a total of 12 per cent of the sample of candidates here would be flagged up as 'unverified' (the 6 per cent who dropped by three stens or more, plus the 6 per cent who increased by three stens or more). So with a verification approach we would be flagging up 12 per cent of candidates as potential 'cheats', even though the differences in their scores would be due simply to the levels of reliability inbuilt in the tests used.

In truth, because we cannot differentiate between statistical random error and actual cheating when explaining such score differences, with a typical verification approach we'd have committed a 12 per cent 'false positive' rate. For more than one in 10 candidates, we may have unfairly labelled them as cheats. Such verification methods therefore often have low credibility with test users. In our view, it is better to use online unsupervised tests to do an efficient screen-out process, then to file these data away and having a separate supervised access version to provide the safeguard of a secure select-in.

To further the simulation research above, we carried out further studies to look at the expected score differences in various other scenarios, all assuming that cheating hasn't taken place. Two normally distributed variables were created which were correlated with each other at two different levels:

- .40 (to simulate the typical correlation seen between two unstructured job interviews);
- .84 (to simulate the typical correlation seen between an unsupervised aptitude test and a follow-up test of greater length).

These additional data sets are represented in the two graphs which follow.

In exactly the same way as we did for our two ability tests, we can now determine the percentage of candidates who would change scores across the two interviews, simply because of the inherent statistical random error that exists for any method that is not perfectly reliable.

For two methods that have a reliability of .40, e.g. two unstructured interviews, 18 per cent of candidates would have no score change between the two interviews.

The following percentages of candidates would do better on the first interview than the second:

- 16 per cent drop by one sten;
- 11 per cent drop by two stens;
- 8 per cent drop by three stens;
- 3 per cent drop by four stens;
- 2 per cent drop by five stens;
- 1 per cent drop by six or more stens.

The following percentages of candidates would do better on the second interview than the first:

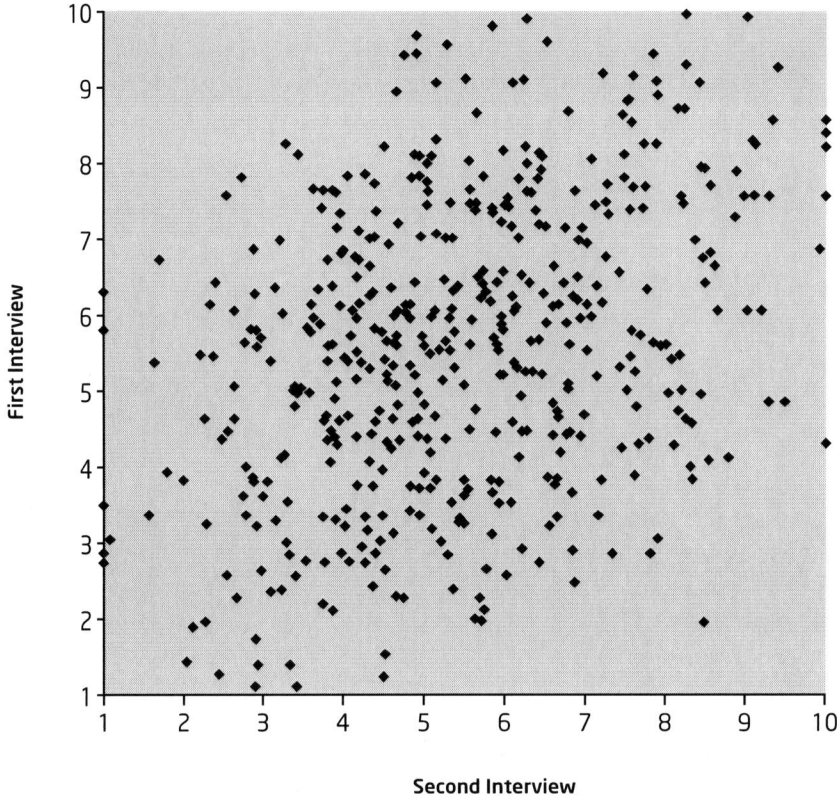

FIGURE 11.2 Simulated concordance of scores between two interviews correlating .40

- 16 per cent increase by one sten;
- 11 per cent increase by two stens;
- 8 per cent increase by three stens;
- 3 per cent increase by four stens;
- 2 per cent increase by five stens;
- 1 per cent increase by six or more stens.

As we can see, where the correlation between the two assessment methods is lower (i.e. there is a lower degree of reliability between the two methods), the percentages of people expected to change scores simply because of the inherent unreliability of the two methods increases dramatically. In the case of two assessments which correlate .40, we'd expect some 28 per cent of our sample to differ by three or more stens across the two methods. Following the verification method, more than a quarter of our sample might typically be flagged up as cheating when we clearly cannot differentiate this possibility from other explanations due to the inherent unreliability of the two assessment methods.

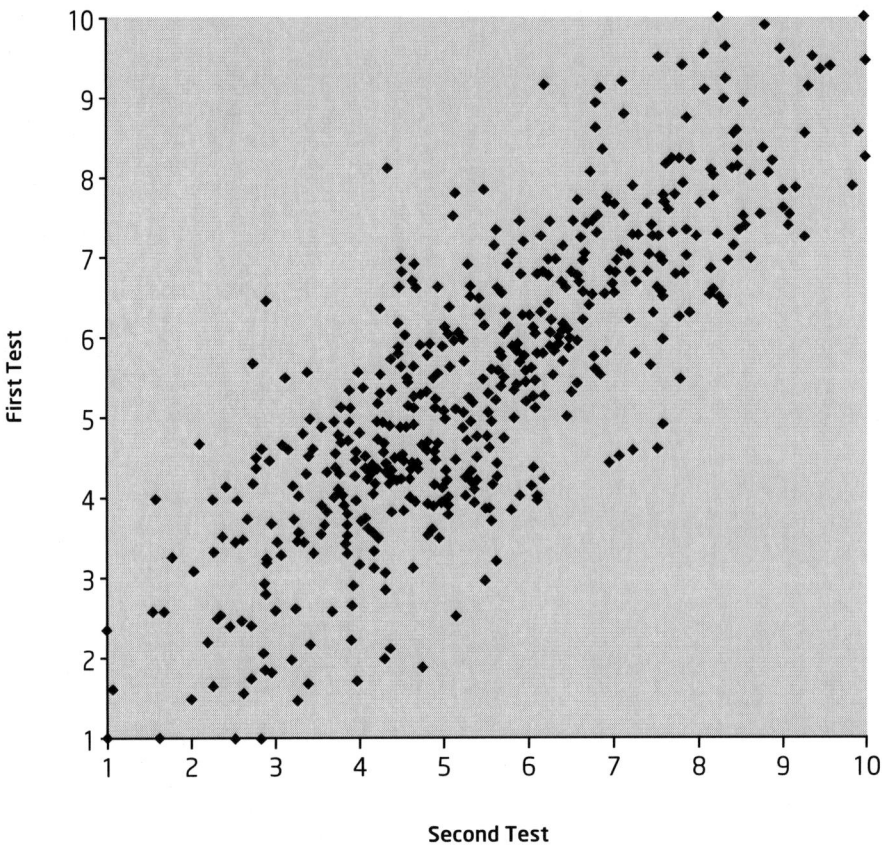

FIGURE 11.3 Simulated concordance between two aptitude tests correlating .84

Again, we can now determine the percentage of candidates who would change scores across the two tests simply because of the inherent statistical random error that exists for any method that is not perfectly reliable.

For two methods that have a reliability of .84, e.g. an ability test delivered unsupervised and then a longer, more reliable ability test delivered supervised, 34 per cent of candidates would have no score change between the two assessments.

The following percentages of candidates would do better on the first test than the second:

- 22 per cent drop by one sten;
- 9 per cent drop by two stens;
- 2 per cent drop by three or more stens.

The following percentages of candidates would do better on the second test than the first:

- 22 per cent increase by one sten;
- 9 per cent increase by two stens;
- 2 per cent increase by three or more stens.

Here, where the correlation between the two assessment methods is high (i.e. there is a high degree of reliability between the two methods), the percentages of people expected to change scores simply because of the inherent unreliability of the two methods decreases. In the case of two assessments which correlate .40, only 4 per cent of our sample to differ by three or more stens across the two methods. Following the verification method, 4 per cent of our sample might typically be flagged up as cheating when we clearly cannot differentiate this possibility from other explanations due to the inherent unreliability of the two assessment methods.

As we have seen, even without any cheating, we can expect substantial numbers of candidates to have considerably different scores if they are tested on more than one occasion. This is simply due to the inherent unreliability of any assessment method and poses considerable challenges for how to deal with these differences in a practical way.

If, following a verification approach, where a score change of a particular size is designed to flag up potential cheats, could we ever safely and reliably eliminate the right individuals from our process? Some candidates will do better on the second assessment and others will do worse. Some will vary a great deal, while others will achieve almost identical scores. How does one go about setting a cut-off to determine what kind of score difference is 'allowed' and what kind of difference is 'cheating'? In others words, how can you be perfectly sure of the difference between two scores with imperfect measurement methods? The problem of setting cut-offs is well-known in many contexts. To return to the 11+ examination, when retested two years later at the age of 13, some 35 per cent of children fell the other side of the cut-off which determined which kind of school they could get into from where they were at 11. This is one limitation of any approach which involves 'verifying' scores – in the case of the 11+ examination, more than a third of students would have been considered to have been placed in the wrong school system if their scores were 'verified' two years later.

Also, what should we do when faced with 'unverified' scores? Should we automatically remove all such candidates from the assessment process or *re*-retest people? The focus on verification can be misleading or can convey to the candidates that they are not trusted, which is unlikely to lead to a positive administrator or candidate experience. For these reasons, verification testing is often viewed quite negatively and discredited by some. As I've already mentioned, a screen-out/ select-in approach, where the two data sets are used independently as sequential hurdles, provides a far neater solution with less of the drawbacks of attempting to interpret differences between scores at the individual candidate level.

To summarise, I would argue that as with most issues in business, we will never have a 100 per cent solution to the cheating problem. Candidates will always find a way to beat the system and are getting increasingly skilled at this. We face a moving target, but simply must stay ahead of the cheats and develop sophisticated ways to prevent cheating.

Retesting job applicants under supervised conditions is perhaps the best method we have for ensuring that individuals cannot cheat their way into a job – which can have serious consequences for an organisation. Given the established and recognised effectiveness of ability tests compared to other selection methods, failure to carry out supervised retesting in an attempt to cut costs in the selection process may turn out to be a false economy.

12

ACCEPTABILITY, COST–BENEFIT AND DECISION MAKING

This paper is based on a presentation I gave in 2015:

> Saville, P. (2015). The bottom line: acceptability, decision making and cost–benefit in selection testing. Presented as part of the Goldsmiths, University of London's Distinguished Speaker Series, March.

The bottom line: acceptability, decision making and cost–benefit in selection testing

Whenever we make decisions based on data, there is a risk that we will get things wrong. Look at weather forecasters – in the UK, the great storm of 1987 wasn't predicted and the UK's Meteorological Office was criticised (Houghton, 1988). However, based on such a single event, would it be recommended that a ship's captain ignore weather forecasts?

We must accept from a practical perspective that whenever we are using tools to forecast future workplace performance, this cannot be done perfectly. Human performance is especially complex and subject to change by a whole host of factors. But if we can do anything at all to reduce the risk of making selection errors, this is typically worthwhile. Happily, psychometric assessments have been shown to be among the best methods for forecasting workplace performance, which I will discuss throughout this presentation.

It is also worth exploring what we mean by 'workplace performance'. Of course, this can vary by industry and even by role. What is good performance in one role could be quite different from good performance in another. However, whenever we are able to compare performance between people in an appropriate, consistent and fair way, we do find that individuals will vary in terms of their performance.

Indeed, there is evidence that the very top performers can be disproportionately valuable to a business compared to others (O'Boyle and Aguinis, 2012). As early as 1928, Hull found that the ratio of output of best to worst performers in a range of manual occupations was as much as five-to-one. In 1968 researchers noticed differences between the productivity of computer programmers and the term '10x programmer', i.e. the idea that top programmers are ten times more productive than the average, entered the lexicon (Sackman, Erikson and Grant, 1968). Some now speak of the 'Ninja Programmer', with reference to the fact that top computer programmers are said to share characteristics with ninjas such as agility, discipline and knowledge. In the world of sport, research has been done to try to find the statistically greatest sportspeople. It was suggested in 2000 by statistician Charles Davis that Donald Bradman, an Australian cricketer, was statistically the greatest of all time, some four standard deviations higher than the 'best of the best'. The remaining top five were soccer player Pelé, baseball player Ty Cobb, golfer Jack Nicklaus, basketball player Michael Jordan and American football player Joe Montana. Though we should now perhaps add the name Jahangir Khan, who, between 1981 and 1986, consecutively won 555 professional matches of squash, the longest winning streak by any athlete in top-level professional sport.

Staying with the world of sport, but equally applicable to the world of business, we know that small differences can mean a lot. When I spoke to former England cricketer Jeremy Snape, he confirmed that small differences in bowling speed can have a huge impact at the fastest level. I asked Jeremy: 'What is the difference the batsman of a ball bowled at 75 to 85 mph, versus one bowled at 85 to 95 mph?' He replied that the former was like going out for a Sunday afternoon drive compared with driving in a Formula 1 race. That is, the extra ten miles per hour, when bowling at very fast speed, is not on a simple linear function. A ball travelling at 95 mph from a fast bowler would result in a typical club batter hardly being able to see the ball. As Daniel Kahneman noted in his book *Thinking, Fast & Slow*, if Tiger Woods in his prime could have improved his performance by just one shot per tournament, his earnings over a year could have increased by more than a million dollars.

Such small differences count for a lot. Sir Dave Brailsford showed this with his theory of 'marginal gains'. He analysed every aspect of cycling and the cyclist, knowing that the difference between Olympic gold and silver could be a matter of just inches. With all of this said, what can we do to use these small differences, thereby increasing the potential return-on-investment from selection activities for a business?

The validity of selection methods

The starting point for estimating whether a selection test for any organisation has any benefit in monetary terms, in other words the bottom line, is the validity coefficient of the test. Validity comes in many guises. These include *face validity*, which concerns whether the test seems reasonable in terms of selecting for the job in question, to the applicant, layperson, a journalist or even a judge. A test of upper-body strength may be face valid and legal for selecting a front row forward at rugby, but not for selecting a graphic designer or board director.

But in cost–benefit analysis the *criterion-related validity* of a selection method – either concurrent or predictive validity – is preferred. Concurrent validity is simply the product moment (r) correlation coefficient between a test and some current measure of job performance (i.e. cross-sectional research), whilst predictive validity is the product moment correlation of a test with future job performance (i.e. longitudinal research). What does a correlation between two variables look like? Figure 12.1 below provides an example of a scatterplot of a correlation between two variables – height and weight. The correlation here is +.76, which is a higher correlation than one could ever realistically achieve with a predictor of job performance. Any author who claims a correlation of an assessment technique much higher than +0.6, such as +0.8 or +0.9, is most certainly exaggerating. This is because no selection method is completely reliable and all measures of job performance, such as 'subjective' ratings, or 'objective' criteria, such as units sold, are imperfect, being influenced by many extraneous and random factors. Though what is 'subjective' versus 'objective' is often difficult to distinguish and artificial.

It is probably no surprise that there appears to be a general trend that heavier people (the points nearer the top of the graph) also tend to be taller people (the points nearer the right of the graph). This relationship, of course, is not perfect and there are plenty of exceptions. Some taller people are lighter than some shorter

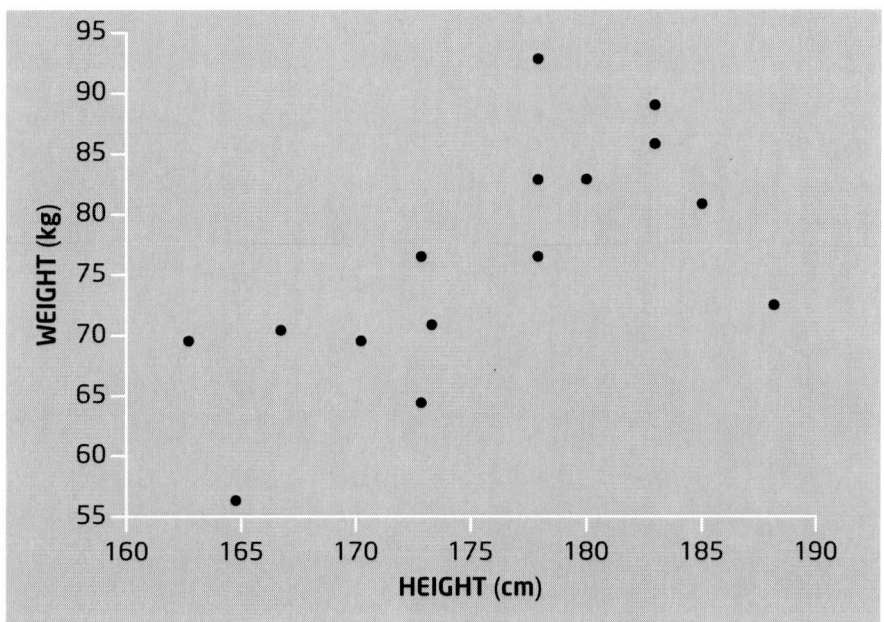

FIGURE 12.1   Scatterplot illustrating a .76 correlation between height and weight

people. This is because there are a number of other factors which impact on the relationship between height and weight, such as age, bone density, nutrition, muscle mass, etc. Our scatterplot merely shows the relationship between the two isolated variables of height and weight and doesn't take into account or offer comment on any of these other factors.

In the example of the relationship between height and weight explored above, running the correlation calculation produces a value of a little above +0.6. This shows a strong positive correlation between height and weight in the example data set. In other words, the two variables are pretty closely related to each other. In general, taller people tend to be heavier. One could predict weight from height (or vice versa) to a pretty high degree of accuracy.

So what about the correlations between different selection methods and job performance? What degree of validity should we expect to see for various kinds of selection method? Figure 12.2 below provides an overview of the validity of a range of different possible selection methods. It is adapted from a number of classic research papers (Schmidt and Hunter, 1998; Robertson and Smith, 2001) which compare the validity of a number of different workplace assessment practices.

In Figure 12.2 you can see correlation coefficients ranging from .00 to .50. In essence, correlation is a technique which represents the strength of the relationship between two different things. Correlations can take values between –1 and +1, where +1 is a perfect positive relationship between two variables.

A correlation of .00 represents no relationship between two variables and, as you can see in this diagram, larger correlation figures represent higher validity.

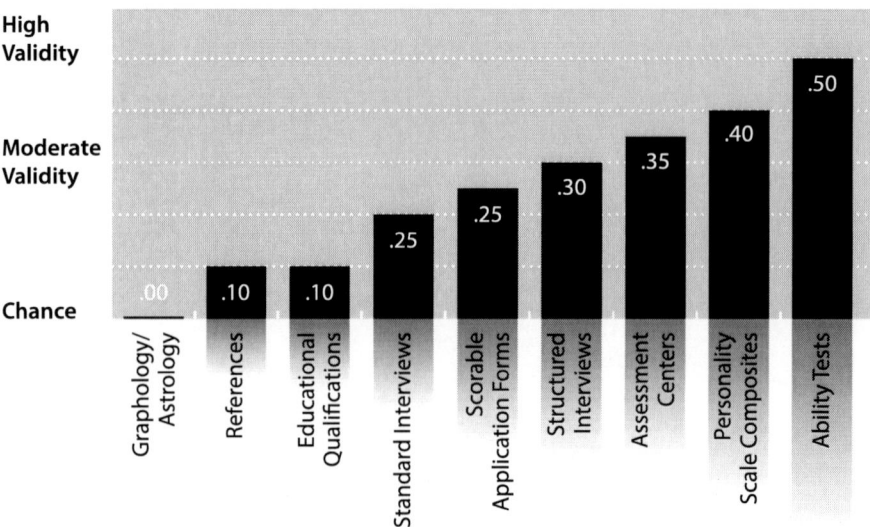

FIGURE 12.2 A comparison of the validity of different selection methods

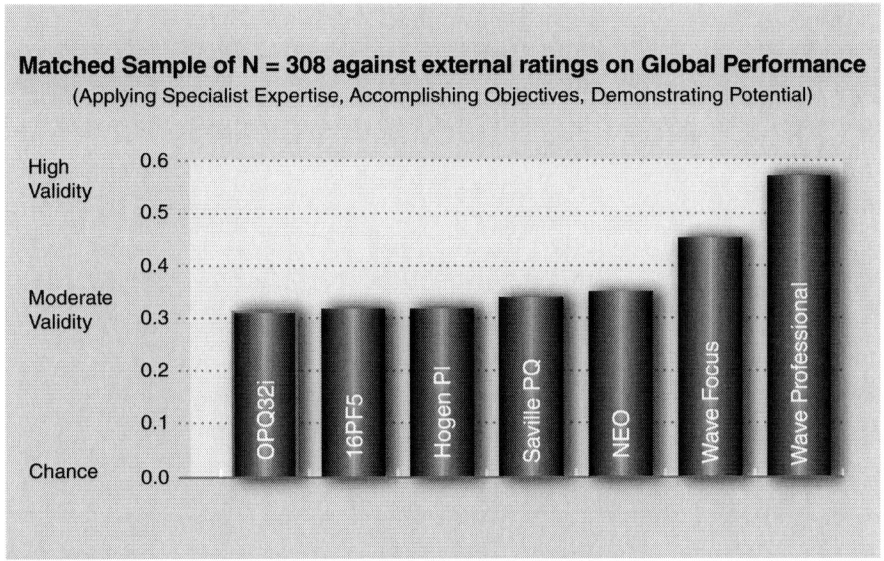

FIGURE 12.3 A comparison of the validity of different personality questionnaires

Ability tests, with a typical correlation figure of around .50, are the most valid method for predicting how somebody is likely to perform in the workplace.

The validity comparison data above cover a broad range of different assessment methods, but what of personality questionnaires specifically? A few years ago I worked with colleagues on a research study where we compared the validity of a range of well-known personality questionnaires. A summary of our findings is provided by Figure 12.3 below.

It is worth noting that since this research was published, other researchers such as Salgado and Tauriz (2014) have published work suggesting that normative questionnaires are the least valid, followed by ipsative questionnaires, and that quasi-ipsative questionnaires (such as the Saville Consulting Wave tools) are the most valid. This work backs up previous work which I carried out in the 1990s (Saville and Willson, 1991) and sits opposite much 'received wisdom'.

The acceptability of selection methods

While the degree to which any selection method can effectively forecast workplace performance is its most important property, the acceptability of the methods – to candidates, administrators and other stakeholders – is also incredibly important. In 2009 I carried out research with my colleague Rab MacIver on 1,000 graduates. We sought their views on certain types of psychometric assessments compared to a range of other assessment methods. We asked the volunteers whether they thought the methods shown in Table 12.1 were useful in selection.

TABLE 12.1 A comparison of the acceptability of different selection methods

METHOD	Is it useful in selection?		
	YES	NO	UNCERTAIN
References	56%	17%	27%
Personality Questionnaires	53%	13%	34%
Intelligence Tests	49%	14%	37%
Interviews	41%	26%	33%
Astrology	22%	50%	28%

As can be seen, psychometric assessments were among the most acceptable to the graduates we surveyed. In more recent years, internet-based assessments have opened up new possibilities. Increasing numbers of companies now look to have their branding reflected in the assessment products which helps attract the best applicants and increases the chances of candidates accepting offers. It seems that acceptable assessments can increase the credibility of an organisation and it is clear that candidates do make judgements about organisations from the assessment materials to which they're exposed. Many organisations have realised that it's a bad thing if the best candidates are turning them down. Figure 12.4 provides two examples of multimedia-driven assessments which have been developed by the team at Saville Consulting to strongly and positively reflect the organisational brands of the clients in question. Much of the appeal of such bespoke assessments is in being able to provide as positive a candidate experience as possible.

Performance and decision making

For years, psychologists have fussed about what a given correlation coefficient means for an organisation in terms of the impact of job performance that they should expect to see having selected candidates on the basis of methods possessing a given level of validity (e.g. .30).

At the National Foundation for Educational Research (NFER), where I started my career, we were concerned that A-Level grades – examinations sat by British schoolchildren aged around 18 – tended to correlate at 'only' .30 with university degree class. Why was the relationship as relatively modest as this? The problem was a practical one: With different examination boards, different universities and different subjects to consider, it meant that the grades and degree classes achieved tended to be relatively inconsistent and hard to compare. Was a 2:1 class degree

FIGURE 12.4 Examples of multimedia-driven selection assessment methods

from a top university really the same as a 2:1 class degree from a less reputable university? There was also the issue to contend with that the vast majority of graduates left university with either a 2:1 or 2:2 class degree. This means that there was a good deal of restriction of range and this, combined with all of the other inconsistency factors, would serve to reduce the 'true' correlations.

While IQ or intelligence tests tend to show the strongest relationship with work performance, we know that personality is important too. Self-reported levels of personality characteristics such as conscientiousness are as good as A-Level grades at forecasting future performance. Nevertheless, as I've said already, psychologists and psychometricians get themselves into much controversy about all of this – even the great ones. Why? The aim of this talk is to explore prediction, decision making and cost–benefit in selection methods. At its core, this is about 'the bottom line' for an organisation. One of the biggest mistakes people make is to confuse *forecasting/ prediction errors* and *decision errors*.

Put simply, some forecasting errors aren't practically important. Take, for example, the case where a hired candidate outperforms expectations – perhaps they exceed their sales targets for a year. While this is technically a forecasting error – we didn't predict this happening – it wouldn't have been a decision error to have hired them. It's also worth pointing out that statistical significance isn't the same as practical significance. On a large enough sample of people, the smallest correlations can be statistically significant, but might have little or no practical implication.

Some scientists have criticised significance testing because it inevitably leads to some interpretation issues around the threshold of statistical significance. For example, a correlation which almost reaches statistical significance and which is having an actual effect might be overlooked because it has not been labelled 'significant' in the test. Equally, some relationships can come out as 'significant' while still having a negligible impact because they are overshadowed by other variables which are even more impactful. A complementary method for evaluating the meaningfulness and importance of correlations is to refer to effect sizes. Cohen (1988) provided some interpretation guidelines for correlations of different sizes. Cohen's suggestion is to refer to correlations of up to $+/-$ .10 as representing no effect, correlations of $+/-$ .10 as a small effect, correlations of $+/-$ .30 as a medium effect and $+/-$ .50 as a large effect. Effect sizes can be a very useful complement to the results of significance testing, providing extra information which helps interpret the likely impact of any correlations seen.

We have to acknowledge too that there is a minefield of equations – some 100 – and their usefulness varies depending on situation and application. For example, many books (and LinkedIn forum users) suggest squaring the correlation of a selection method with the criterion (i.e. job performance). This provides what is known as the Coefficient of Determination. Using this method, a .30 correlation would suggest a 9 per cent improvement based on selecting using that given method. But in truth this is just a measure of common variance, not an indication of the improvement in decisions that can be made, i.e. a utility measure. Or, perhaps better still, some suggest to use the Coefficient of Forecasting Efficiency – which you should Google if you're interested! Again, this is based on a squaring of the correlation coefficient.

Another approach from the 1930s is Taylor-Russell tables. Taylor and Russell wanted to respond to frequent criticisms in the 1930s of low predictor-criteria correlations in psychometric assessments, that is, that psychometric assessments didn't relate very closely to job performance. To do this, they demonstrated that assessments can still be useful even when correlations are low. Their crucial contribution was to highlight the importance of two other key variables that often get overlooked:

Success (base) rate – the number of people currently considered successful as a ratio of all applicants hired (e.g. 60 per cent base rate = 60 per cent of hired applicants go on to be 'successful'). There can be a degree of subjectivity in working out what the base rate is because it is not always easy to know how to define success in a given role. There's no simple solution to this – defining the base rate needs a lot of thought to make sure the information which comes from utility analysis is credible and useful.

Selection ratio – the number of posts to total number of applicants (high selectivity = a low selection ratio).

Taylor and Russell (1939) illustrated these variables in 'Taylor-Russell tables', which demonstrate that the greatest gain from using an assessment comes when it has: high validity, a low base rate (low success currently from using the assessment – i.e. you have a problem) and a low selection ratio (i.e. you have lots of applicants and can be highly selective about who is chosen from the assessment process). Even coefficients as low as .10, under the right circumstances, can give a useful return-on-investment by the Taylor-Russell approach. However, the problem of Taylor-Russell tables is finding the 'true' base and success rates.

Subsequent researchers, including Cronbach and Gleser (1965), confirmed what I mentioned before; that the squaring of the correlation coefficient is the common variance, but not cost–benefit return at all. Such researchers also showed that cost–benefit is actually linear to the validity coefficient, not its square. Thus, they showed that financial return was in fact proportional to the validity coefficient. Despite all of this established research, there are still a number of individuals who state that return-on-investment is proportional to the squared correlation.

Next came the prediction equation. By this, predicted workplace performance = assessment validity x assessment score expressed as a Z-score. A Z-score, of course, represents the number of standard deviations an individual is above or below the mean of a distribution of scores. For example, imagine a selection test with a validity of .44 and a person scores at = +2. This is a high score which in a normal distribution corresponds to about the 98th percentile.

$$\hat{Z}_y - .44 \times 2 = .88$$

Therefore, the individual here would be estimated to have a work performance level of +.88 when expressed in Z-scores. This is nearly a standard deviation above the group mean score. However, because this outcome is expressed in Z-score units, it may not be that useful. What is .88 of a standard deviation worth in terms of increased work effectiveness for the hired individual? Also, we must acknowledge that there is a standard error around this prediction:

Standard Error of Estimate = Square root of 1 − (Squared validity coefficient)

So:

$$SE_E = \sqrt{1 - r_{xy}^2}$$

At the 68 per cent confidence level we can say that the above candidate will perform between −.30 and +1.70 standard deviations (SDs_ from the mean. This is a quantification of prediction error, but not all is a decision error. I'd argue, in fact, that half of this prediction error (anything which exceeds the prediction) is good decision making!

The prediction equation is useful in trying to estimate how a given individual will perform, but cannot be used to estimate the utility or return for a whole group of individuals. Perhaps the most well-known measure of utility, which attempts to deal with some of the limitation of earlier methods, is the Cronbach-Gleser equation, based on the work of Brogden (1949) as shown below:

$$\pounds \text{ or } \$ \text{ gain} = r_v . \bar{Z}_x . SD_y . N - C$$

r_v = validity coefficient (correlation coefficient with job performance) on the test

$\bar{Z}_x$ = mean Z-score on the assessment for selected applicants

SD_y = standard deviation of the job performance criterion ($\pounds$)

N = number of selected applicants

C = cost of the assessment programme.

In order to illustrate how this is used, let us give an example of an assessment process, with some details as below:

> Number of applicants = 200
> Number selected (N) = 50
> Validity coefficient (r_v) = +.40
> Mean Z-score on the test of the selected candidates ($\bar{Z}_x$) = +1
> SD of profit on the job performance criterion in \$ (SD_y) = \$20,000
> Cost of the testing programme (C) – @ \$80 per head = \$16,000.
> We can then put these numbers into our equation, as shown in Figure 12.5.

The gain to the employer here is estimated at \$384,000 per annum that the selected people remain in their roles.

Cronbach found that any financial gain at all from an assessment method easily overshadowed the cost of testing, which could be lower than \$100 per person tested. Especially given that there are so many potential costs of poor selection, it seems eminently sensible to use valid selection methods. Just some of the many potential impacts of poor selection practices include:

- Unnecessary recruitment and selection costs.
- Poor job performance.
- Poor retention and high staff turnover.
- Lost training costs.
- Lost opportunity costs (e.g. lost sales revenue).
- Wasted time spent managing poor performers.
- Reduced revenues/fewer customers.
- Reduced morale.
- Candidate litigation.

$$\pounds \text{ gain} = (r_v . \bar{Z}_x . SD_y . N) - C$$
$$= (.40 \times 1 \times \$20,000 \times 50) - \$16,000$$
$$= \$384,000$$

FIGURE 12.5 Worked example of the Cronbach-Gleser equation

- Legal issues associated with poor selection (e.g. a charge of corporate responsibility if a serious accident is caused by someone who was inappropriately selected).
- Discontent in the workplace.
- Company failure.

Clearly calculating financial benefits and return-on-investment is a complex area, which has taxed many great researchers over the years. In response to the Cronbach-Gleser equation, for example, some have raised objections or suggested refinements, which have become progressively more complicated and esoteric. I've even heard it suggested that we need to find a way to take into account that the best performers get paid more than others, so companies will have to pay more tax for having successful people, and that the best performers often travel more – both of which are costs that need to be taken into consideration . . .

Because of the complexity of the whole area of research, the work of Latham and Whyte (1994) came as no surprise. They found that utility information 'reduced the support of managers for implementing a valid selection procedure, even though the analysis indicated that the net benefits from the new procedure were substantial'. They also noted that managers 'may be suspicious of consultants who claim to accurately estimate the dollar value of their recommendations'. I would agree and add that, in my experience, intricately calculated utility analyses are often not required. Simply pointing out to board members that taking the wrong person at a senior level can be very expensive tends to be enough to have the desired effect.

There is an interesting area of debate regarding whether such statistical (or actuarial) methods of comparing candidates are better than expert judgements about who is likely to be the best. Meehl (1954) wrote a classic book called *Clinical vs. Statistical Prediction: A Theoretical Analysis and a Review of the Evidence*, which found that mechanical models of data combination tended to outperform expert subjective judgements by clinical practitioners. As was to be expected, this caused something of a stir amongst clinical practitioners at the time, but these findings are far from isolated.

Indeed, Grove et al. (2000) carried out a meta-analysis on a total of 136 different studies which were published over a period of around 60 years. On average, mechanical prediction techniques such as the use of standard equations were around 10 per cent more accurate than clinical expert predictions. The authors found that this trend held across general medicine, mental health, personality, education and training settings, regardless of the nature of the expert judgements, the types of judges used, the experience of the expert judges or the types of data that were being combined. The authors posited that people exhibit a range of biases and inaccuracies in their judgements (as is well known) and this likely contributes to the general trend seen. There is also some evidence that people are more honest when they are being scored by a computer rather than another person (cf. Phellas et al., 2012). It is likely that some of the impression management behaviours which we see in face-to-face interactions are reduced when there is no person assessor involved in the process.

What is clear is that there are some recommendations one can give to increase the potential for return-on-investment of a selection method. Using valid and cost-effective assessment methods early on in a process is important.

With even a relatively modest validity of .44, for example, under typical conditions you are more than three times as likely to correctly select someone in the top third of work performers from a pool of people who achieve the top third of assessment scores compared to when the pool of people represented the bottom third of assessment scores.

To explain this point, my colleague Rab MacIver simulated data on 10,000 people where there was a .44 correlation between an assessment score and a measure of workplace performance. Rab then divided the 10,000 cases into three according to their scores on the assessment. The top third of scores represented the 'High Assessment Score' group, the middle third of scores represented the 'Medium Assessment Score' group and the bottom third of scores represented the 'Low Assessment Score' group.

Rab then compared the percentage of people within each of these groups who were also in the top third, middle third and bottom third for workplace performance. Below I show the percentages of each of the top and bottom thirds for assessment scores who fell into each third for workplace performance:

Top Third of Assessment Scores

- Percentage in Top Third of Workplace Performance – 51.50 per cent.
- Percentage in Middle Third of Workplace Performance – 31.60 per cent.
- Percentage in Bottom Third of Workplace Performance – 16.90 per cent.

Bottom Third of Assessment Scores

- Percentage in Top Third of Workplace Performance – 16.90 per cent.
- Percentage in Middle Third of Workplace Performance – 30.30 per cent.
- Percentage in Bottom Third of Workplace Performance – 52.80 per cent.

This shows the real impact of validity whereby selecting the highest performers on an assessment with a validity of .44 means you are much more likely to successfully get a high performer (51.50 per cent) versus a low performer (16.90 per cent). This can be compared to what would happen if you were trying to identify someone from the top third of performance without using any assessment method. In such a case you'd have a one in three (approximately 33.3 per cent) chance of selecting a top performer at random. By introducing an assessment method with a validity of .44, you are in effect halving your risk of making a serious selection error (i.e. accidentally taking a low performer when you want to take a high performer) from 33.3 per cent to 16.9 per cent.

These data also show the converse situation whereby selecting people without screening their assessment performance means you are likely to make more selection errors and recruit more people who are likely to be poor performers

(52.80 per cent) than high performers (16.90 per cent). In many cases, small changes in validity or performance can have quite profound effects on the accuracy and usefulness of your assessment process. Remember that Kahneman (2011) calculated that Tiger Woods in his prime could have improved his performance by just one shot per tournament, his earnings over a year could have increased by more than a million dollars.

As I explored at the start of this talk, the acceptability of the methods used is also incredibly important and shouldn't be overlooked – you don't want to risk losing the best applicants because of your selection process. The cost of testing people virtually disappears and gets quickly eaten up when compared against the potential for financial gain if you recruit the best people. And the more selective you can be amongst candidates, the greater your potential for gain.

Another way of thinking about the potential benefits and risks of good or bad selection can be illustrated in an expectancy table. In the table below, a group of individuals have been categorised as either high or low performers in terms of management effectiveness. They have also been categorised into the top third, middle third or bottom third of performers in terms of their scores on a test of verbal reasoning. You can see that in the top third of test scores there are relatively more people who are high-performing managers than low-performing managers. In the middle third of test scores there are an equal number of high- and low-performing managers. In the bottom third of test scores there are relatively more people who are low-performing managers than high-performing managers.

This is important. We can see that for a test with this level of validity – here a relatively modest +0.30 – selecting from within the group of top test performers will greatly increase your chance of also choosing someone who's also a high performer (expressed here in terms of management performance). Conversely, if you choose not to select from within the top test performers and instead settle for someone who's in the bottom third of test performers, you have a relatively greater

TABLE 12.2 An expectancy table based on a verbal reasoning test and management performance data

Verbal Reasoning Scores	Management Performance					
	Low		High		Total	
	N	%	N	%	N	%
Top Third	38	25	112	75	150	100
Middle Third	75	50	75	50	150	100
Bottom Third	105	70	45	30	150	100
	218	-	232	-	450	100

chance of choosing someone who's also a low performer. So using a test with established validity can both increase your chance of making good selection decisions (i.e. selecting someone who's a high performer) and reduce the chance of making selection errors (i.e. selecting someone who turns out to be a low performer).

The simple message is that a valid assessment can reduce the risk of serious selection errors. I've often found that such expectancy tables, which show the practical impact of the theory I've discussed, are easier to explain to managers than the kinds of equations we've also touched upon.

Lastly, I'd just like to reflect that the future of utility and cost–benefit research may well end up focusing on broader constructs than the gains to a team or organisation. Indeed, I've been working with Tom Hopton and the eminent economist from Durham University, Brian Snowdon, who was unlucky enough to share a flat with me whilst at the University of Leicester.

Cronbach, Hunter and Schmidt and others have developed utility/cost–benefit equations in industrial psychology to estimate the dollar/pound return to an organisation if selection in employment were improved by X per cent. It would be interesting to speculate on what would be the impact on the economy if we could improve getting the right person in the right job and increasing average output by, say, 10 per cent? In personal correspondence I raised this with Brian Snowdon and he agreed that while there has been work that attempts to measure improvements in efficiency of an economy at the aggregate level, this has tended to focus on improved efficiency (more competition, technological progress, etc.) rather than improved labour allocation at the micro level. He explained to me that Solow (1957), a Nobel laureate, attributed up to two-thirds of US growth in the early twentieth century to improved efficiency.

Brian Snowdon suggested that since the total output of an economy is '$Y = E \star q$' (where Y = GDP, E = employment and q = average productivity) then, by definition, getting the right people into the right jobs must raise average productivity and total GDP. He concluded that better job selection should raise E and q.

Our initial investigations into this have suggested that countries which use psychometrics more often tend to be more developed according to the Human Development Index and tend to have a higher GDP. This is, of course, a correlation – so it doesn't imply causality. There is likely to be an association here between countries with higher living standards being able to afford to use techniques such as psychometrics, so this probably isn't surprising.

Okun's law describes a relatively stable relationship between GDP and unemployment – whereby every 1 per cent increase in unemployment reduces GDP by 2 per cent. So, conversely, a 1 per cent increase in employment is likely to increase output (as defined by GDP) in the range of 2 per cent . . .

Our challenge is to find a sensible way from the utility equations we use in assessment to look at the impact at the level of national economies. So far we've been looking at what we can learn from economics and 'Growth Accounting' in particular. Of specific interest is the Productivity Growth formula offered by Abel and Bernanke (2005), shown in Figure 12.6.

$$\frac{\Delta A}{A} = \frac{\Delta Y}{Y} - a_K \frac{\Delta K}{K} - a_N \frac{\Delta N}{N}$$

Output growth, $\Delta Y/Y$, can be broken into three parts:
1. that resulting from productivity growth, $\Delta A/A$,
2. that resulting from increased capital inputs, $a_K \Delta K/K$, and
3. that resulting from increased labor inputs, $a_N \Delta N/N$.

FIGURE 12.6 Productivity Growth formula presented in Abel and Bernanke (2005)

Output growth – represents the increased number/value of outputs in the time period under investigation.
Capital growth – represents the increased capital in the time period under investigation.
Labour growth – represents the increased number of employees in the time period under investigation.

Once you have all of the above values, it should be possible to work out productivity growth (i.e. the amount of growth not explained by capital or labour). So, as you can see, we're working on it!

Conclusion

On a practical note, many of the equations covered in this paper do produce results that, at times, seem too good to be true. I've built up my businesses on two main factors in my employees – intelligence and drive. In order to maximise the return-on-investment of your selection decisions, I believe you should reward people well and not micro-manage them. It is important for creating a culture of success that people take pride in what they do and that everybody gets involved in order to satisfy customers.

From the perspective of a business leader looking to maximise return-on-investment, it is critical to show enthusiasm and generally to have a vision, but no fixed plans that can shackle progress. I would also recommend keeping bureaucracy low and creating a culture of integrity and trust which, although will be abused by a few, most people will appreciate. Staff development and mentoring is key – ideally to the point where you are nurturing people to be better than you. As far as possible, your team should be given the opportunity to gain knowledge of their field through experience and 'stars' should be given early responsibility, but coupled with a 'my door is always open' philosophy for when they need support. The more stars you have the better, but to retain and develop them, you will also need to be prepared to take tough decisions at times.

For now I'd just like to leave you with a simple thought, commonly attributed to Bill Gates: 'Hire the smartest people you can get!'

Many thanks for your time.

References

Abel, A. B. and Bernanke, B. S. (2005). *Macroeconomics*, 5th edn. Boston, MA: Pearson Addison Wesley.

Brogden, H. E. (1949). When Testing Pays Off. *Personnel Psychology*, 2, 171–83.

Cohen, J. (1988). *Statistical Power Analysis for the Behavioral Sciences*, 2nd edn. Mahwah, NJ: Lawrence Erlbaum Associates.

Cronbach, L. J. and Gleser, G. C. (1965). *Psychological Tests and Personnel Decisions*. Urbana: University of Illinois Press.

Davis, C. (2000). *The Best of the Best: A New Look at the Great Cricketers and Their Changing Times*. Sydney: ABC Books.

Grove, W. M, Zald, D. H., Lebow, B. S., Snitz, B. E. and Nelson, C. (2000). Clinical versus mechanical prediction: A meta-analysis. *Psychological Assessment*, 12(1), 19–30.

Houghton, J. T. (1988). The Storm, the Media and the Enquiry. *Weather*, 43, 67–70.

Hull, C. L. (1928). *Aptitude Testing*. London: George G. Harrap & Co. Ltd.

Kahneman, D. (2011). *Thinking, Fast & Slow*. Farrar, Straus & Giroux.

Latham, G. P. and Whyte, G. (1994). The futility of utility analysis. *Personnel Psychology*, 47, 31–46.

Meehl, P. E. (1954). *Clinical vs. Statistical Prediction: A Theoretical Analysis and a Review of the Evidence*. Minneapolis: University of Minnesota Press.

O'Boyle, E. and Aguinis, H. (2012). The best and the rest: Revisiting the norm of normality of individual performance. *Personnel Psychology*, 65, 79–119.

Phellas, C. N., Bloch, A. and Seale, C. (2012). Structured methods: Interviews, questionnaires and observation. In C. Seale (ed.), *Researching Society and Culture*, 3rd edn. London: Sage, pp. 181–205.

Robertson, I. T. and Smith, M. (2001). Personnel selection. *Journal of Occupational and Organizational Psychology*, 74, 441–72.

Sackman, H. H., Erikson, W. J. and Grant, E. E. (1968). Exploratory experimental studies comparing online and offline programming performance. *Communication of the ACM*, 11(1), 3–11.

Schmidt, F. L. and Hunter, J. E. (1998). The validity and utility of selection methods in personnel psychology: Practical and theoretical implications of 85 years of research. *Psychological Bulletin*, 124(2), 262–74.

Salgado, J. F. and Tauriz, G. (2014). The Five-Factor Model, forced-choice personality inventories and performance: A comprehensive meta-analysis of academic and occupational validity studies. *European Journal of Work and Organizational Psychology*, 23(1), 3–30.

Saville, P. and Willson, E. (1991). The reliability and validity of normative and ipsative approaches in the measurement of personality. *Journal of Occupational Psychology*, 64, 219–38.

Solow, R. M. (1957). Technical change and the aggregate production function. *Review of Economics and Statistics*, 39(3), 312–20.

Taylor, H. C. and Russell J. T. (1939). The relationship of validity coefficients to the practical effectiveness of tests in selection. *Journal of Applied Psychology*, 23, 565–78.

INDEX